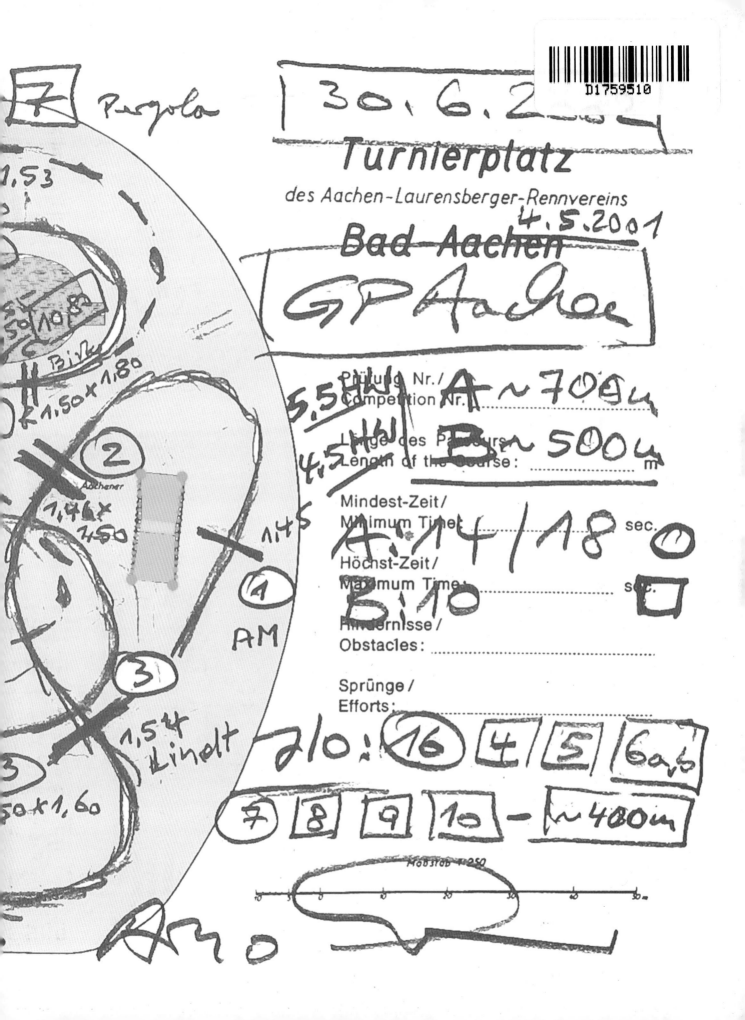

Pergola

30.6.2...

Turnierplatz

des Aachen-Laurensberger-Rennvereins

4.5.2001

Bad Aachen

GP Aachen

Prüfung Nr. / Competition Nr. A ~700m

Länge des Parcours / Length of the Course: B 500 m

Mindest-Zeit / Minimum Time: A: 14 / 18 sec.

Höchst-Zeit / Maximum Time: B: 10 sec.

Hindernisse / Obstacles:

Sprünge / Efforts: 10: 16 4 5 6a/b

7 8 9 10 - ~400m

Maßstab 1:250

PENCOED COLLEGE LIBRARY

00514529

COURSE
DESIGN

PENCOED COLLEGE
LIBRARY

COURSE
DESIGN

*Historical Roots, Theory, Practice,
Aesthetics, Ethics and State of the Art*

ARNO GEGO

In co-operation with Christa Heibach

PENCOED COLLEGE LIBRARY

CLASS No. 798·24 GEG

COPY 00514529   PRICE £50·00

REQ. LRC047   DATE May 2011

J. A. Allen
London

Translation from German to English by
Isabella Draper-Züllig, Romanshorn, Switzerland

Lectors of the original German text:
Marlen Clemens, Vaals, NED
Marlon Gego, Raeren, BEL

© Arno Gego 2006
First published in Great Britain 2006

ISBN-10: 0-85131-929-7
ISBN-13: 978-0-85131-929-2

J.A. Allen
Clerkenwell House
Clerkenwell Green
London EC1R 0HT

J.A. Allen is an imprint of Robert Hale Limited

The right of Arno Gego to be identified as author
of this work has been asserted by him in accordance
with the Copyright, Designs and Patents Act 1988

A catalogue record for this book is available from the British Library

Design by Judy Linard
Edited by Lesley Young

Printed by Kyodo Printing Co (S'pore) Pte Ltd, Singapore

CONTENTS

APPENDICES

FOREWORD

HRH THE INFANTA DOÑA PILAR DE BORBÓN

Not many sports are as attractive as the equestrian disciplines. I see several reasons for this: horse riding and care involve nurturing a relationship with a beautiful animal which deserves admiration and respect; our sport is also one of the very few where women and men compete on equal terms, from novice class to Olympic level; it has also an innate affinity with nature and is environment-friendly.

Arno Gego has a passionate – though scientific – approach to the equestrian sport. Praised course designer and founder of the Aachen School of Course Design, Arno has conducted numerous courses around the world, supporting the education of the new generation of course designers. There are very few publications on the subject, and we are especially grateful to Arno for sharing his wide experience with us.

The book you have in your hands is a comprehensive manual on course design. It includes not only theoretical and practical information on the construction of jumping courses, but also interesting information on the history, evolution and ethics of equestrian sport. On behalf of the FEI, I wish all success to this essential reading for all professionals and horse lovers.

HRH The Infanta Doña Pilar de Borbón
Honorary President of the FEI

PREFACE

Equestrian sport has a very special appeal for many people. It is the only form of sport which has been part of the Olympic Games since 680 BC, shortly after the Games first began in Greece in 776 BC [159]. It is the only form of sport in which men and women participate together, with equal chances of winning. It is the only form of sport in which a human athlete and an animal athlete compete as a team to win Olympic medals.

A more recent development in equestrian sport, thanks in particular to the intense efforts made by the FEI under the leadership of its president, Her Royal Highness Infanta Doña Pilar de Borbón, has been its considerable growth over the last ten years. This can be seen through:

- an increase in FEI disciplines (there is now competition in jumping, dressage, driving, eventing, vaulting, reining and endurance);

- an increase in universality: more and more countries from all continents are now gradually progressing towards the Olympic standard;

- an increase in the number of sports horses;

- an increase in the number of people and horses who are involved in competition and leisure riding [134].

It is clear that equestrian sport is attracting more attention and is seen as unique because the horse is considered to be one of the most aristocratic of animals with a special historical significance in the culture and development of the human race [140]. Furthermore, equestrian sport belongs to the group of sports based on nature and ecology. This group of sports is regarded as so important that a new institute has been established at the German Sports University in Cologne to promote greater understanding of this field of endeavour.

Consequently, the triangle formed between nature, animal and human athlete determines the way equestrian sport identifies itself, which can be understood in terms of the closest affinity with the animal and nature. Any artifice would be counter-productive.

Jumping at Olympic level is primarily an outdoor sport, as is horse racing, golf, skiing, the MARATHON, the Tour de France and even football. Indoor jumping tournaments allow competitions to be organised in winter or during spells of bad weather, but they are, at best, only an alternative to the traditional outdoor tournaments and they cannot replace the standard of an outstanding outdoor GRAND PRIX at the world's most important tournaments.

Jumping and other equestrian disciplines are in fierce competition with other types of sport when it comes to attracting the interest of the public, the media, sponsors and other types of support. There is a serious danger that jumping could lose its appeal, with a resultant decline in spectator interest, if huge images, bright logos, ideas and important concepts become mixed up and misused in second-class tournaments without reaching the corresponding standard of the great GRAND PRIX. It would be as if, for example, someone filled a wine bottle with red lemonade and then labelled the bottle as a classic Bordeaux wine.

Equestrian sport – with jumping at the top of the list – can only win if it continues to develop on the basis of its historic natural roots and high classical principles.

Course design is an important part of the general school of jumping which involves:

- horse breeding;

- an established system for training and schooling horses and riders;

- well-defined systems and structures of tournaments and competitions;

- good course design;

- high quality and quantity of tournaments;

- the interest and respect of the media;

- the interest and respect of sponsors.

One of the greatest contributors to the success of good tournaments is good course design. The road to becoming a skilled and experienced international FEI course designer requires a long and demanding period of work as an assistant, consolidating skills learned first at fairly small, then medium-sized and finally large national tournaments. Practical experience at many smaller tournaments, as well as personal riding experience in the saddle (in jumping classes of 1.40 m and above), and learning from leading international instructors are an essential part of the career of any FEI candidate or international course designer. Becoming an international course designer demands a great deal of enthusiasm, passion and patience.

On the other hand, course design is such a fascinating and creative task that many young, open-minded and flexible riders do become motivated to take up such a career – and not only men, for women are welcomed and positively encouraged. At the present time there are certainly not enough good course designers worldwide, especially for the sport at the grass roots and for smaller tournaments where young riders and novice horses can be aided to develop and progress on well-built, rhythmical courses.

Both jumping and course design continuously evolve and progress, as can be seen, for example, from the remarkable developments and advances in the quality of contemporary footings (grass and sand), and from the stricter safety requirements demanded over the last 20 years.

As the available literature on course design is, to put it mildly, limited, this book is intended for those who are interested in becoming course designers. Riders, trainers, coaches, judges, stewards, organisers, sponsors, journalists and other followers of equestrian sport may also find much to interest them. All the relevant literature known to me is listed in the bibliography.

INFLUENTIAL FORCES IN EQUESTRIAN SPORT

For many years, I had the privilege of working closely with many of the best teachers such as:

Colonel Hans-Heinrich ('Micky') Brinckmann (born 1911), a riding instructor since 1960 who had a formative influence on the sport as well as being a style-setting course designer since 1964. Brinckmann was a rider at the Deutsche Kavallerieschule in Hannover from 1935. He won the Rome GRAND PRIX before the start of the Second World War in 1939, won the Aachen GRAND PRIX twice, and also won many other internationally important jumping competitions.

He spoke several languages, was a philosopher and an author of fiction and poetry, and loved music, great paintings and literature. He was a great communicator and a master of 'treading softly'. After the Second World War, he went to Cairo in the 1950s to prepare the Egyptian team of military riders for their participation in the 1960

Olympic Games in Rome where they won fourth place in the Nations Cup, a feat which created a small sensation at the time and bears eloquent witness to Brinckmann's qualities as a trainer.

In 1976, Brinckmann seemed to be the only person on the jumping committee of the German National Federation who believed in Alwin Schockemöhle and he insisted on nominating Alwin for the 1976 Olympic Games in Montreal. Schockemöhle went through to become individual Olympic champion with 0 faults, and 12 penalties (three knock downs) ahead of the silver medal winner Michel Vaillancourt!

For around 20 years from 1960 onwards, Brinckmann had a decisive influence on jumping in Germany and worldwide:

- as course designer of the CHIO Aachen (figure 0.1) and other top tournaments;

- as German national trainer and an international consultant;

- as an outstanding personality in jumping.

Figure 0.1: *Arno Gego (left) and H.-H. Brinckmann during the World Jumping Championships, Aachen 1978. Photo by Robert Jolicoeur, Canada, Course Designer of the Olympic Games, Montreal 1976.*

Unfortunately, he never wrote down his knowledge, his thoughts and experiences. As early as 1962 he asked me whether I could produce the drawings for a book that he intended to publish but, sadly, the planned work was never written.

Dr h.c. Bertalan de Némethy of Hungary [114] gained a diploma at the Royal Hungarian Military Academy. Later, he was appointed as a teacher at the Royal Military Cavalry School and he also took part in the three-day event at the 1936 Olympic Games in Berlin. He, too, accumulated personal experience in the Deutsche Kavallerieschule in Hannover. After the Second World War, he worked first as a trainer in Denmark and then as the national show-jumping coach of the US equestrian team in Gladstone, New Jersey. He developed jumping as a sport in the USA and had outstanding success with his team at many international championships and GRAND PRIX, including the Olympic Games.

He, too, was a refined and multilingual gentleman with an excellent education. He was the course designer of the 1984 Olympic Games in Los Angeles. Natural schooling, the best style and free forward movement of well-trained horses were his hallmark.

> THE GROWING QUALITY OF THE HORSES HAS
> SPEEDED UP THE DECLINE OF US EQUESTRIAN
> SPORT ... TODAY, THERE IS NO ONE WHO STILL
> PUTS ACROSS WHAT BERTALAN DE NEMETHY
> WAS TEACHING THEM. IT MAKES ME SAD,
> BECAUSE DE NEMETHY'S METHOD IS THE BEST
> THAT EXISTS TO THIS DAY.

(Albert Voorn of the Netherlands, Olympic runner-up in Sydney 2000 [177])

Pamela Carruthers of Great Britain [032] was a former international show-jumper who became one of the outstanding course designers of the second half of the last century.

Firgure 0.2: *From left: Pamela Carruthers, Hauke Schmidt, H.-H. Brinckmann and Arno Gego, Olympic Games, Munich 1972. Photo by Szimay.*

Figure 0.3: *Bertalan de Némethy at CHIO Aachen (circa 1970). Photo: private collection.*

She designed and built the famous Hickstead (England) showground in the 1960s, and the showground in Calgary (Canada) some ten years later.

Pamela's work (figure 0.2), like that of Brinckmann and de Némethy (figure 0.3), took as its base the classical roots and history of the sport, but at the same time all three were extremely influential innovators in contemporary jumping and course design.

MY OWN CAREER AND PERSONAL ACKNOWLEDGEMENTS

From 1965, I worked at the jumping stadium of the CHIO Aachen (figure 0.4), first as an assistant and, from 1974, as a course designer in a team with Micky Brinckmann and Horst Ense. From 1981, I was chief course designer, including a spell with Olaf Petersen, from 1983 to 1986, as a colleague of equal standing.

During my career I have worked successfully with almost all of the official international course designers of the FEI and with very many national, candidate and international FEI course designers and judges around the world.

I would like especially to acknowledge the support of my former employers:

- Fähse & Co., Düren, Germany (1963–69)

- Deutz AG, Cologne, Germany (1969–91)

Figure 0.4: *Together for over 40 years: Arno Gego and CHIO Aachen, Germany. Photo by ALRV.*

- Pulsaar S.A. de C.V. Monterrey, Mexico (1991–2000)

and have greatly appreciated their trust and understanding of my passion for equestrian sport.

I have been inspired, encouraged and supported by the Mexican Olympic rider Alfonso Romo, for 15 years one of the most important supporters and visionaries of jumping.

I am grateful for having had the trust and support of the FEI and of national federations, tournament organisers and colleagues across the world in designing new facilities, arenas, stadiums, etc., and in developing new tournaments, including new Derby designs, such as La Bagnaia in Italy, Pavarotti International in Modena, Italy, Monterrey in Mexico, Istanbul in Turkey, Luxembourg, Valkenswaard in the Netherlands, or in acting as advisor to organisers such as the CSIO La Baule in France.

Above all, I am grateful for always enjoying the support of my family.

MY OWN PHILOSOPHY OF EQUESTRIAN SPORT

It may surprise readers to find that I relate equestrian sport to the fine arts of literature, architecture, painting, music, theatre and landscape design which, until now, have rarely been connected with course design. It is worth noting, however, that music in particular has always played an important role in riding [073], for example, in military and other parades, classical riding institutions, manège riding, presentations of dressage and quadrilles.

After some misgiving, Olympic dressage did at last acknowledge this and, in 1986, thanks to the special vision and effort of Dr Joep Bartels [016] (first in World Cup dressage, s'Hertogenbosch, the Netherlands, 1986), the combination of horse and music was revived with great success in the form of the Kür or freestyle to music. When staged and choreographed to a high standard to deliver what has been advertised, gala evenings, such as 'horse and music', have become increasingly popular in Europe.

This more recent development in equestrian sport may also help to establish a similar qualifying relationship between jumping and course design. The traditional, classical term of 'equitation' (the art of riding)[023/140/152/154/184] deserves to be revived in order to pinpoint clearly the high standard and level of knowledge, ability, performance, aesthetics, ethics, fairness, horsemanship and human ideal required.

So it may not come as a surprise that, in later years, I have frequently found new inspiration in the work of various artists concerned with painting, architecture and music. The arts are a particularly rich source of inspiration in jumping and course design.

In this context, it is remarkable to discover how many artists who excelled at one art form also took up other art forms, as the following examples illustrate.

EQUESTRIANISM IS PART OF 'NATURE-BASED SPORT AND ECOLOGY' AND STANDS FOR
- NOBILITY
- ELEGANCE
- TRADITION
- BEAUTY
- MUSIC
  AND
- ART

(Persuasion of the author)

- The twelve-tone musician Schonberg was also a painter [194].

- The architect Le Corbusier was also a painter and designer [094].

- The Olympic champion William C. Steinkraus is a musician and man of letters [166].

- Wassily Kandinsky, one of the major painters of the last century, was a lawyer and economist and also passionately interested in staging plays [047/087/088}.

- The painter Marc Chagall had strong links with other art forms such as literature and poetry (he worked on Bible illustrations, for example), architecture (murals and stained-glass windows for the churches of Assy in France, 1957; stained-glass windows for the cathedral of Rheims in France, 1974) and music (murals for the new Metropolitan Opera House in New York, 1965)[036].

- There are many other examples of multi-disciplinary artists, such as Henri Matisse (lawyer), Ernst Ludwig Kirchner (architect), Andy Warhol (art history, sociology, psychology and design) or El Lissitzky (architecture).

THE AIMS OF THIS BOOK

Of course, this book is primarily concerned with the theory and implementation of course design and its interdependency with jumping. It is my intention:

- to contribute to a better understanding of the roots of equestrian sport [006];

- to pay tribute to the potential of equestrian sport as a medium of cultural inspiration [017/042/083/159];

- to help to increase the appeal of jumping;

- to make links, albeit modest, between course design and other artistic spheres such as landscape design, arts and crafts, painting and music;

- and, most of all, to make a contribution to the theory of course design.

In 1982, together with Hauke Schmidt, a former successful Nations Cup rider and pupil of Brinckmann [057], I published a book entitled *Parcours-Gestaltung* (Course Design) which was addressed particularly to the new generation of course designers. The degree of interest in this subject can be gauged from the fact that around eight translations into various languages were produced without the authors' co-operation. That book covered both outdoor and indoor tournaments. This book concentrates primarily on outdoor tournaments.

It also deals with competition sport and, without neglecting the basic questions of course design, also looks critically at the development, status and future of international jumping. It takes as its base the teachings of the great military equestrian schools of jumping and of such influential personalities as Brinckmann and de Némethy.

AUTHOR'S NOTE

In conclusion, the following should be noted.

1   The author uses the term tournament (German: *Turnier*, French: *tournoi*) in order to stake an absolutely clear claim to the quality and image, and thus the class, of an equestrian event.

In the English-speaking parts of the world, people often talk in a very loose way of 'shows' (cattle shows, dog shows, chicken shows, pig shows, etc.) and thus, unintentionally but inevitably, devalue equestrian sport with the use of the description 'horse show'. Thus the term 'show' lacks any qualifying value.

At this point, in view of the increasingly international nature of the sport, it is worth stressing the importance of the quality of the language used in and about

Table 0.1: *Language and terminology – 'Noblesse du Sport'*

| FEI Languages (for almost 100 years) | | Non FEI Language |
French	English	'Slang'
Concours (tournoi)	*Tournament, event*	*Show (?)*
Première manche	*First round*	*First leg (?) (f.e. Eurosport)*
Inspection/contrôle vétérinaire	*Veterinary inspection*	*Jog (?)*
Concours hippique	*Equestrian tournament or event*	*Horse show (?)*
Baréme A au chrono	*Table A on time*	*Speed class (?) – wrong!*
Parcours de chasse - baréme C	*Speed class, Table C*	*?? (confusion?)*
Obstacle	*Obstacle*	*Fence*
Stade	*Stadium*	*Ring*
Distance courte	*Short distance*	*'Quickie' (Eurosport)*

equestrian sport (table 0.1). A culture lives through its language, and language is a major element in determining culture.

The FEI has very successfully defined many important terms in such a way that they contain much affinity, tradition and potential for identification in both official languages. Many FEI terms are even close to the Spanish language (*obstaculo, concurso, manga, etc.*).

2   This book uses the system of metric units which is the only system of internationally agreed units (ISO standard).

3   This book summarises the rules for the sport, especially at the grass-roots level, and the middle level of national and international tournaments (approximately 1.20 m to 1.45 m) as shared by most leading international course designers, and is aimed at the middle-level course designer.

The examples relating to the great Olympic sport discussed in this book are intended to give a more rounded picture of the teaching material, and to familiarise the new generation of international course designers with the tasks of international competitive sport. They must, however, never be used to justify lack of experience and maturity to produce audacious copies of top-level courses in the sport at the grass roots.

4   Throughout this book I have used the term 'he' when talking about course designers. This is done simply to avoid the clumsiness of the expression 'he or she' repeated endlessly throughout the text. Women are positively encouraged and welcomed at all levels in the profession of course design and no discrimination is intended by the use of the masculine pronoun 'he'.

Arno Gego, 2006

1 THE HISTORY OF EQUESTRIAN SPORT AND THE DEVELOPMENT OF SHOW-JUMPING AND COURSE DESIGN

The known history of the ancestor of the modern horse, eohippus, dates back about 50 to 60 million years, long before the first appearance of our own ancestor, *Homo sapiens*, whose evolution is thought to have begun around 50,000 years ago [017/083/140].

However, it was only with the invention of the wheel (figure 1.1) around 4,000–3,500 BC in Mesopotamia, the 'land between two rivers', the Euphrates and the Tigris, that the horse entered history's field of vision [083/140].

The roots of equestrian sport reach far back into antiquity, and there is much early evidence of it in the Near East, the Middle East and the Far East [017/042/083/140].

The oldest literature dealing specifically with the subject of horses was discovered in an archive of clay tablets in Bongazköy in Turkey and dates from around the sixteenth century BC. This text covers both the training of chariot horses and the breaking in of imported horses [006].

Figure 1.1: *An early type of wheel* [083].

Reports of races on horseback and in chariots appeared in India and Persia as early as 1000 BC [006/140]. At the same time, various horse races, equestrian games and chariot races were also held in many Asian countries, from Central Asia through China to Japan. The Medes and Persians are believed to have invented the game of polo which later spread to India and, from there, was taken up by British sportsmen.

The first chariot race with horses (*quadriga*) at the Olympic Games in Greece took place in 680 BC (figure 1.2). The term 'hippodrome' comes from the ancient Greek word *hippodromos* and translates as 'race track for horses'. It refers to a sports stadium in which horse races took place: at first chariot races but later also horse races under saddle. The sports complex of ancient Olympia is known to have had a hippodrome [159].

During the time of the Roman Empire, the size of the hippodrome was imposing [206], measuring 600 m in length and 200 m in width. These dimensions give us some idea of the important position occupied by equestrian sport at the Olympic Games of antiquity. As still happens today with the human 100-m sprint, the finalists of the *quadriga* races were selected by competing in several preliminaries before reaching the winning round, viewed by a maximum of 320,000 spectators.

The first chariot pairs races took place at the ninety-third Olympic Games in 408 BC, and later horse races with jockeys were also included.

As well as being a sporting competition, Olympia was also a place of intellectual exchanges and contests in which writers, poets, rhetoricians (public speakers) and other thinkers addressed the public directly about their work and their concerns. So the early Olympic movement in Greece was not just a matter of competition and sportsmanship, but a complex movement in which the promotion of youth, science, poetry, politics, art, aesthetics and society was actively represented alongside the sport of the adult elite [159].

Xenophon, military commander and pupil of the Greek philosopher Socrates, wrote a noted work as early as 400 BC, entitled *On the Art of Horsemanship* [184]. Chariot races were also popular in later times among the Etruscans and the Romans

Figure 1.2: *Pelops and Hippodameia on a* quadriga *(fifth century BC) [159].*

and in the Middle Ages the martial games of the aristocracy dominated tournaments [093] (figure 1.3).

Because of its importance in the cultural history of so many peoples, the horse has always held a place of special significance through the millennia:

Figure 1.3: *Tournament in the arena of the Vatican City, Rome, Carneval 1565 [093].*

- for mobilising the military (the predominant task of the horse until the Second World War);

- for general transport;

- to a limited degree for the purposes of sport, prestige and status (such as festival processions, chariot races, horse games, ring spearing, etc.) even in more recent history;

- as a means of travel for the aristocracy and other rich persons of high rank;

- in sport (until the Second World War almost exclusively among the aristocracy but later also among military riders);

- in later centuries as a replacement for oxen and mules in agriculture, as draught animals for pulling ploughs, harrows, etc.

Horse races have been held in Chester, England since 1511. It quickly became a British national sport and was first introduced in Europe in the nineteenth century.

As the importance of court stables and royal and military riding schools grew (figure 1.4), a number of treatises on riding were published from the sixteenth century onwards, by, for example:

- Federico Grisone of Italy, *Gli Ordine de Cavalcare*, Naples (1552);

- Pignatelli, head of the Naples Equestrian Academy, a pupil of Grisone;

- Antoine de Pluvinel of France, a pupil of Pignatelli, *Manège du Roi* (1623) [075];

ANYTHING FORCED OR MISUNDERSTOOD, CAN NEVER BE BEAUTIFUL.

(Xenophon, Greece, 400 BC)

THIS IS THE FUNDAMENTAL NOTION OF CLASSICAL BEAUTY; BEAUTY BASED ON HARMONY, ORDER, MODERATION AND THE FOLLOWING OF NATURE!

THE VERY NOTIONS THAT MEN OF THE 17TH CENTURY – AND WITH THEM PLUVINEL – STRESSED.

(Le Manège Royal, [215])

- the first Duke of Newcastle in England contributed a major publication [075] in 1657, although this was soon outdated because of the crude methods it advocated;

- in 1733, François Robichon de la Guérinière of France (1687–1751), commander of the Louis XIV riding school at Versailles, wrote a major text entitled *Ecole de Cavalerie* which is still regarded as an important work today [075];

- James Fillis (1834–1913) published a work entitled *Breaking and Riding*. Fillis was an artist and a successful circus rider, but his success in the field of classical equitation was rather short-lived, although his horses could canter on three legs, for example, and also backwards [140].

AT THE BEGINNING OF THE EIGHTEENTH CENTURY, EUROPEAN EQUITATION WAS ALMOST EXCLUSIVELY UNDER THE INFLUENCE OF FRANCE. AT THE TIME, THE GREAT MASTER OF RIDING, DE LA GUERINIERE, WROTE ONE OF THE MOST IMPORTANT BOOKS ON HORSEMANSHIP OF ALL TIMES [023/075], WHICH HAD AN ALMOST REVOLUTIONARY IMPACT. HIS WORK DISTINGUISHES ITSELF BY ... ITS SPECIAL CLARITY!

(Alois Podhajsky of Austria, third in dressage at the 1936 Olympic Games in Berlin [154])

Figure 1.4: *A medieval knight in tournament north of the Alps (Ritterspiele) [093].*

EQUESTRIAN SPORT IN PERFECTION IS AN ART LIKE BALLET, DANCING, THEATRE OR CONCERT.

(Georges Louis Leclerc Buffon, (1707–88), natural scientist)

Round about the eighteenth century, manège riding assumed a certain importance among the upper classes in European cities, but was later rejected, in France and Italy for example, as a useful basis for military cross-country riding because it lacked naturalness.

The Campagne School (table 1.1), which developed in the eighteenth and nineteenth centuries, particularly suited military horses because it combined dressage-type training and the 'forward school' (*sempre avanti*) in the best possible way.

Gustav Steinbrecht [163] of Germany was considered to be the only early German representative of the high school of dressage and was reputed to be able to combine dressage and the forward school in a perfect way.

De la Guérinière called his school Ecole de Cavalerie and this strongly influenced the development of the Campagne School. Of course, the mounted military units, the cavalry, had long perfected jumping on horseback in order to get over natural obstacles in the countryside (ditches, hedges, walls, gates, etc.). Fox-hunting, which had been practised in the British Isles in particular since the eighteenth century, also required horses to jump over natural obstacles.

Table 1.1: *The development of 'Campagne' riding 1700–1900*

de la Guérinière/FRA 1733, 'Ecole de Cavalerie'

(Haute) Ecole de Dressage

'Riding to War'

Cross-country Riding

General von Seydlitz/GER and others in the 18th/19th century up to Caprilli (main activities 1892/1902)

School of 'Campagne-Riding'

Features of Military Horses

- Gymnastic ability
- Balance
- Obedience
- Impulsion
- Speed/*Vitesse*
- Superior Cross-country abilities
- '*Sempre avanti*' – (Caprilli) Endurance

The famous Royal Cavalry School in Saumur, France [083/099], with its celebrated Cadre Noir, was founded around 1789, based on a smaller, earlier establishment in the same place.

The Grand National steeplechase, the most important and most difficult hurdles race in the world (length approx. 7,190 m [4 miles/836 yards] with 32 obstacles) was founded in 1836 near Liverpool, England.

However, it is the First Horse Show of the Royal Dublin Society in Ireland in 1864 that is considered to be the birth of modern equestrian sport, and thus also of show-jumping. It was also the first time that two jumping competitions were held which were designed to test the suitability of horses for fox-hunting [006].

Just two years later, in 1866, the first *Concours Central* took place in Paris over a period of several weeks. From 1872 onwards, this was supplemented by the *Concours Régionaux* in Bordeaux, Vichy, Nancy and Lille, organised by the '*Société Hippique Française*' [006].

These *concours* heralded the birth of modern equestrian sport which triggered a large number of new and very different equestrian activities in Europe, especially in Italy, Austria, France, Belgium, Germany, the Netherlands, Switzerland, Spain and the former Czechoslovakia.

In the USA, too, the development of modern equestrian sport started around 1870–80. Upperville in Virginia, Lakefield in Connecticut and Springfield in Massachusetts all claim to have been the 'first' place to host modern competitions [006].

In the early years, the programme usually comprised six different jumping classes, including:

- high jump;

- long jump;

- knock out/fault and out.

Comparison of the early high jump records (table 1.2) shows (figures 1.5 and 1.6) the enormous appeal and importance attached to this discipline in the USA. This may in part have been due to the aspirations of a new, young country where horse breeding was not run on traditional European lines and there was no culture of sporting aristocracy.

The first National Horse Show took place in 1883 in Madison Square Garden in New York, one of the earliest indoor events.

Progress towards modern equestrian sport continued until the turn of the century in 1900, and a large number of new tournaments were now held regularly; for example, in Barcelona, Berlin, Brussels, Lisbon, London, Lucerne, Maastricht, Rome, Spa Francorchamps, Turin, Vienna, etc.

Table 1.2: *Early high jump records in the USA and Europe*

Place		Horse	Rider	Height (m) Official Test	Unofficial Test
1883 1884 1888 1891	New York/USA National Horse Show, Madison Square Garden	Leo	USA USA USA USA	1.83 1.98 2.08 2.16	-- -- -- --
1902	1. CHI Torino/ITA	Meloppo	Capt. Frederico Caprilli	2.08	--
1902	Richmond/VI/USA	Heatherbloom	Dick Donelly/USA	2.40	--
				--	2.49
				--	2.515
1904	San Sebastian/ESP	Conspirateur	Capt. Crousse/FRA	2.23	--

Figure 1.5: *1902 Richmond, VI, USA. Dick Donelly, USA with Heatherbloom. Official measurement 2.40 m – unofficial 2.49 and 2.515 m [006].*

Figure 1.6: *High jump in San Sebastian, Spain 1904 (2.23 m) [006].*

As well as the New York National Horse Show, a small number of other tournaments were held overseas, for example in Buenos Aires.

The historical roots of individual tournaments were quite different.

- Aachen, Germany: horse races in the nineteenth century [107]

- Dublin, Ireland: horse breeding, military, fox-hunting/cross-country

- Paris, France: horse breeding and military

- Spa Francorchamps, Belgium: no traditional links to horses (no horse breeding in Belgium at that time)

- Yverdon, Switzerland: horse races and horse breeding

to mention but a few.

In Italy, from 1892, Lieutenant Federico Caprilli [006], a riding instructor in Tor di Quinto, achieved sensational success and caused a great stir with his new style of jumping (figure 1.7), preferring a light, forward seat. After initial resistance, his new jumping school in Italy quickly and successfully established itself, but was still strongly opposed in the northern European countries, especially by the military (figure 1.8) and traditionalists who clung to their 'die-hard' attitudes.

In 1842, even before Caprilli, an equerry of the duchy of Nassau, Karl Kegel, had produced a book [006] about the *Latest theory of horsemanship, based on common-sense principles*, and in this he wrote about the new 'approach when crossing obstacles and ditches'. His teaching concurred with Caprilli's in regard to leaning forward when jumping, but was not yet accepted in his own German environment which was dominated by the military approach.

Spa Francorchamps in Belgium did not feel the need to follow tradition and attracted attention from around 1900 with new ideas and initiatives.

Figure 1.7: *Lt Federico Caprilli of Italy [111].*

- As early as around 1900, prize-money of 100,000 francs was awarded for jumping competitions alone (this was a considerable amount of money).

- This is where the triple bar was invented (figure 1.8).

- This is where an open ditch (Trakehner) 1.5 m deep and with a 1.25 m high wall behind it was first used.

- Various other combined, fixed natural obstacles (for example, an Irish bank with small water ditches in front and behind) echoed the natural outdoor environment.

Figure 1.8: *Traditional (stiff) jumping style. (Left) at Spa, Francorchamps, Belgium 1899, showing the newly invented triple bar [006].*

Figure 1.9: *Fitness, courage and beauty [220].*

These innovations gradually spread throughout Europe.

At the end of the nineteenth century, the first important equestrian magazines were published, such as:

- 1884 *Horse and Hound,* Great Britain;

- 1894 *Le Sport Universel Illustré,* France ;

- 1900 *St. Georg,* Germany.

By the turn of the century, a rich and varied programme of equestrian events was already in place within the various disciplines:

- the 'military', today called eventing (figure 1.9);

- dressage;

- jumping;

- driving;

Figure 1.10: *The Olympic Games, Stockholm 1912* [221].

- endurance;

- high jump;

- long jump.

In 1902, the first Concorso Ippico Internazionale di Torino took place in Turin in Italy. Thanks to the great successes of the Italian jumpers, the *sistema Caprilli* (style of Caprilli) gained worldwide recognition. However, after the shattering defeat of his military jumpers in Turin, the German Emperor imposed a ban preventing German jumpers from competing abroad. The Russians, too, distanced themselves from Fillis's teachings.

Also in 1902, the first Championat du Cheval d'Armes took place in Paris. This was an early form of present-day eventing. In 1905, a three-day eventing competition was organised for the first time in Brussels. This event was now called a 'military', a term that remained in usage in Germany until the end of the last century and has only recently been replaced with the term *Vielseitigkeit* (French: *concours complet*).

After nearly ten years of isolation imposed by the German Emperor, an International Equestrian Tournament was held in Frankfurt in 1910 (the first CSI in Germany), with guests from Belgium, Austria and Hungary. The Germans had by now given up their antiquated jumping style in favour of Caprilli's style and were able to register corresponding successes.

Some sources believe that equestrian sport was represented for the first time in the modern era at the 1912 Olympic Games in Stockholm [006/096] (figure 1.10). The jumping course ran over 19 obstacles up to a maximum height of 1.40 m, with a 4-m wide water jump. The treble combination led across a wall to a water jump to a wall and the distance between each of the obstacles was 8 m.

The Swedes were outstanding. Baron Clarence von Rosen of Sweden had developed an Olympic equestrian sports programme that formed the basis for today's three-discipline concept. Only dressage was not yet represented as a team competition.

However, Lenz [096] claims that it was not at the 1912 Stockholm Olympics that equestrian competitions were included for the first time in the modern era, but that:

- at the Olympic Games in Paris (14 May to 28 October 1900, organised in conjunction with the World Exhibition), the disciplines of prize jumping (now show-jumping), high jump and long jump, were already on the programme;

- while at the Olympic Games in London in 1908, even polo was on the programme as a discipline for the first time, though it was only repeated again at Olympic level in 1920, 1924 and 1936;

- vaulting was included as an Olympic competition for the first and last time in 1920 at the Olympic Games of the modern era in Antwerp, in response to a request from the host country, Belgium, and was called 'artistic riding';

- the disciplines of record high and long jump were important at the end of the nineteenth and during the first half of the twentieth centuries but this declined to a large extent later on (table 1.3).

On 28 May 1921, the FEI was founded at the Olympic Congress and its head office was established in Lausanne, Switzerland. The eight founding countries were Belgium, France, Italy, Japan, the Netherlands, Norway, Sweden and the USA. The language of the IOC, FEI and most international federations was French.

COMPETITION HORSES

For millennia, until the Second World War, the development of the art of riding was predominantly shaped by military imperatives because the horse was the only animal able to give man clear military advantages. This situation persisted until motor-powered inventions of the modern era, such as the automobile, aircraft, all-terrain

Table 1.3 *High jump and long jump records in the twentieth century*

Year	Place	Rider	High Jump Height (m) official	Long Jump Distance (m) official
1912	Vittel/FRA	--	2.36	
1933	Paris/FRA	Lt de Castries/FRA	2.38	
1938	Rome/ITA	Capt. Guitierrez/ITA	2.44	
1947	Argentina	Lt Jorge Fraga P./ARG	--	7.70
1947	Quillota/CHI	Lt Alberto Laraguibel/CHI	2.47	
1951	Spain	Lt Lopez del Hierro/ESP	--	8.30
1975	South Africa	André Ferreira/RSA	--	8.40

vehicles and long-distance weapons, completely changed the face of armed forces and of warfare itself.

Until that time, however, most rulers and nations were forced to accept that horse breeding and schooling and horsemanship were extremely important strategic factors in the winning of military battles.

Commanders needed horse breeds that were suitable for use in battle and were:

- well trained under saddle and/or for drawing a carriage;

- obedient, with maximum suitability for cross-country riding;

- easy to manage;

- blessed with stamina;

- undemanding;

- adaptable in every respect (climate, fodder, type of deployment, etc.);

- 'team players or partners' that would go through 'thick and thin';

to cite only a few essential characteristics.

Another extremely important aspect during the nineteenth and twentieth centuries was the representation of the military at the highest level of the sport. The best military officers were not only expected to be the best in combat, but also the best in equestrian sport!

It is against this background that we should consider:

- the objectives of the Campagne School;

- the significance of the optimum combination of the art of dressage (High School) and the Forward School;

- the very high standards of the military riding schools before the Second World War, especially in Argentina, Brazil, Chile, Czechoslovakia, France, Germany, Great Britain, Ireland, Italy, Japan, Mexico, Poland, Portugal, Romania, Spain, Sweden and Switzerland.

From the time when Caprilli first began his work in Italy, at the end of the nineteenth century, to the start of the Second World War in 1939, the general school of jumping made significant progress in theory and practice in many countries. This is essentially due to the development and endeavour of the many military riding schools, whose task it was to participate successfully in international equestrian tournaments for the glory of their home country. Especially in Europe, the number of tournaments increased steadily. The Nations Cup and the GRAND PRIX at tournaments such as Aachen, Dublin, Rome, Lucerne, Nice, Allenstein, London (later Hickstead), Fontainebleau and

Figure 1.11: *Freiherr von Langen, master and aesthete, Olympic winner in dressage, Amsterdam 1928; also winner of many GRAND PRIX in jumping and military (eventing) [222].*

many others enjoyed great prestige. Prominent civilian riders, for example Freiherr von Langen (figure 1.11), were the great exception to the rule in the 1920s.

The dominance of military riding in Europe before the Second World War can be seen from the example of Belgium [024], where some 'civilian riders', referred to as the *Habits Rouges* or red coats, united in the mid-1930s in order to:

- organise tournaments for civilian riders in Belgium;

- organise participation in tournaments abroad (*Club des Habits Rouges de Belgique*) [024/104].

- Following the Second World War, 'rural' riding formed the basis for the continuation of equestrian sport and breeding but it is worth remembering that of the 54 starters in the jumping test at the 1936 Olympic Games in Berlin, 51 were military riders.

It is interesting to note that, to this day, many important large outdoor tournaments, such as Aachen, Calgary, Falsterbo, Hickstead, La Baule, Monterrey, St Gallen and Valkenswaard, all take place in rather small towns and villages, while large indoor competitions are often held in the great cities, such as Amsterdam, Berlin, Brussels, Geneva, London, New York, Paris, Toronto and Washington. There are good reasons for this.

The development of show-jumping, since the beginning of the nineteenth century, essentially has three important roots (table 1.4):

Table 1.4 *The development of jumping sport (a simplified explanation)*

- riding to hunt (including fox-hunting);

- outdoor military riding (figure 1.9), with many different challenges (topography, natural obstacles such as lakes, water courses, fences, walls, paddock gates, open or forested country, firm or wet ground, etc.);

- flat races and later also hurdles races (steeplechases).

It is important to be aware of this when analysing the development of course building in the last century.

Early examples (figure 1.12) lead to the following observations.

- The lines of the courses are simple (the Olympic Games in Amsterdam in 1928 and in Berlin in 1936).

- The obstacle designs are largely borrowed from nature and the landscape (something often lacking today!).

- The tracks of big jumping classes are long and some have more than 20 jumps (normally 1.30 to 1.50 m [1.60 m] high and up to 2.20 m wide).

- The alteration of the line is minimal, as is the number of changes of rein.

The 1925 Aachen GRAND PRIX had no change of rein, despite a 'bold loop' in the final part. The line of the course, oriented along the perimeter, reveals the importance of horse-racing in Aachen in the nineteenth century [107/109/174].

Course design was not considered very important in the first half of the last century, as can clearly be seen from table 1.5.

- In 1937, the CHIO Aachen had 39 judges and other members of the Ground Jury (predominantly aristocracy and military), and there was only one man [109] (retired equerry Wilhelm Morgen) responsible for obstacles!

It should be said at this point that course design was not a traditional responsibility in competition sport, but a new one, the importance of which has only slowly been recognised. This also explains why, in both theory and practice, course design definitely lagged behind jumping until the start of the second half of the last century.

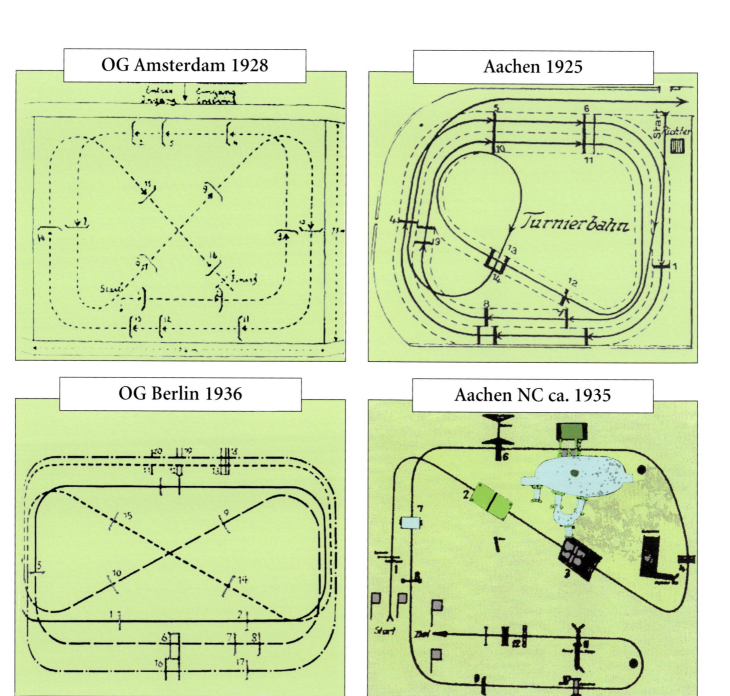

Figure 1.12 *Early lines of major GRAND PRIX and Nations Cup, 1925–36.*

THEORY IS KNOWLEDGE,
PRACTICE IS ABILITY.
BUT KNOWLEDGE SHOULD ALWAYS
PRECEDE ACTION.

(Alois Podhajsky, Olympic medal winner Berlin 1936, and
longstanding director of the Spanish Riding School in Vienna)

Table 1.5: *Judges and course designers, CHIO Aachen 1937 and 2002*

1937	2002 (FEI Officials)
• 19 Judges (4 countries) • 20 Members of Appeal Committee (19 Countries) • 1 Gentleman for 'obstacles' Most of them have been military officers	• 5 Judges • 2 Assistant Judges • 3 Judges for national competitions • 3 Members of Appeal Committee • 1 Course Designer • 6 Co-course designers (including 3 women) • 6 Guest Course Designers (from Belgium, Brazil, Mexico, Iran and Spain)

Until that time course building was usually referred to as obstacle building and was regarded as a manual task which was not sufficiently challenging for higher ranking officers. This image changed noticeably after the Second World War when high-ranking military officers began to take up course design.

General Lombardi of Italy (winner of the Aachen GRAND PRIX in 1930), Colonel Brinckmann of Germany (figure 1.13), Dr de Némethy of the USA, Colonel Hamon of France, Colonel Anselm of Great Britain (all former members of great military riding schools), Pamela Carruthers of Great Britain and others were instrumental in pushing course design forward between 1950 to 1955, especially with regard to:

- more movement and variety in the track (musical, flowing lines);

- new ideas for obstacle design and more variety in the obstacles (different ones for each big showground);

- emphasising the extreme importance of large, grass stadiums;

- the creation of new, large stadiums with permanent natural obstacles (for example, Calgary, Hickstead, Monterrey and Valkenswaard);

- the promotion and development of large showgrounds of world stature.

Figure 1.13: *Col. Hans-Heinrich (Micky) Brinckmann, CSIO Rome 1939 [111].*

The study of a few randomly selected course lines, from 1952 to the present (figures 1.14–1.23) gives an example of the development of course design, and especially of the track, from initially simple to more flowing and more individual lines which are also increasingly the signature of individual course designers.

What is also remarkable is that the influence of former members of once famous military riding schools persisted far into the second half of the twentieth century in influential positions of management in equestrian sport (judges, course designers, trainers, officials, etc.).

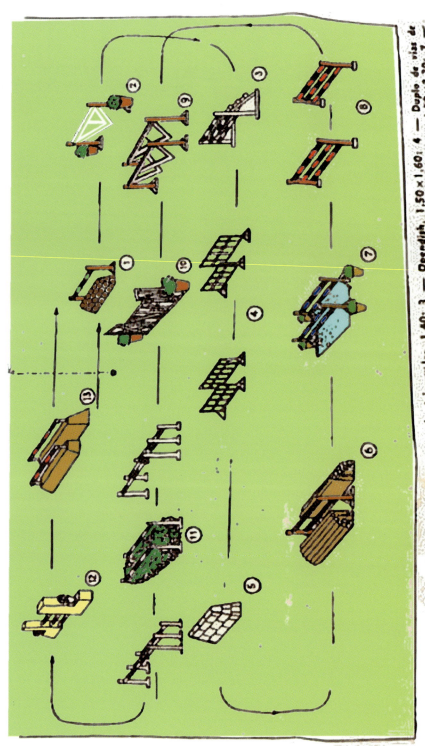

Figure 1.14: *GRAND PRIX, Lisbon, Portugal 1952.*

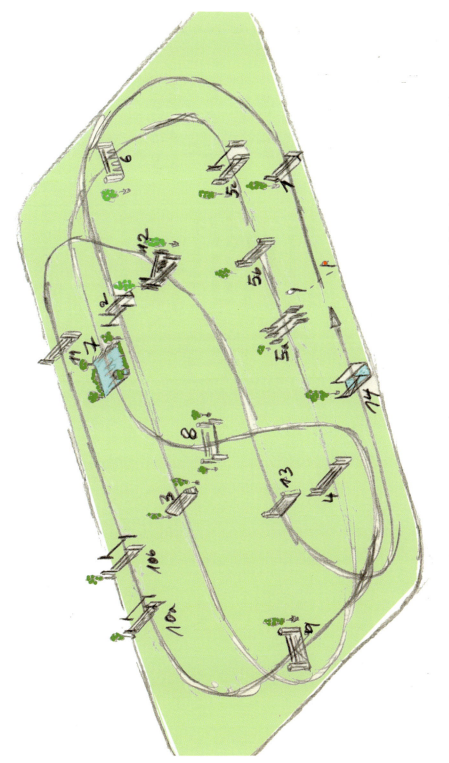

Figure 1.15: *Olympic Games, Rome 1960, Nations Cup. Course designer: Gen. Lombardi. (Freehand drawing: Arno Gego, 1962)*

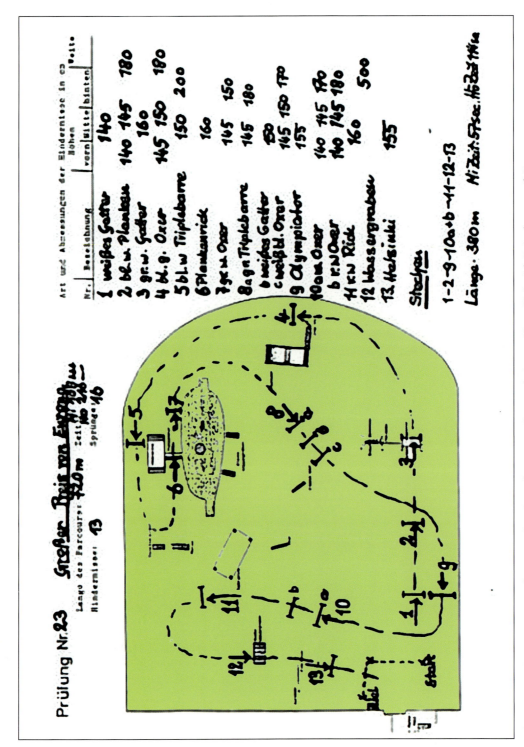

Figure 1.16: *GRAND PRIX of Europe, CHIO Aachen 1968. Course designer: Hans-Heinrich Brinckmann of Germany.*

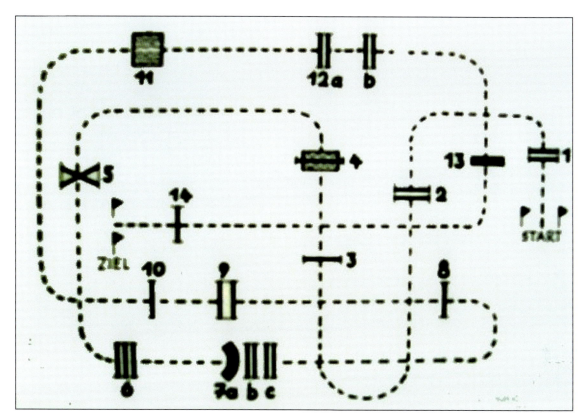

Figure 1.17: *Nations Cup, Olympic Games, Mexico City 1968. Course designer: Col. Ruben Uriza of Mexico.*

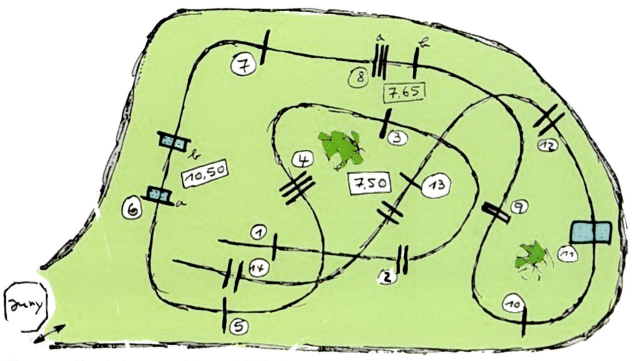

Figure 1.18: *Olympic Games, Munich 1972, individual competition, first round. Course designer: Hans-Heinrich Brinckmann of Germany.*

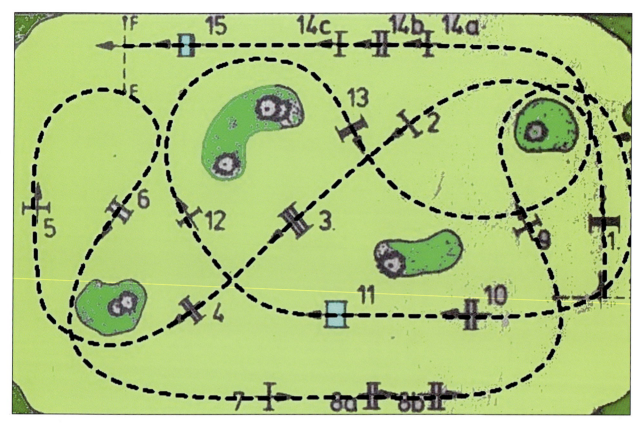

Figure 1.19: *Olympic Games, Seoul 1988, Nations Cup. Course designer: Olaf Petersen of Germany.*

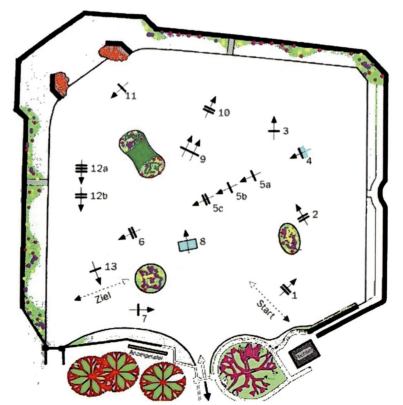

Figure 1.20: *Olympic Games, Atlanta 1996, Nations Cup. Course designer: Linda Allen of the USA.*

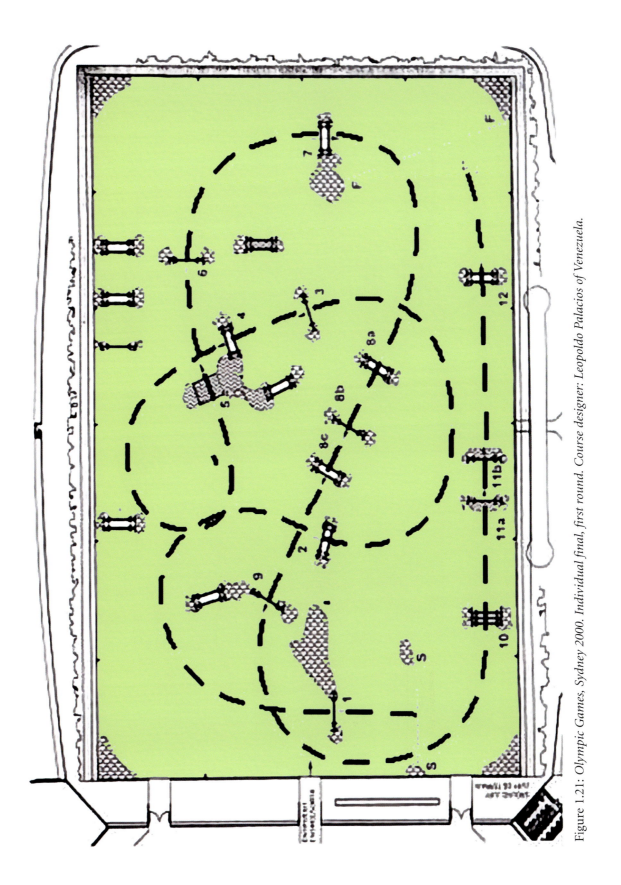

Figure 1.21: Olympic Games, Sydney 2000. Individual final, first round. Course designer: Leopoldo Palacios of Venezuela.

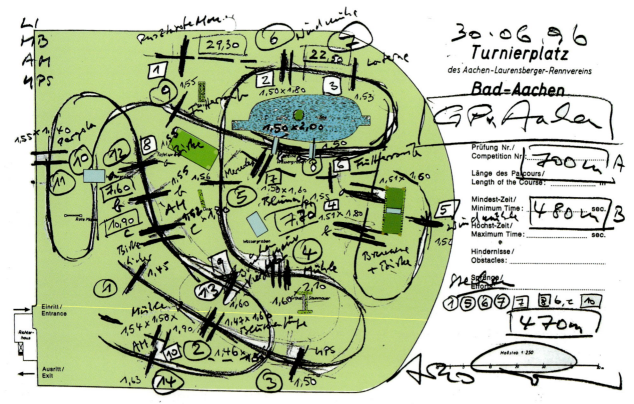

Figure 1.22: GRAND PRIX of Aachen, CHIO Aachen, Germany 1996. Course designer: Arno Gego.

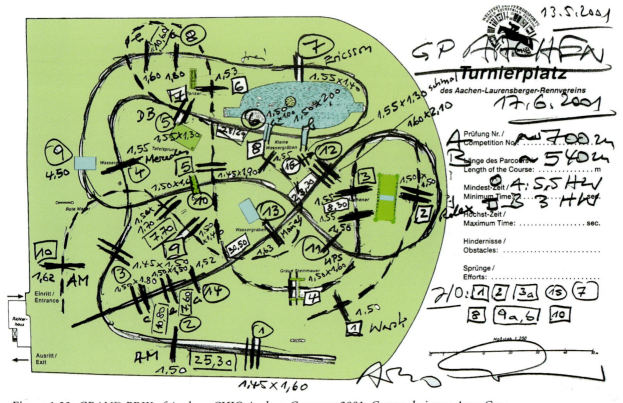

Figure 1.23: GRAND PRIX of Aachen, CHIO Aachen, Germany 2001. Course designer: Arno Gego.

2 THE DEFINITION AND AIMS OF COURSE DESIGN

Ever since athletic contests were first invented, there has also been a need for judges, referees, appeal committee members, etc. to adjudicate about outright victory or to agree on the ranking of winners and losers [159/186].

At the top level of sports such as golf, Formula 1 motor-racing or steeplechasing, there are experts who individually design, create and build the appropriate sports fields, tracks, showgrounds, etc. [189].They mostly work as a team, consisting, for example, of landscape or sports ground architects and experts in the particular sports discipline. In show-jumping, jumping stadiums, showgrounds, etc. are designed and created according to the same principles.

What they all have in common is that, ideally, traditional showgrounds, stadiums, etc. are developed gradually, without losing their character. Venues which best reflect this gradual development are the showgrounds in Aachen, Calgary, Monterrey and Rome, or the tennis courts at Wimbledon.

Major changes or complete redesigns only take place if there are important reasons, such as safety or capacity. Moving the venue is usually the kiss of death, as the example of moving from Madison Square Garden in New York to an anonymous indoor arena in Newark, New Jersey, has proved over the last 15 years.

The difference between show-jumping and most other types of sport is the addition of a dominant, individual design component.

- The course designer designs and creates an individual course, with all the specific requirements for each jumping competition.

- For 'his course', the course designer takes responsibility for specifying all the technical, physical, psychological and emotional aspects, specifically the dimensions, distances, visual aspects, colours, length of the course, rhythm, focal points, individuality, positioning and space design, knock-down behaviour, symmetries, overall presentation, etc.

The course designer is therefore the one person solely responsible for the quality, standard, requirement profile, fairness and originality of every single jumping competition, and is expected to demonstrate a high degree of creativity while also safeguarding the sport's traditions and fair play. In addition to a thorough knowledge of the sport, this involves an understanding of aesthetics, ethics, history, culture and, in the best cases, even art.

Figure 2.1: *Olaf Petersen (left) and Arno Gego, CHIO Aachen 1985. Photo: private collection.*

The course for a GRAND PRIX, for example, involves the building of a course in a given tournament situation, which will form the basis for a jumping competition whose design is very much determined by:

- the competition format;

- the line of the course (*musicalité des lignes*);

- the distribution of obstacles, types of obstacles and combinations;

- the optimum use of space (grid);

- ideas for decoration and colour;

- dimensions and distances;

- dramatic ideas (a planned progression of tension).

As the basis of a very detailed MASTERPLAN, it is not unlike the creation of a musical score.

The MASTERPLAN is a product of intellect (thinking) and emotion (feeling), and determines the rhythm and alternative choices of obstacles, as well as the quality, appeal, uniqueness and tension of the sport from the point of view of the spectators and athletes.

Figure 2.2: *Jon Doney of Great Britain (left). Photo by Christa Heibach*

Figure 2.3: *(From left) Arno Gego, Linda Allen, Harry Cornford and Javier Fernandez, CSIO Mexico 1988. Photo: private collection.*

The tournament situation referred to above might be described by:

- its historic status and image;

- its FEI/NF status as a showground and jumping stadium;

- the class and importance of the event, the jumping competition and the quality of the competitors;

- the amount of prize-money;

- the layout and design, dimensions and condition of the footing in the actual jumping area (grass, sand, permanent natural obstacles, etc.);

- the structure of the jumping arena's periphery (position of judges' box, entrance/exit, show secretary's office, competitors' stands, hospitality, press, sponsor area, distribution of stands, observation points, lawns, etc.);

- the position of the practice arena, stables, parking areas, restaurants, etc.;

- the infrastructure in general (short or long distances etc.), landscape, greenery, décor;

- other factors that will influence the atmosphere.

Certainly, not all tournaments, courses and MASTERPLANS can meet the standard described here. However, perfect course design is an art form that draws on landscape design, arts and crafts and painting and music, using the foundations of jumping as a base – it is choreography for jumping!

As is the case with many other creative tasks, the course designer is at the interface of a large number of other, very different influences (table 2.1) which inform his work. A course designer working at a given showground goes through the following major creative stages in the process of building a complete course ready for competition.

Table 2.1: *The theoretical structure of course design*

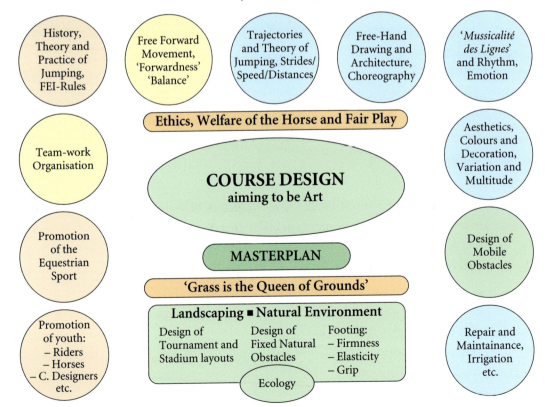

1 **Internalising (inwardly digesting) the showground** with all its complex individual details, such as:

- size of the showground, geometry, type, dimensions and position of permanent (natural) obstacles;

- soil condition in different weather conditions;

- topography, gradient of land and minor surface undulations;

- micro-climate over the sports area and general weather conditions;

- changes in light conditions through the day during the competition period (especially the path of the sun);

- position of the judges' box, entrance and exit;

- distribution of spectators at the main events;

- position of TV cameras, visibility;

- visibility of the course for the spectators;

- scope, technical features and quality of the obstacle material;

- position of the storage area for the obstacle material and means of transport (low-pressure tyres to protect the ground);

- general design of décor;

- technology and organisation of maintenance of the obstacle material and the surface, including an automatic sprinkler installation.

No doubt there will be many other aspects. Nobody should be more familiar with a showground than the course designer.

It goes without saying that many of the aspects referred to above either do not exist on a flat sand arena or are of less importance. That is just one reason why natural grass surfaces are more interesting from a sports point of view as well as being more challenging than small sanded arenas.

Figure 2.4: *(From left) Christa Heibach, Harry Cornford and Arno Gego, CSI Monterrey, Mexico 1994. Photo by John Weier.*

Internalising a showground may require many visits, with inspection from different perspectives, and it may sometimes take several years until sufficient knowledge has been acquired.

The possession of a totally accurate surveyor's plan is by no means proof of adequate knowledge or internalisation. A jumping stadium is not a drawing board!

2 Preparing a course MASTERPLAN

Just like a score by a composer, so a freehand MASTERPLAN (produced with the help of a soft pencil and an eraser) is the creative result for a course designer (figure 2.5). It is a unique piece of work and will contain all important information including, among other things:

- the track, for two rounds where appropriate;

- the distribution of the obstacles (grid, covering the outer track);

- types of obstacles;

- dimensions;

- major distances;

- main colours and obstacle material;

- distribution of the main obstacle material, designs and sponsors' obstacles;

- the track for jump-offs;

- approximate lengths of course (first and second round and jump-off).

The MASTERPLAN for an outstanding GRAND PRIX-level competition may well

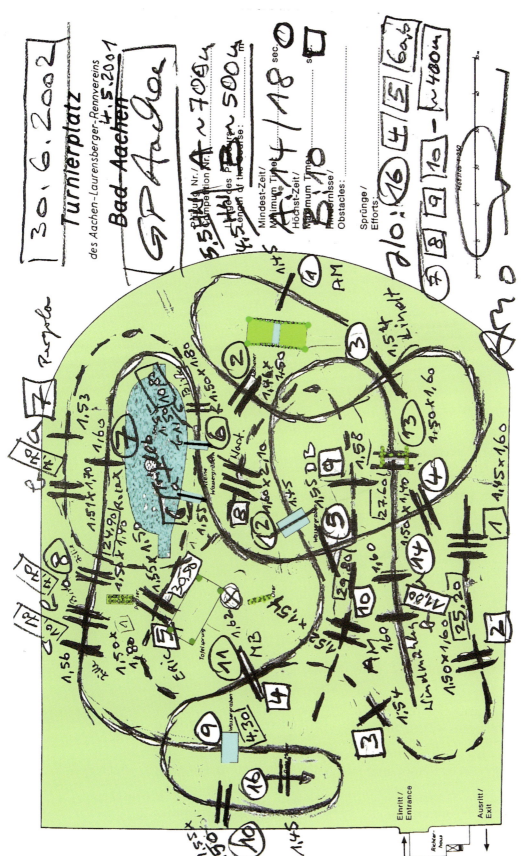

Figure 2.5: *GRAND PRIX of Aachen, CHIO Aachen 2002. Course designer: Arno Gego.*

Figure 2.6: *Ron Southern (right) and Arno Gego, CSI-W Palm Beach 2004. Photo by Christa Heibach.*

take days or weeks to produce. 'Only "idiots" always have a quick solution' (Le Corbusier) [094]. The MASTERPLAN demands a high degree of sensitivity and intellectual effort.

A most interesting theoretical approach to the design process of a course landscape in a major outdoor jumping stadium can be gleaned from the thoughts of landscape architect Robert Thayer [170] (figure 2.7):

1   From a subjective, three-dimensional structure of ideas (A) with the co-ordinates of:

   • perception

   • function and

   • symbolism,

there results a dynamic

2   intellectual-emotional interaction of the course designer (B) which leads to

3   the theoretical model of a stadium course landscape (C), which is clearly influenced, if not actually dominated by the polarity of:

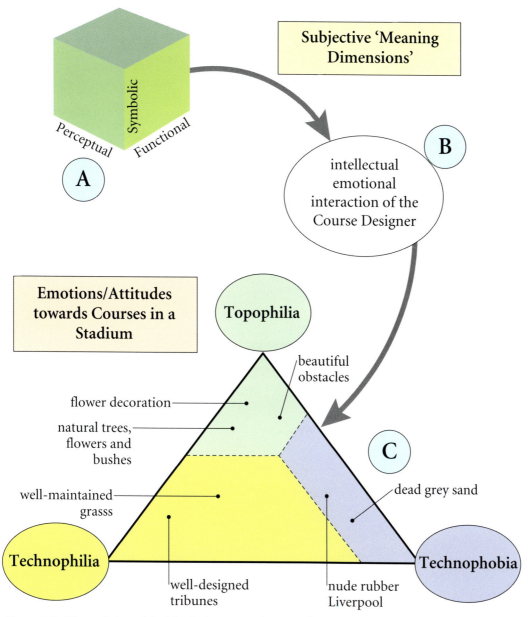

Figure 2.7: *Theoretical model of the design process in natural surroundings (after Robert Thayer).*

- topophilia (roughly, a positive attitude to the landscape);

- technophilia (roughly, a positive attitude to technology); and

- technophobia (roughly, an aversion to technology).

This theoretical construct then forms the basis of the concrete MASTERPLAN for the course of a top-level jumping competition, as, for example, a GRAND PRIX.

AN ARTIST WHO WORKS WITHOUT ANY
THEORY IS LIKE A SKIPPER WHO RISKS
EMBARKING ON THE OCEAN WITHOUT A
RUDDER AND WITHOUT A COMPASS!

(Leonardo da Vinci, 1452–1511)

This theoretical concept, taken from landscape design, is interesting and remarkable in many respects.

1   The course designer's work can be enriched by stimuli and intellectual approaches if he also looks at related areas such as:

- technology

- design

- landscape architecture

- music

- painting and other art forms.

2   The model described by Robert Thayer is in harmony with the claim that equestrian sport is a nature-based sport.

3   The absence of topophilia clearly shows the inferior role of indoor equestrian sport, and the 'instability of a two-sided pyramid', no matter what the names, labels, logos, etc. may be.

Indoor sport is important and has its own value but it is not of Olympic stature. On the other hand, a view expressed by Jorge Johannpeter, rider and horse breeder from Porto Alegre, Brazil, is interesting. He attributes the great successes of the European riders at the Olympic Games and other top-level championships to the existence of many indoor competitions. Because of their frequent experience in indoor competitions, European horses have to be better trained, better schooled, more agile and more flexible in order to be consistently successful on small jumping arenas of between 1,200 and 3,000 m^2. This argument cannot be dismissed. However, neither should the positive effect of participating in a large number of competitions in Europe and the proximity of a highly developed horse breeding industry be underestimated.

Figure 2.8: *(From left) Arno Gego with Viktor Hauser, President CSIO Lucerne, and Paul Weier cosmopolitan hippologist. Photo by CHIO Aachen.*

3 Marking out the course

Marking out the course on the basis of the MASTERPLAN is the next creative stage.

- In the main arena, the course designer has by now internalised the arena layout sufficiently to walk along the intended track and specify the position of the obstacles (marked by poles), combinations and distances, which are then checked by staff with a tape measure.

- Before obstacle building starts, the course designer again checks the anticipated general layout before giving the go-ahead for the building of the obstacles.

Because of their generally low degree of complexity, course design and construction on small sand arenas, especially indoor arenas, take much less time and are simplified, often being reduced to the effective distribution of light and small hired obstacles.

4 Last checking inspection

On his last round, the course designer checks each detail, from start to finish, together with his co-course designer and assistants, looking at factors such as:

- knock-down behaviour ('manual check');

Figure 2.9: *(From left) Javier Ferndandez, Arno Gego and Leopoldo Palacios CSI at Monterrey, Mexico 1994. Photo by John Weier.*

- ground conditions;

- lines (are the obstacles really in alignment – a frequent building error!);

- visual aspect;

- dimensions;

- distances (one last check of combinations with a tape measure – measuring only the middle line – essential in order to verify planned distances);

- length of the course (a co-course designer or assistant measures the course at the same time);

- position of start and finish;

- checking the track of the jump-off course;

- visibility from the judges' box etc.

In isolated cases, this inspection round can also be done jointly with the ground jury (this was often done in GRAND PRIX-level competitions at the CHIO Aachen, with the chief judge Dr Dohn and, earlier, Ernst Gössing).

Because of the tight schedule of indoor shows, the inspection round is usually reduced to a few minutes' checking by the course designer and an assistant. However, fewer aspects will need to be checked here than at a large showground.

On the rare occasions when perfection is achieved, course design can come close to what the director of a dance academy in Mexico City called 'choreography for show-jumping'.

In some languages, it is difficult to find the proper terminology for a course designer (see table 2.2). It goes without saying that only terminology that reflects the main creative aspect of course design is acceptable.

The course designer is a creative designer and not someone who just 'puts up' the obstacles. National and international course designers should state this claim with confidence.

The course designer is someone who sets the rhythm of a course, who plans the tension and excitement for the spectators and competitors, preferably even in the preliminary round and also in smaller competitions, not just in the jump-off of a GRAND PRIX.

In addition, the course designer has a major input in the visual presentation of the showground, as part of the overall presentation of an equestrian tournament's character, which, in its totality, should be as distinctive, original and unique as possible. Hickstead would not be so interesting if it was identical to La Baule, Aachen to Rome, Calgary to St Gallen or Monterrey to Valkenswaard.

The foremost guide for the visual, architectural and aesthetic design of obstacles and courses should be a reference to nature and the natural environment, especially if the showground has a very distinctive character, a natural feel or a specific 'personality'.

The course designer's tools (table 2.3) are identical to those of the artist [153]:

Figure 2.10: *Last visit of Fritz Thiedemann (born 1918) to 'his CHIO Aachen 1988'. Photo by Susanne Gossen.*

Table 2.2: *The terminology for 'course designer' in different languages*

	Language	Creativity-oriented Terminology	Handcraft-oriented Terminology ('man with hammer')
1	Dutch	*- ? -*	*Parcours-bouwer*
2	English	*Course designer*	*Course-builder*
3	French	*Chef-de-piste*	*Constructeur*
4	German	*Parcours-Chef*	*Parcours-Bauer*
		Parcours-Gestalter	
		Parcours-Designer	
5	Italian	*Direttore di campo*	*- ? -*
6	Portuguese	*Desenhador de percoursos*	*Armador*
7	Scandinavian	*- ? -*	*Banebygger*
8	Spanish	*Diseñador de pistas*	*Armador*

- line

- form

- light

- colour

- space

- grid/frame

- symmetry (asymmetry).

These tools draw ingredients such as the landscape, the showground, the grass surface, flowers, wood, water, etc., into a general composition which is then presented in a complex MASTERPLAN which contains a large amount of information – starting with the course line (figure 2.5).

During this process, the course designer focuses in particular on the following objectives:

Table 2.3: *The design tools of the artist and/or course designer*

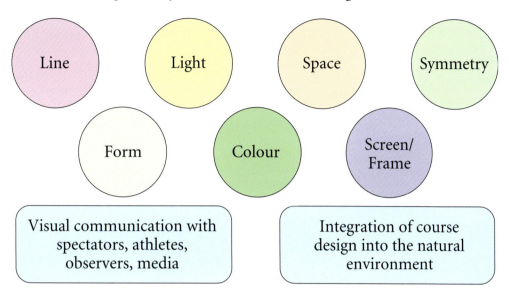

1   creating an attractive sport that appeals to spectators;

2   using interesting and rhythmical lines and aesthetically pleasing obstacles;

3   promoting the free forward movement of the horse;

4   developing and supporting young riders and horses at the grass roots of the sport and instilling a feeling for rhythm and free forward movement;

5   giving young riders and horses positive experiences and confidence (the challenges of top-level sport should most definitely not be transferred to sport at grass-roots level – after all, the training of young piano players doesn't begin with the music of Chopin which is very difficult and only for real masters of the piano);

6   verifying the type of competition, class, dimensions and rules;

7   balancing the different competition requirements, such as:

   ● physical and mental condition;

   ● scope and stamina;

   ● submissiveness (obedience);

- jumping ability;

- the horse's agility and talent for clean jumping;

- the rider's ability (physical and mental fitness, level-headedness, sensitivity with regard to the respective type of horse, horse management, etc.);

8   a maximum of variety and diversity, avoiding repetition;

9   introducing distance-related tasks only if horses and riders are prepared for them, and then only to a level at which they are sufficiently experienced to be able to handle them in a way that is pleasing to watch – a perceptive comment from Pamela Carruthers;

10   avoiding the risk of accidents (safer sport);

11   the course designer does not create problems; rather, he sets tests that can be solved in the context of the particular competition;

12   and not least:

- The responsible, master course designer works with a team of qualified co-course designers and assistants (table 2.4).

- Ideally, his team will include women and men because as course designers women have qualities that are often alien to men, such as a greater feeling for beauty, naturalness and overall presentation. Furthermore, women who are motivated to pursue a career in course design are usually keen and reliable.

- The occasional masculine phenomenon of machismo and alcohol is counter-productive.

13   the 'ideal' course designer is *primus inter pares* (first among equals) and conducts himself accordingly.

In addition to a sound knowledge of all sport and design aspects, the course designer must also be a good organiser, communicator, team player and teacher (table 2.5) in order to:

Table 2.4: *Course design CHIO Aachen 2002 – my dream team*

Function	Name	FEI-Status *	City	Country	CHIO since	Languages
Course Designers	Prof. Dr. Arno Gego **	O	Aachen	GER	1965	G,F,E, (I,S,P,Dutch)
	Werner Deeg **	O	Feuchtwangen	GER	1992	G,E,
	Christa Jung **	I	Heilbronn	GER	1985	G,,E, (F)
	Michael Gockel **	I	Duisburg	GER	1986	G,F,E,
Co-course Designers	Christa Heibach **	C	Aachen	GER	1988	G,E,(I,S,Dutch)
	Olaf Petersen jr **	C	München	GER	2000	G,E,F,(S)
	Ferdi Rosellen	I	Kerpen	GER	1986	G,(E)
	Mehves Trak **	I	Istanbul	TUR	1997	Tur,F,E,(G)
Guest Course Designers	Avelino Rodriguez Miravalles	O	Gijon	ESP, Course Designer WEG Jerez de la Frontera/ESP, 2002)		
	Luc Musette	I	Brüssel	BEL		
	Ali Mohajer Iravanloo	C	Teheran	Iran		
	Hossein Shaffiee	C	Teheran	Iran		

*   O   = Official International Course Designer
     I   = International Course Designer
     C   = Candidate International Course Designer
     N   = National Course Designer

**   Experience with computer-graphics and design

- actually translate theory into practice and produce, together with the team of co-course designers, assistants and construction workers, courses that have been meticulously planned, while also adhering to a timetable and ensuring the greatest quality of design;

- create a completely new overall image every time (rather like designing a stage set);

- integrate the interests of the media (particularly television) and sponsors (especially in regard to sponsored obstacles) in a fair, restrained and sympathetic way and to a high standard;

Table 2.5: *The hierarchy of responsibility*

Choreography	Team	Stage Scenery	Media, Sponsors	Development
• Concept of lines 'musicalité des lignes'	• Co-course designers, assistants and team of helpers	• Overall picture	• Communication	• New arenas, new footing technologies
• Optics, design, distances	• Communication	• Optical presentation in detail	• Sponsor-fences (max. 4 ?)	• Maintenance of footing
• Dimensions, rhythm	• Co-operation	• Accentuation	• Camera management	• Obstacle material
• Dynamics multitude, variety	• Organisation of course building	• Variety and changes from day to day	• Timetable	• Motives, themes, colours
• Dramaturgy	• Timetable		• TV transmission schedule	• Improvement of organisation
• Variety and changes from day to day	• Promotion of young course designers world-wide			

- supply the top-level jumping competitions (GRAND PRIX, Nations Cup and Derby), through one or two rounds and a jump-off, with a high degree of dramatic tension, right to the last rider and the last obstacle;

- concentrate primarily on his chief task which is to facilitate 'the maximum of good sport'. The course designer is modest and represents an 'attitude of mind' (Le Corbusier). He does not chase the media, he is a personality, a gentleman, a 'créateur'. Master designers like Brinckmann and de Némethy are paramount examples.

Of course, the course designer must also be an autonomous individual who, within the powers his status gives him, is able to make quick, independent decisions in the context of frank advice from his team.

1   When making decisions alone, without the team, a very experienced course designer will make very few mistakes (perhaps in only two or three situations out of a hundred).

2   However, the same course designer, following a frank discussion with his qualified team, will undoubtedly make even fewer mistakes!

3   We are not talking here about a course designer/builder (a 'high priest of poles') whose main aim is to combine his commercial interest with course design, and who:

   ● hires out obstacles;

   ● hires out stabling;

   ● insists on long-term contracts with tournament organisers;

   ● builds courses with 2- to 3-m poles;

   ● provides no wall, no Liverpool, no water;

   ● preferably has no décor;

   ● but does everything in 'no time' with technically skilled 'soldiers'.

   ARCHITECTURE IS NOT A 'JOB' TO 'MAKE QUICK MONEY', BUT IT IS A 'VOCATION' AND 'PERSONAL EXPRESSION OF SPIRIT' – IT IS THE LIGHT TO CHASE AWAY 'IGNORANCE AND STUPIDITY'!

   (*Le Corbusier, 1887–1965 [094], one of the most important architects of the twentieth century*)

   THIS SENTIMENT MIGHT ALSO BE VALID FOR COURSE DESIGN.

4   By contrast, a responsible course designer who is committed to quality will never try to extract personal financial gain from the task entrusted to him, but will act from honourable principles. A good course designer can, of course, expect to be paid appropriately, but he can in no way be bought.

5 A 'course builder', who takes on 50 or 60 tournaments a year and then sends members of his team to some ten or 15 tournaments and deals with the rest in person, will disqualify himself in the long run. Course design can certainly be a life's work, but it should never be the sole source of income, if only to give creativity a chance to flourish. Very few artists, and we wish, to a modest degree, to count the good course designer among them, are in a position where they can constantly combine high quality with high quantity.

A course designer's team should be characterised by:

- excellent professional qualifications, experience, modesty, FEI status and multi-lingual ability;

- passion and the ability to work in a team;

- professional independence;

- a relationship with the course designer based on total trust;

- individual team members who possess the talent to become course designers in their own right.

I had the honour of working for many years with the world's best, internationally experienced colleagues and teams at the CHIO Aachen, the Olympic Games, various championships and many great tournaments. Each year at the CHIO Aachen there were always some guest course designers in addition to the permanent team, including many well-known names (see appendix 2). All have remained friends, yet each always retained his or her independence and distinctive style.

The course designer is thus a creative designer who does justice to all expected requirements and plans his design from a sort of bird's eye view, similar to town planners and landscape designers.

A course is not just a sequence of obstacles on a given track. A good course has as its base a soul, a positive emotion:

- 'Feeling good after the ride is more important than a prize.' (*Bertalan de Némethy*) [114]

- 'Composure comes from working on one's own personality, and this unpaid effort is not an easy exercise. This service is an achievement which is rare in [today's] arid service industry in Germany.' (*Nickel*) [118]

- When the elderly conductor Arturo Toscanini was asked after an opera rehearsal why he had twice asked the two best soloists to repeat their performance, he replied, sitting relaxed in his armchair: '*Manca emozione*' – 'It lacked passion'. A high C alone does not make a world-famous tenor!

- 'There are so many well-trained singers with beautiful voices who master their repertoire. But in the end, a decisive factor for success is how much of his own personality a singer can invest in his singing performance.' *(Luciano Pavarotti)* [143]

- This truth can be unconditionally transposed to course design.

Course design is something quite special, a creative task worked to a high standard, with the greatest excellence when it comes to:

- professional expertise;

- creativity;

- ethics and fair play;

- independence and courage;

- aesthetics and artistic potential;

- modesty;

- absolute independence.

Course design done as a favour, constant repetition of ideas, avoiding classical competition obstacles (for example, Liverpools or water jumps), manipulating and disregarding the minimum speed stipulated in the schedule, neglecting or minimising the spread of obstacles, dispensing with variety and variation, including permanent natural obstacles and knock-down elements other than just poles, the absence of great tracks, any type of counterfeit (the 'red lemonade in the Bordeaux wine bottle') are counter-productive and detrimental to the quality of the sport at all levels.

ART IS NOT THE BREAD, BUT THE WINE OF LIFE!

(Jean Paul, 1763–1825)

The required personality profile of an international course designer can be summarised as follows:

- a mature personality, cultured, multilingual (Anglophone FEI officials should also speak a second language);

- professional experience as a show-jumper;

- 'miles under the belt' (experience gained by being responsible for designing and creating many smaller or medium-sized tournaments, many years of experience as an assistant, with sufficient professional proximity to an expert course designer, and other experience, gained, for example, as an instructor, trainer, coach, etc.);

- total respectability, incorruptibility, integrity, reliability, talent, passion, diplomacy and the ability to work in a team;

- professional and financial independence from course design; otherwise there is a danger of infringing the principles of ethics and fair play (see FEI rules and chapter 3);

Figure 2.11: *A dream team of international course designers, CHIO Aachen 2002. (From right) Olaf Petersen Jr, Michael Gockel behind Christa Jung, Arno Gego, Christa Heibach and Werner Deeg (Mehves Trak and Ferdi Rosellen are missing). Jury: Dr Hanno Dohn, Sven Holmberg and Kazuya Hirayama. Photo by Lucasz Jankowski/POL.*

- an internationally known course designer is normally a representative of an established school – autodidacts are the rare exception; (surgery is also not for autodidacts);

- and it goes without saying that an international course designer will have mastered freehand drawing (just like an architect), and is also a good teacher who encourages the younger generation.

UNFORTUNATELY, IN THE LAST DECADES, THERE HAS BEEN A REGRETTABLE NEGLECT OF THEORETICAL KNOWLEDGE, AND SUPERFICIALITY IS INCREASING AT A FRIGHTENING PACE IN ALL DISCIPLINES OF EQUESTRIAN SPORT.

(Podhajsky) [154]

TRAINING THE NEXT GENERATION

It is striking that the great majority of course designers fail to participate in any type of further training, attending seminars, etc. as soon as they have attained their FEI status. Such conduct should not be accepted. It is high time for the national federations and the FEI to act. It would be worth considering making it obligatory for international course designers to participate in ongoing training or other seminars at regular intervals, perhaps every three years, if they want to retain their status.

Those in positions of responsibility, for example the leading international course designers, have a moral duty to pass on their knowledge, their new findings and experience, not only verbally but by writing them down, publishing them and putting them up for discussion, as is common practice in all forms of science and art. That is the only way to encourage debate, the serious dissemination of knowledge and progress.

3 ETHICS, FAIR PLAY AND EQUESTRIAN SPORT

With the growing importance of money prizes, advertising and the media in most sports, the danger of manipulation or cheating in equestrian sport has also increased [011/125/127/132] through such practices as:

- doping of the horse and/or athlete;

- maltreatment of horses in the form of rapping and other types of abuse that hurt the horse;

- other measures not appropriate to the horse, which are intended to improve performance;

- conflicts of interest for participants of a commercial or other nature;

- knowingly procuring an advantage for individual athletes, teams or other interest groups either before or during a tournament.

The FEI has laid down binding ethical rules for the welfare of horses.

FEI CODE OF CONDUCT

1   In all equestrian sports the welfare of the horse must be considered paramount.

2   The well-being of the horse shall take precedence over the demands of all interested parties and commercial concerns.

THE EUROPEAN PHILOSOPHERS – WITH FEW EXCEPTIONS – HAVE BEEN AWARE THAT NO ANIMALS HAVE BEEN WALKING OVER THEIR ETHICS.

(Albert Schweitzer, 1875–1965)

3   All handling and veterinary treatment must ensure the health and welfare of the horse.

4   The highest standards of nutrition, health, sanitation and safety shall be encouraged and maintained at all times.

5   During transportation, adequate provision must be made for ventilation, feeding, watering and maintaining a healthy environment.

6   Emphasis should be placed on increasing education in equestrian practices and on promoting scientific studies in equine health.

7   In the interest of the horse, the fitness and competence of the rider or driver shall be regarded as essential.

8   All riding and training methods should take account of the horse as a living, sentient creature and must not include any technique considered by the FEI to be abusive.

9   National federations must establish adequate controls in order that all persons and bodies under their jurisdiction respect the welfare of the horse.

10 National and international rules and regulations in equestrian sport, regarding the health and welfare of the horse, must be strictly adhered to, not only during national and international events, but also during training; such rules are to be regularly reviewed.

The above code of conduct was extended in 2003 [127] in order to close any loopholes and to ensure high moral standards regarding ethics and fair play.

In order to prevent more widespread indirect influence on performance or results, not only on the part of competitors, officials (i.e. judges, course designers, stewards, veterinarians, etc.), organisers and federations, but also by horse owners, trainers, spectators and the media, at its general meeting in Doha, Quatar in April 1999, the FEI decided to adopt binding guidelines for 'Fair Play and Equestrian Sport' which should be seen as a supplement to the above-cited code of conduct [132].

It appears, however, that there are still unresolved questions to be considered. Most officials at riding and driving events, such as judges, stewards and veterinarians, continue to perform their tasks on a voluntary basis while working in another profession that is independent of equestrian sport. The same also applies to most officials at the Olympic Games.

They are remunerated with a fixed daily payment and expenses (travel, hotel, food, telephone, parking tickets, etc.). As a rule, they are autonomous and independent officials with the status of an expert.

Among a section of course designers, however, there is a growing trend towards so-called 'professionalisation', that is, one or several activities in equestrian sport serve exclusively as a means of earning a living. Often, their activity is supplemented by the sale and/or hire of show supplies of some kind, so that, in certain cases, a huge economic dependence on, say, riders or organisers is created.

It is not a question of denying the course designer an appropriate fee. Such a fee is certainly justified on the basis of the considerably great investment of time and effort alone. Rather, the questions that arise are of ethical significance. Is it right for a course designer to be economically dependent on his activity to such an extent? Is there not a question of a conflict of interest here? Is a full-time course designer really still autonomous and independent in his decisions?

Such a person would need truly amazing abilities if they wanted to design courses for 40 to 50 different tournaments at different levels every year, all with spirit, variety, innovation, uniqueness, independence, intensity and autonomy! Even with only 30 different tournaments a year, the problem still exists.

These are new questions which the responsible bodies of the national federations and the FEI must tackle in order to adopt workable ethical rules. In some cases in Europe, it can already be observed that certain judges, stewards or course designers will not be invited to the next tournament, perhaps because they:

- are not – one might almost say – 'answerable' to the organiser (they might refuse, for example, to change the competition schedules during the tournament, contrary to the organiser's/marketing manager's demands);

- stewards may prove themselves unwilling to be manipulated;

- course designers may refuse to allow themselves to be manipulated by individual riders or organisers ('leave out the water jump' – 'don't make the oxers so deep', etc.).

Further questions concerning ethics and fair play may arise.
1   Should a sponsor be allowed to dictate the location of a CSIO in any country?

2   Is not the influence of the riders' representatives inappropriately great if rules that
    have governed the sport for more than 100 years are eliminated, as for example:

    ● a ban on triple bars in combinations (is that perhaps a problem for rapped
    horses?);

    ● a severe restriction on the type of obstacle placed over water jumps (which, like
    other natural obstacles, have represented the charm of top-level sport until
    today);

    ● a ban on water jumps in indoor arenas.

3   On the other hand, nobody from among the media, the riders, organisers or federa-
    tions speaks out when an exceptional horse is for years – in a way recognisable to
    any expert – being mercilessly ridden into the ground by what can only be called
    an egotistical rider (where are the ethics and fair play in this?).

4   Nobody, not even a representative of the associations or the equestrian press,
    comments, questions or opens a debate if one of the world's most highly remuner-
    ated GRAND PRIX tournaments is staged on the best new Lava grass surface, but
    the course consists only of poles – above all without a water jump, without walls,
    without an upper plank, without a second round, without any natural obstacle, to
    mention just a few factors. And where does that leave the independent position and
    the responsibility of the course designer and the organiser?

5   Nobody speaks out when fine horses are effectively maltreated through the use of
    poor, unharmonious tracks and perhaps continual extreme distance problems in
    the range of below 18 m.

6   Nobody speaks out when badly built water jumps at championships discredit
    show-jumping with penalty rates of up to 50 per cent or more.

7   Nobody speaks out when a big indoor series final leads almost exclusively along a
    course that scarcely varies and consists mostly of poles, a testimony to unsurpass-
    able monotony – no Liverpool, no wall, etc.

8   No equestrian journalist speaks out when mostly self-promoting course designers,
    working on new, Olympic-status showgrounds, counter their fear of too many clear
    rounds by brashly increasing the speed requirement, in defiance of the existing

statutes, from 400 m to 430–440 m/min. – an outrageous case of manipulation in show-jumping and a true violation of the ethical principles of equestrian sport!

Ethics and fair play in equestrian sport have gained increasing importance in the recent past. For a course designer, the following guidelines should be seen as beyond question.

- The course designer is demonstrably an honest person who respects all moral principles of ethics and fair play.

- He has a natural instinct for maintaining a discreet distance from athletes, trainers, owners, team leaders, etc. – and yet can still be their friend.

- He does not allow any conflict of interest. He does not allow any confusion of his responsibility as a course designer with whatever type of business or other interests he has either inside or outside of equestrian sport.

- He neither offers himself directly or indirectly as a course designer, nor 'invites himself': he is invited!

- And if he is invited, he will not try to persuade the organiser to accept a long-term contract! (The referee in a national or international football championship does not expect a long-term contract either!)

- He will train qualified younger course designers, both men and women, and will promote them to the best of his ability.

It is interesting to note that manipulation, bribery and other methods of exerting subtle influence to achieve an advantage are not just a contemporary phenomenon, but were the subject of discussions at the Olympic Games in ancient times [186].

CODE OF ETHICS OF FEI COURSE DESIGNERS

Analogous to the Code of Ethics of Engineers [125], one could envisage a code of ethics to read as follows.

The fundamental principles
FEI course designers will uphold and advance the integrity, honour and dignity of course design and equestrian sports by:

1   using their knowledge and skill for the enhancement of the welfare of equestrian sports;

2   being honest and impartial and loyally serving organisers, competitors, spectators, owners, sponsors and the media, and respecting the rules of ethics and fair play;

3   striving to increase the competence and prestige of the art of course design;

4   supporting the FEI, national federations and technical committees.

The fundamental canons

1   Course designers shall hold paramount the safety, health and welfare of horse and rider.

2   Course designers shall perform services only in the areas of their competence.

3   Course designers shall issue public statements only in an objective and truthful manner.

4   Course designers shall act for organisers as faithful agents or trustees, and shall avoid conflict of interest.

5   Course designers shall build their reputation on the merit of their services and shall not compete unfairly with others.

6   Course designers shall act in such a manner as to uphold and enhance the honour, integrity and dignity of equestrian sports.

7   Course designers shall continue their professional development throughout their careers and shall provide opportunities for the development of those course designers under their supervision (men and women).

Another important aspect of ethics is the question of how 'honoured personalities of the sport' – athletes, officials, organisers, long-term employees, etc. are treated by the federations, associations, event organisers, etc.

To conclude, a quotation from Mahatma Gandhi 1869–1948 [055] says it all:

> ONE CAN MEASURE THE GREATNESS AND MORAL PROGRESS OF A SOCIETY BY HOW IT TREATS ITS ANIMALS.

4 OLYMPIC JUMPING IN COMPETITION WITH OTHER LEADING SPORTS DISCIPLINES

Equestrian sport (particularly riding and driving) has many exclusive attributes which form the basis for strengthening its position when compared with other sports disciplines. Moreover, equestrian sport is one of the nature-based sports par excellence.

Unfortunately, for some time there has been a trend towards watering down and diminishing show-jumping, which threatens the position of equestrian sport at the international level and could have a detrimental effect on its future development.

A GRAND PRIX is a *great*, not a *small* prize! Misleading labels have quite often been attached to GRAND PRIX, particularly in recent times.

The GRAND PRIX of Aachen, Calgary and Rome, to name just a few with outstanding reputations, have for years been staged according to the classical format of Olympic individual jumping:

- two different rounds, maximum height of 1.6 m, speed 400 m/min., single jump-off if required.

The international prestige of some GRAND PRIX is more or less equal to that of an Olympic individual competition. However, this can only apply if the standards are also 'Olympic'.

Some course designers try to qualify the demands placed on courses at major GRAND PRIX.

1 Far more tournaments take place now than in the past.

2 The effort required by competitors may be carefully measured, and the GRAND PRIX participation of top horses should be restricted and carefully conserved.

3 A commercial representative of the course design fraternity may promise, rather immodestly, that he will, at last, 'build more intelligent and technical courses'.

4 'The spectators won't even notice it from the outside ...' – It is a fundamental mistake to underestimate the expert knowledge of the spectators; this is especially true for traditional tournaments which have a large and loyal following.

5 '... but the riders will be very aware of it!'

6 The course designer who favours a 'change of philosophy' and a 'leap forward into the modern world', decides that 'solid-looking, high obstacles represent an outdated requirement profile'. This set of arguments has been out of date for 20 years (see chapter 14) [190/193].

On another occasion, the same source might let it be known that:

● to produce penalties in show-jumping, the course designer has to 'disturb the rhythm of the horses'! Could that not, in fact, be called sadism? Whose 'school' is this?

1 In a GRAND PRIX, the riders and horses are set solvable problems that can be mastered by the best competitors (height, width, variety and variation of the requirements, visual aspects, distances, condition of rider and horse on long courses, physical and mental fitness, water jumps and water ditches, and possibly other natural obstacles).

2 The course designer is not interested in 'disturbing the horses' rhythm', but, rather, he sets achievable tasks for the best and does not produce problems.

3 'The beauty of jumping is best expressed by the free forward movement of the horses.' (Albert Voorn, and seconded by Berthalan de Némethy and Pamela Carruthers [032/177/178])

4 To avoid the less pleasing sight of weaker competitors, GRAND PRIX competitors have to qualify in preliminary competitions. This is the normal practice at the Olympic Games and in other championships.

The basic principles of riding and driving must apply to every level, from novice youngsters to competitors at the Olympic Games.

I have made this point so forcibly and quoted so extensively in order to document the groundlessness of the arguments put forward by some extremely business-minded, dangerous and 'obliging' representatives of the course design fraternity.

WHAT DO GRAND PRIX LOOK LIKE IN OTHER SPORTS DISCIPLINES?

1 The requirements of a MARATHON are always the same. It is run over a distance of 42.195 km. Nobody would dream of shortening the length of the course by 10 km so that MARATHON runners will get the opportunity to run ten times a year instead of only two or three times.

2 With 100-m sprinters like Carl Lewis, no thought was given to the possibility of reducing the requirement from 100 m to perhaps 50 or 80 m, so that 100-m Olympic champions can produce Olympic results not just two or three times a year, but could perhaps compete ten times a year instead.

3 World boxing champions fight only a few times a year – perhaps only once – and yet they have to maintain an extreme training programme throughout the year.

4 Top dressage horses compete in perhaps six to eight important competitions a year. Nobody would dream of reducing the requirements for GRAND PRIX, GRAND PRIX SPECIAL, GRAND PRIX KÜR (freestyle to music), for example by eliminating the piaffe so that GRAND PRIX horses can compete more often in dressage.

5 Even Deister, the famous mount of Paul Schockmöhle only competed 12 times a year in major tournaments – and he still won more GRAND PRIX than many others.

There are some riders who believe that a GRAND PRIX should involve only one round, plus jump-off, so as to be gentle on the horses, and an incomprehensibly large number of show organisers comply with this demand! This might seem to be perfectly all right, except for the fact that a final with one round, plus jump-off, does not constitute a GRAND PRIX.

Wimbledon would not be Wimbledon if it did not have the world's best tennis players competing against each other. Tennis is a sport in which the best players are not let off the hook. Tennis rackets are not getting larger, the nets lower and the balls lighter! A Wimbledon victory is comparable to an Olympic victory. It is the high point of the tennis year! Misleading labels do not help any sport to develop positively and gain in prestige.

Equally, a Tour de France – the world's most difficult cycle race [121] – can only be won once a year and that victory requires an incredible amount of training, team spirit, strategy and discipline.

Nobody would dream of reducing the Tour de France to a well-commercialised, media-intensive tour around Paris just to save the cyclists' strength for the next great race that was to start in three days' time!

Equestrian sport, especially show-jumping, is a special Olympic discipline. A sport of outstanding beauty, appeal and uniqueness, it demands a lot of imagination, energy and idealism to use the strengths of show-jumping to juxtaposition it even more successfully against other types of top-level sport [124/134/192](table 4.1).

Show-jumping will only gain ground if it develops noticeably in the following directions:

Table 4.1: *Areas of individual experience in different sports for men and women*

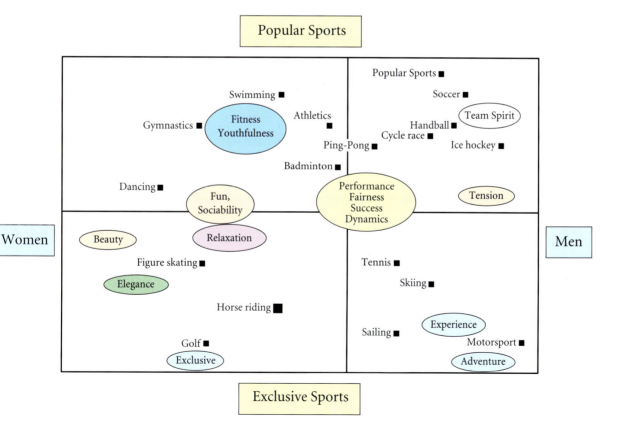

- ethics and fair play;

- the clear predominance of outstanding natural grass stadiums;

- convincing role-model riders and stars (for example the conduct of Jan Ulrich in the 2003 Tour de France when Armstrong was falling, in that he stopped and waited);

- the measured use of GRAND PRIX horses;

- by maintaining classical principles and Olympic requirements in top-level tournaments and the variety of course designs (including natural obstacles, varied dry or water ditches, walls, gates, etc.), to develop and contribute towards;

- an end to coarsening and brutalising jumping by applying the wrong standards and curtailing the proper requirements (sometimes in response to enormous pressure from competitors); for example, the severe restriction of the type of obstacle used over water jumps, triple bars in combinations, water jumps in indoor arenas, ignoring the maximum requirements concerning the spread of obstacles by putting pressure on course designers, etc.);

Table 4.2: *The extremes of course design (antipoles)*

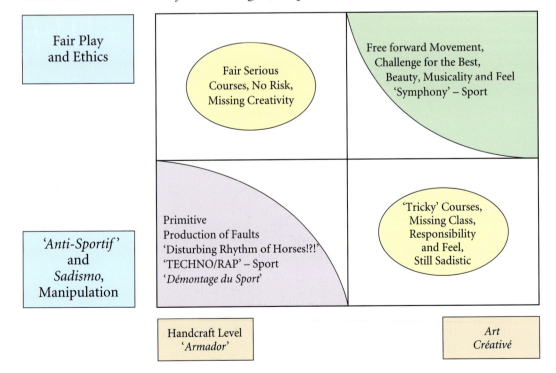

- stopping the inappropriate glorification of indoor sport which is secondary to Olympic outdoor sport;

- reducing or eliminating other types of misleading labelling and the neglect of classical principles.

Show-jumping has so many positive attributes in its favour that it is worth fighting for the best methods of working and making people aware of the critical connection between excellence and principles. The difference between good and bad is often quite slight (table 4.2).

5 FIRST-CLASS TOURNAMENTS

A first-class tournament means 'the best tournament at its level'. This can, for example, be:

● a regional tournament;

● a national tournament;

● an international tournament;

● one of a very few international tournaments of outstanding importance.

If they deserve this attribute, the latter may have virtual 'Olympic status'!

As course designers, in everything we do we must start from an ideal vision in order to transfer as much as possible of this ideal to our practical task of developing a new tournament and/or creating the course design of a planned or existing tournament.

The status of great, outstanding tournaments (table 5.1) rests predominantly on personalities, images and traditions. This is true, for example, of such important tournaments as:

● Aachen

● La Baule

● Calgary

● Donaueschingen

● Dublin

- Hamburg

- Hickstead

- Lisbon

- Rome

to mention only a few.

Important tandem tournaments such as:

- St Gallen/ Lucerne in Switzerland

- Fontainebleau/Dinard in France

- Barcelona/Gijon/Madrid in Spain

at which the Nations Cup is held annually in turn, show that achieving world renown requires total focus. Aachen and Wimbledon are typical examples, each in its own way and despite all their differences.

The more recent examples of:

- Falsterbo, Sweden

- Gera, Germany

- Monterrey, Mexico

- Valkenswaard, the Netherlands

show that if there is an extraordinary commitment by major personalities with vision, ideas, enthusiasm and energy, it is possible to develop outstanding tournaments in the space of a few years.

On the other hand, other recent examples, such as:

- CSIO Luxembourg 1977–96

Table 5.1: *First-class tournaments – the interdependence between riders, spectators, the media, sponsors and the internal infrastructure*

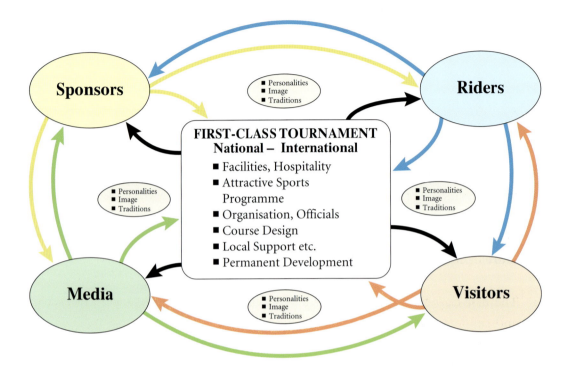

- CSIO Modena, Italy 1991

- CSI Bodensee, Germany since 1998

show that where an important tournament is dependent on one single influential personality, its long-term survival often cannot be guaranteed.

If one looks at the question of how a new, important tournament should be developed, one comes up with interesting results (table 5.1).

First of all, the riders/athletes think that they are the most important element in a tournament. However, that is not the case! The actual ranking of importance is as follows.

1   A first-class tournament is the showcase of the sport for the public.

- Without tournaments and organisations, there would be no competition sport, no competition riders, etc. at today's high commercial standard.

- Without tournaments, there would be no public, no media, no money.

2　The first-class tournament therefore rests on:

- personalities (with great ideas)

- images

- traditions.

3　It is seen as welcoming, has its own distinctive showground, an attractive sports programme, a friendly, efficient tournament organisation where everyone co-operates, with well-chosen officials, assistants, helpers and an outstanding course design (tournament-specific, independent and with varied obstacle material and decoration).

4　One cannot compensate for an unsatisfactory sports programme or save the tournament standard by using other types of shows.

5　The first-class tournament stands a good chance of generating local enthusiasm and support if it is based on the above-cited structure. A first-class tournament does not exist on its own, but has the support of the community, local companies, shops, families and individuals.

Only if the internal organisation of a first-class tournament is coherent and strong can the tournament organiser enthuse the media, at least the local media, about the tournament and only then will spectators and visitors be interested in the planned event and be curious enough to visit the tournament. A major tournament must be visitor-friendly in the following respects:

- adequate parking facilities close by;

- short distances to walk;

- children- and family-friendly;

- low or no entrance charges – children (if at all possible) free;

- acceptable prices for food and drink.

A top tournament thrives on lots and lots of visitors to create a 'full house'! However, no equestrian tournament can be primarily funded by its visitors.

1   A first-class tournament can only be considered accepted and confirmed as such if the main events (for example, the Nations Cup and GRAND PRIX) are well attended and supported!

2   Only if the above conditions have been met will it be possible to attract the interest of regional television.

3   If the tournament is so important that it attracts high visitor numbers and is transmitted on television, then it will most likely to be able to attract sponsors.

4   If all these requirements have been met, then the organiser does not need to worry about attracting top-class riders.

5   Riders who have to be paid for their participation do not constitute a top-class tournament. A top-class tournament invites top-class riders, but it does not pay a 'star bonus'.

An equestrian tournament will only become important and top class if it takes place regularly, that is:

● annually;

● at the same time each year;

● in the same place and on a major, independent showground;

● if it can attract many visitors and sufficient media interest;

● which requires a well-qualified field of competitors, a high sports standard (course designer, varied and independent obstacle material/decoration) and an attractive sports programme with appropriate prizes;

● top tournaments concentrate their main programme on the most popular time of the day and on a few hours per day;

● an excess of starters, classes and entertainment in a daily programme is always counter-productive and quickly leads to boredom or devalues the tournament!

● at a first-class tournament, 'lesser competitions' are best located on secondary arenas, as has been done in different ways at tournaments such as Calgary, Hickstead and Monterrey, each of which have several secondary arenas.

Every good tournament, whether small or large, needs local support, preferably over many years. This contributes little to the budget but is important for the atmosphere. Top tournaments have a large number of voluntary helpers who support the tournament, not for money but out of sheer idealism. Such volunteers make a significant contribution towards an inviting and friendly atmosphere. The 1984 Olympic Games in Los Angeles, and the 2000 Games in Sydney had the support of excellent volunteers, as did the CSIO Calgary and Spruce Meadows.

The observations made so far on the subject of first-class tournaments alone should give some idea of the complexity of the matter, which is also reflected in the financial and budget structure (table 5.2).

Table 5.2: *An example of the mechanics of the financial structure of important tournaments*

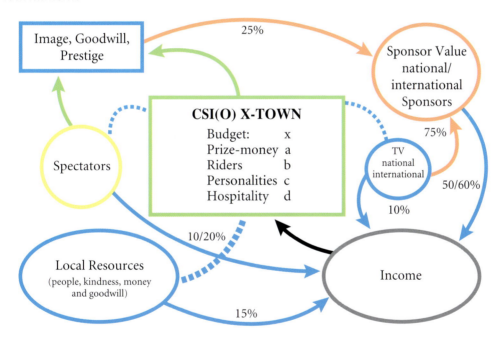

The connections shown here and the relative importance of individual sources of finance are given purely as examples and can, of course, vary considerably in each individual case.

L'anee Hippique, the traditional yearbook of equestrian sport which was thankfully revived by BCM, Best in the Netherlands a few decades ago, regularly conducts surveys of riders and officials in order to compile listings of the world's best tournaments.

The result of the last statistically detailed rankings for outdoor jumping tournaments in 1998 [007] is shown for some leading events in table 5.3. Extra information is presented visually, in addition to the chosen rankings, such as:

● total prize-money;

● total number of visitors;

● total of the world ranking points of the 40 best competitors in the respective GRAND PRIX (a significant indicator of the field of competitors).

What transpires from this is that the world's top riders are clearly keen to enter the most important tournaments.

Table 5.3: *Portfolio of selected outdoor jumping events, 1998*

If we summarise the criteria for a first-class tournament, a simplified list of specifications could look roughly as follows:

● a unique, charismatic, distinctive showground with a grass surface outdoor stadium and permanent natural obstacles;

- visitor capacity not greater than the number of visitors at the main event; it must be at least close to being sold out on the Saturday or Sunday;

- first-class sport, no misleading labels, with a top course of world-class standard;

- an interesting supporting programme, with lesser competitions preferably on secondary arenas;

- a multilingual, knowledgeable stadium announcer (who should be a horseman) with a distinctive, strong voice, empathic and able to adapt to any situation, a good speaker but not someone who talks too much;

- sophisticated, emotional music and a presentation that 'gets under the skin' and appeals to all generations.

A top tournament on a charismatic showground with many visitors, a good atmosphere and an ambiance that brings together and enthuses all social classes will have enough appeal to interest the media and sponsors.

It goes without saying that the whole environment of such a tournament should be welcoming, starting with the volunteers (figures 5.1–5.4), the entrance, signposting and parking, short distances to walk, entertainment for children, different types of food and drink, the stable area, the training arenas, the press centre/stand, television, the show office, guests of honour – friendliness everywhere.

However, an international, leading tournament will not remain first class just because it is traditional and has survived successfully for many years. Age in itself is not a credit nor a guarantee of further success. Successful tournaments only stay successful if they constantly develop, in small but perceptible steps – if they stay 'young at heart'.

I have often said, in a jocular way, 'Show me an aerial photograph of an Aachen GRAND PRIX and I'll tell you what year it was.' Why? Because every year there is a small change or development, and the tournament stays young as a result.

In the equestrian sports scene, and to some extent in the media, the true value of outdoor tournaments is frequently confused with that of indoor events. One consistently successful rider in the indoor World Cup final even said, about two years ago, after an average ranking at an important outdoor tournament around September, that he had deliberately made a slow start since the main season only begins in October (which is the indoor season)!

My earlier evaluation of each of the six best outdoor and indoor tournaments speaks for itself, even if one only looks at the accumulated value of prize-money or the visitor numbers alone (table 5.4).

5.1

5.2

5.3

5.4

Figures 5.1–5.4: *Some of my stadium dream teams. The Malteser Hilfsdienst arena party – World Championships, Aachen 1986. Photo by Gloria Transparente International. Arena party, CSIO Istanbul 2003. Photo by Christa Heibach. The jumping crew, arena party, CSI-W Winter Equestrian Festival, Palm Beach 2004. Photo by Christa Heibach. The Malteser Hilfsdienst, arena party, CHIO Aachen 1998, centenary anniversary of the ALRV. Photo by Christa Heibach.*

Table 5.4: *Accumulated potential of world leading events 1998–99*

Type of event	Number of events	Total prize-money		Spectators		Attractivity weighting * spect. x money	
		US $ 000	%	number	%	10³	%
Indoor	6	1,494	28	313,700	35	469	12
Outdoor	6	3,785	72	565,000	65	3,326	88
Total	12	5,279	100	878,700	100	3,795	100

* Attractivity weighting = accumulation of total prize-money x spectators x 10³

I have already commented on the interesting fact that the major outdoor tournaments do not, as a rule, take place in large cities but, rather, in smaller locations.

- La Baule, a town attracting summer tourists who like bathing, only has 11,000 regular inhabitants in winter.

- The English hamlet of Hickstead probably contains not many more than six houses.

- Aachen has more visitors than inhabitants.

- Valkenswaard has only slightly more than 30,000 inhabitants.

- Calgary is quite a small town by North American standards.

- Donaueschingen, Gijon, Lucerne or St Gallen are not large.

Equestrian tournaments in small towns attract more attention and focus. In the big city, they risk being lost in the competitive struggle with a large number of other events.

Indoor tournaments, which in Europe are predominantly winter events, may well be governed by different laws.

6 ON DESIGNING ARENAS AND STADIUMS

BASIC REFLECTIONS ON OUTDOOR ARENAS

The grass arena, the jumping stadium or, indeed, the sand arena that is used all year round, are the focus for the sport and the centre of sports activities during the event. It is therefore important that the arena has the maximum natural appeal; for example:

- a unique and distinctive shape, position and natural environment;

- it is well cared for, with colourful flower/garden design;

- the arena surroundings have a friendly and natural aspect;

- there is a natural attractiveness to the showground as a whole, resulting from successful landscape design.

General rules of attractiveness apply to the design of arenas, irrespective of the category of event.

1   Arenas should be as broad as possible, in the proportions shown below where the breadth or width is greater than half the length.

$$B > \frac{L}{2}$$

B = breadth or width

L = length

This will ensure a maximum of variety for the course. The wider the better! Only

GOD CREATED PAPER IN ORDER TO DESIGN ARCHITECTURE ON IT!

(Alvara Aalto, Helsinki, 1898–1976, important European architect)

wide arenas are interesting. Long, narrow arenas are rather boring.

2   The most interesting arenas tend not to be rectangular, but to have their own characteristic shape.

3   Ideally, they are embedded in an existing landscape.

4   Attractive arenas gain special character and uniqueness by having a number of permanent natural obstacles appropriate to the size of the area.

Table 6.1 shows the dimensions and status of some internationally important tournaments, some of them Derby competitions, held on a grass surface. Many of them owe their special, unique charisma to the presence of interesting, permanent natural obstacles.

Since the introduction of all-weather grass surfaces (Lava technology, which was first used in 1992–93 in Modena in Italy and Monterrey in Mexico, see p. 104), there is no reason for letting the beauty of our sport drown in dead grey sand (figure 6.1). Sand is simply stones ground into dust. Sand can only justify its use on arenas that are also used for daily training. Therefore, large and internationally important arenas are characterised by:

- a grass surface;

- an interesting, individual shape and layout;

- permanent natural obstacles.

At this point, the critical observation must be made that all the jumping competitions of the modern Olympic Games, from 1912 in Stockholm to 1972 in Munich, took place on grass, but that from 1976 in Montreal to 2000 in Sydney – with the welcome exception of Moscow in 1980 [021/096]– all jumping competitions were held on sand!

Barcelona 1992 and Sydney 2000 were particularly negative examples because they missed the great opportunity of presenting our sport appropriately. Course designers and technical delegates were, unfortunately, not successful in turning their suggestions and ideas into practice in the face of a rigid Olympic organisation.

Table 6.1: *Sizes of classical GRAND PRIX grass stadiums*

Location/Country		Natural Obstacles	Approximate Size of Main Stadium		Relative Width	Number of Stadiums/ Rings/Arenas			
		estd.	m x m	m²	%	Jumping	Dressage	Other	Indoor
CSI Hamburg	GER	18	98 x 146	14,300	67	1	1	1	1
CSIO La Baule	FRA	11	80 x 120	9,600	67	1L*	1	1	--
CHIO Aachen	GER	10	125 x 155	18,000	80	1L*	1	1 driving	2 (27 x 70)
									(20 x 50)
CSIO Calgary	CAN	10	110 x 180	19,800	61	6	--	--	1 (30 x 70)
CSIO Hickstead	GBR	10	121 x 166	20,000	78	5	1	1 pony	--
CSI Valkenswaard **	NED	10	90 x 125	11,250	72	3(1L) *	--	--	2 (36 x 66)
									(25 x 70)
CSI Monterrey	MEX	3	90 x 125	11,250	72	6L*	--	--	1 (45 x 70)
		7	75 x 150	11,250	50				
CSIO Falsterbo	SWE	6	75 x 150	11,250	50	2	1	1 hunter	--
CSI La Bagnaia	ITA	5	120 x 143	14,500	84	1	--	--	1 (25 x 50)
CSI Donaueschingen	GER	4	90 x 120	10,800	75	1	1	1	--
CSI Lanaken	BEL	4	90 x 100	9,000	90	2	--	--	1 (25 x 60)
CSI Juiz de Fora	BRA	4	90 x 100	9,000	90	1	--	--	1 (20 x 40)
CSI Wiesbaden	GER	4	80 x 140	11,000	57	1	1	--	--
CSI Buenos Aires (Club Hipico Argentino)	ARG	3	70 x 110	7,700	64	1	--	--	1 (25 x 60)
CSIO Dublin	IRL	3	120 x 200	23,000	60	3	1	3 hunter	1 (30 x 70)
CSIO Roma	ITA	3	75 x 150	11,000	50	1	--	--	--
CSI(O)Barcelona	ESP	2	66 x 127	8,380	52	1	--	--	1
CSIO St Gallen	SUI	2	130 x 150	18,000	87	1	(1)	1	--
CSI(O) Gijon	ESP	2	70 x 100	7,000	70	1	--	--	--
CSI Palm Beach	USA	2	120 x 120	14,400	100	1	--	5	--
								2 hunter	
CSI(O)Modena	ITA	1	76 x 130	9,880	58	1L*	--	1	1 (30 x 70)
CSI Gera	GER	1	70 x120	8,400	58	1L*	1	--	1 (25 x 60)
CSI Aach	GER	0	75 x 100	7,500	75	1L*	--	1	2 (20 x 60)
									(20 x 40)

* L = Lava-footing-technology (Lava is volcanic and hygroscopic material) ** includes 1 jumping ring (Lava) and 1 big indoor arena

So it is even more gratifying that Olaf Petersen [146-149], the course designer of the 2004 Olympic Games in Athens, together with Freddy Serpieri of Greece, first vice-president of the FEI, was able to persuade the organisers to create a Lava-grass jumping stadium. This was a remarkably positive and constructive contribution towards increasing the appeal of international show-jumping in the media and among the public. It has set a good example and will help to introduce positive change in the show-jumping environment.

KEY PRINCIPLES FOR RESTORATION WORK ON GOLF COURSES

'IF THERE IS NO CLEAR, LOGICAL GOAL AND NO IMPORTANT NECESSITY FOR CHANGE, A GOLF COURSE ARCHITECT HAS ONLY ONE ALTERNATIVE:

SAY NO!'

(European Institute of Golf Course Architects, Yearbook 2002/2003)

Figure 6.1: *Sand or grass? That is the question! Photos by Christa Heibach.*

To lead on from the discussions in the previous chapter, the question of the size of the main stadium and the possible capacity for visitors will be further explored here.

There are some rather simple rules of the connection between:

- stadium size;

- spectator stand capacity;

and

- visitor numbers.

Such rules can be simply summarised as follows.

- There should be a healthy relationship between the size of the main stadium and the number of visitors on the main day (usually Sunday).

- Stand and visitor capacity should be guided by the number of visitors present at the main event. Vital target: sold-out stadium on the Sunday!

- While it is a shame if some visitors to the main event have to be disappointed because they are unable to buy a ticket ahead of the day, it is better than to accept a half-full stadium at the main event which creates a negative image!

Figures 6.2–6.9 show the different angles and layouts of various important arenas, where each one has its own characteristic and unique shape.

Figure 6.2: *CHIO Aachen 2002. Photo by ALRV.*

Figure 6.3: *CHIO Aachen 1998. Photo by Susanne Gossen.*

Figure 6.4: *Main Stadium CSIO Spruce Meadows, Canada. Photo by CSIO Spruce Meadows.*

Figure 6.5: *Main Stadium CSI Valkenswaard, the Netherlands. Photo by CSIO Valkenswaard.*

Figure 6.6: *Stadium CSI Monterrey, Mexico. Photo by CSI Monterrey.*

Figure 6.7: *Piazza di Siena, CSIO Rome, Italy. Photo by Christa Heibach.*

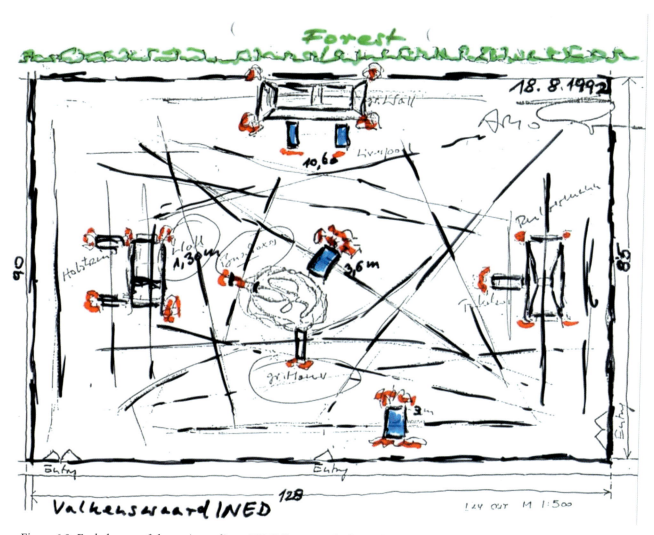

Figure 6.8: *Early layout of the main stadium CSI Valkenswaard, the Netherlands. Shape given by trees and water ditches.*

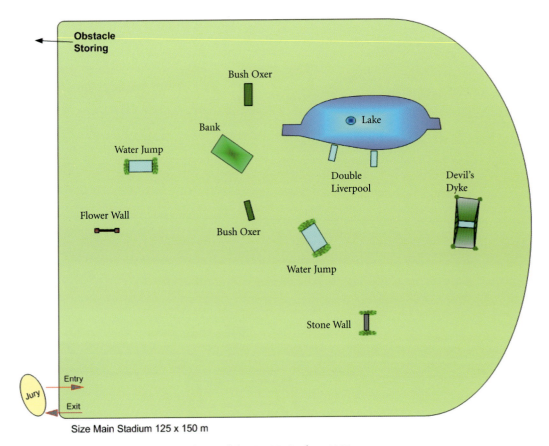

Obstacle Storing

Bush Oxer

Lake

Bank

Water Jump

Double Liverpool

Devil's Dyke

Flower Wall

Bush Oxer

Water Jump

Stone Wall

Jury

Entry

Exit

Size Main Stadium 125 x 150 m

Figure 6.9: *Layout of the main stadium of the CHIO Aachen 2002.*

MIXED GRASS-SAND SURFACES

Until around the middle of the last century there were some outdoor arenas which consisted, on the one hand, of a grass surface with some shrub and tree groupings in the inner area and, on the other hand, of partly integrated sand tracks (figure 6.10) which ran through an 'inner' green surface with a generous outer track on sand. These were found, for example, in the Belgian Cercle Equestre du Fort Jacot and in Essen, Germany, the home ground of the legendary rider and Chef d'Equipe Gustav Rudolph Pfordte.

The entire area had some permanent obstacles (approximately 30 in Fort Jacot), which formed the basis for courses on existing and/or freely variable tracks, and the generous outer track with its sand surface provided the flexibility to offer many different tracks and uses, such as daily training, dressage training or classes and show events.

These arenas formed an interesting combination between training and competition areas – a bit of this idea can still be recognised today in Wiesbaden in Germany and Lexington in Kentucky, USA.

Such grounds stand out positively when compared to those made exclusively of dead grey sand!

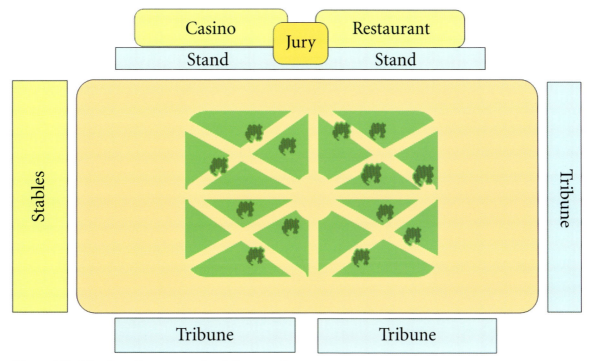

Figure 6.10: *Mixed sand/grass arena for daily use and tournaments.*

GUIDELINE FIGURES FOR ARENA SIZES

Outdoor tournaments take place on different sizes of arena (see table 6.2):

● small

● medium

● big

● very big.

In practice, most arenas are small sand areas which are predominantly used as training arenas. They have the advantage that it is easier to fill them with spectators during tournaments.

Their disadvantage is that they can hold little more than just one course if one wants to maintain a clear view of the arena. This means that each course has to be built where the main event will be held, which is different to big tournaments. So, after each jumping class,

Table 6.2: *Stadium size and capacity of built courses (out of doors)*

Size of Stadium					Obstacle Capacity		Capacity of Courses	
Type	m	x	m	= m²	number of fences	average area m²/fence	number of courses that will fit	courses/ha
Small	50	x	90					
	60	x	100	6,000	17	350	1.2	2
	80	x	80					
Medium	90	x	100					
	80	x	110	9,000	21	430	1.5	1.7
	95	x	95					
Big	80	x	140					
	100	x	120	12,000	26	460	2	1.7
	110	x	110					
Very big	120	x	130					
	120	x	150	18,000	35	510	2.5	1.4
	135	x	135					

a new course has to be built. Added to this, there is frequently spatial conflict between:

- the prize-giving and lap of honour;

- the building of a new course;

- any show presentations on the arena.

Another drawback of small arenas is the more intensive use of the ground (table 6.4), which results in additional maintenance work during and between jumping classes.

Table 6.3: *Stadium size and capacity of fixed natural obstacles*

Stadium Size	Area m x m	Area m²	Width %	Capacity of fixed obstacles *	Average area m²/obstacle
Small	60 x 100	6,000	60	1…2	6,000/3,000
Medium	83 x 120	10,000	69	3…4	3,333/2,500
	92 x 130	12,000	71	6…8	2,000/1,500
Big	107 x 140	15,000	77	8…10	1,875/1,500
	120 x 150	18,000	80	10…12	1,800/1,500

* bank, devil's dyke, double Liverpool, etc. each counting as one obstacle

Table 6.4: *Intensity of soil stress: the related length of the course depends on the stadium size*

Arena/stadium type	Size of jumping area		Related length of the course (m/ha)					
			Length of the course (m)					Derby
	m x m	m²	300	400	500	600	800	1,300
Indoor	20 x 40	800	3,750	5,000	6,250	--	--	--
	30 x 60	1,800	1,670	2,220	2,780	3,330	--	--
	40 x 80	3,200	940	1,250	1,560	1,880	--	--
Outdoor	60 x 100	6,000	500	670	833	1,000	1,330	--
	70 x 110	7,700	--	520	650	780	1,039	--
	90 x 100	9,000	--	440	560	667	890	--
	100 x 120	12,000	--	330	420	500	670	1,080
	125 x 155	19,375	--	210	260	310	410	670

TECHNOLOGIES FOR JUMPING SURFACES

Show-jumping has made considerable progress in the last 25 years thanks to:

1   the systematic breeding of outstanding jumping horses;

2   enhancing the safety for rider and horse through the easier knock down of the upper obstacle parts, use of better safety cups, etc.;

3   selecting the best facilities and materials for large, outstanding jumping classes;

4   the globalisation of show-jumping through the successful sharing of know-how and sports horses (promoting the universality of show-jumping in line with the aims of the IOC);

5   particularly in the last 15 years, a clear improvement in the surfaces – both sand and grass (figure 6.11).

The technology behind jumping surfaces has now made such advances that outdoor tournaments on both sand and grass can be held in all weather conditions without having a negative effect on the sport and without additional risks due to the weather. Some outstanding examples of this development include:

1   The sand surfaces of Toubain-Clement of Paris, which are based on a mixture of quartz sand and geo-textile. The Toubain-Clement surfaces have been adopted throughout the world with more success than any other competitors' products. These surfaces are extremely suitable for training arenas and small competition arenas. However, like many other sand surfaces, they have two disadvantages:

    ●   they are not grass surfaces;

    ●   the light-coloured sand gives off a strong glare in bright sunlight and increases the stadium temperature. (The ground can, however, be dyed, for example, green.)

2   The Lava technology for grass surfaces was introduced at our initiative by landscape designer John Weier of Luxembourg (initially in Pavarotti, Modena, Italy 1992–93, La Silla, Monterrey, Mexico 1992–93, La Silla, Valkenswaard, the Netherlands 1996).

While alternatives exist for sand surfaces, Lava technology is, until now, the only

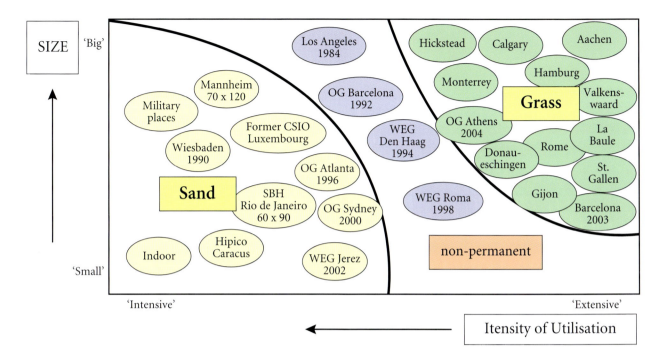

Figure 6.11: *Sizes of equestrian stadiums, footing and intensity of utilisation.*

known technology for a grass surface that meets all requirements such as:

- firmness

- grip

- elasticity

- water absorption capacity

in all weather conditions.

CONDITIONS OF FOOTING

'AS WE SHALL SEE ... CLINICAL STUDIES AGREE THAT BREAKDOWN MAY BE RELATED MORE TO STRAIN AND OVERUSE THAN TO TRACK CONDITIONS OR [THE] FREQUENTLY BLAMED "BAD STEP".'

(*Stephen Budianski*)

First-class tournaments demand first-class surfaces. Tournaments such as Aachen, La Baule, Donaueschingen Gera, Modena and Monterrey, as well as the 2004 Olympic Games in Athens, have successfully introduced Lava surfaces (see figure 6.12).

Profile Structure:

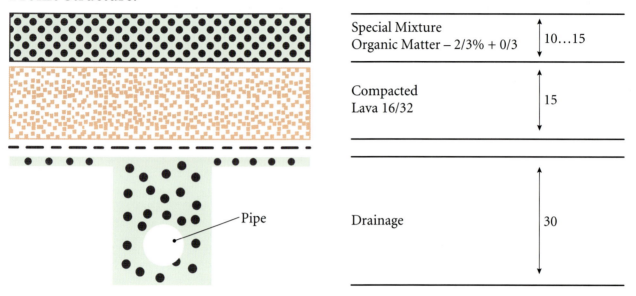

Figure 6.12: *Lava technology for grass footing (simplified), introduced for the first time at the Olympic Games in Munich 1972, but with a different specification.*

The choice between the alternative surfaces of grass or sand depends mainly on two parameters:

1   the size of the arena;

2   the intensity of use (from daily to once a year).

Both types of arena surface obviously need regular maintenance work such as:

● levelling/flattening;

● compacting;

● watering;

- manual maintenance during the jumping competition;

- (usually) specific autumn maintenance.

There is no great difference in the investment cost for the sports arena or for regular maintenance. Sand surfaces usually require more water.

The following information may help to give the reader a better understanding of Lava technology.

1   Lava is a material of volcanic origin.

2   Lava is either:

- ground into sand (for example 0/3); or

- coarsely crushed (for example 6/50).

3   Lava is hygroscopic and has the capacity to store water (up to approximately 10 per cent of its volume); the remaining water drains off into the subsoil as with normal sand.

4   Lava has an amorphous surface; it mixes in with other substances and does not roll or clump.

5   Lava compounds therefore exhibit an elasticity that can be observed when driving over them with a roller (for example of 1.20 m diameter).

- The roller presses the surface down while passing over it.

- The surface springs back up as soon as the roller has passed.

6   Lava ground is cultivated as an organically extremely poor soil, so that the grass roots are forced to search for nutrients deep down in the ground, creating long roots that make the grass firm and stabilise the soil.

7   However, the Lava ground must always be kept moist in order to retain its firmness and also give 'grip' on the surface.

8   Organic substances on the surface of a Lava ground, such as leaves, mown grass,

weeds, etc., must be carefully removed from the surface in autumn by quick cross-raking using a heavy, sharp spring-tine harrow.

9   The most important maintenance work during the tournament is regular watering as required, and rolling the surface in between jumping classes.

10 Compacting of the soil is dealt with before the show season by loosening it with the help of Vertidrain-technology (with controlled tines). Subsequent light sanding with Lava sand improves the soil's water absorption capacity.

Organisers who want to improve and/or renew their competition surfaces should get advice from independent experts (usually landscape designers). These people are experts who will accept responsible for the quality of the result. The prime interest of construction companies lies elsewhere.

To conclude this section:

1   Grass is the queen of jumping arenas …

2   and green sand, although green, is still not grass!

TECHNICAL AIDS FOR GROUND MAINTENANCE AND OBSTACLE TRANSPORT

Sports surfaces demand regular maintenance and care. This is particularly true for competition arenas which must be expertly maintained according to a fixed yearly schedule as well as during the sports event itself. Here, too, it is advisable to consult an expert or an experienced landscape designer who will prepare an exact plan which sets out in detail all the necessary measures such as:

- care and maintenance;

- sprinkling/watering;

- fertilising;

- plant protection (against insects, worms, microbacterial pests, weeds, etc.);

in a complete annual plan.

An extra plan is drawn up for maintenance work required during a tournament and directly afterwards, including the availability of green-dyed sand to repair damaged grass surfaces.

Figures 6.13 and 6.14 show some typical implements for the care and maintenance of arenas and riding surfaces.

Figure 6.13: *Small tractors with low-pressure turf tyres and large rollers (about 1.20 m in diameter and possibly filled with water) are useful tools especially in grass arenas. Ground stamps are useful for small surface repairs. (Right) A self-propelled mowing machine. Photos by Christa Heibach.*

Figure 6.14: *Other useful tools: (above left) a small tractor with six turf tyres and a loading platform; (above right) a rear-carrier for loading sand or other material; (below left) a wheel-barrow; (below right) a leveller for sand arenas. Photos by Christa Heibach.*

7 TYPES OF JUMPING CLASSES AND MINIMUM SPEEDS

In jumping, the horse is the rider's equal partner, and a horse/rider combination can only achieve a genuine and sustained performance if both partners have the benefit, either individually or preferably together, of instruction and schooling that is appropriate and builds up their skills gradually. This applies particularly to the horses, as they cannot speak and so cannot directly defend themselves against inappropriate training.

One would do well to remember the following saying:

- A rider without a horse is just a human being;

- but a horse without a rider is still a horse.

Marten von Barnekow [015], former top-level rider at the legendary Kavallerie-Reitschule in Hannover [111], described simply and convincingly how, and through what stages, young horses are prepared for great performances in show-jumping. De Némethy's views are also worth reading [114].

Table 7.1 describes the maximum dimensions of obstacles for individual age categories, based on recent experience!

In addition:

- dressage-type basic schooling (flat work);

- gymnastic exercises with the help of cavalletti etc. [003/097];

- regular hacking and negotiating smallish, natural obstacles, including experience with natural water (puddles, streams, small lakes, etc.);

Table 7.1: *Orientation figures for obstacle dimensions in different types of classes and minimum age of horses*

Type of class	Minimum age of horses in years	Maximum height * m	Minimum height ** m	Maximum spread parallel *** m	Water jump max. m
Youngsters by age and experience	5	1.10	1.00	1.40	2.50
		1.20	1.10	1.50	3.00
	6	1.30	1.20	1.60	3.50
Classical	7	1.40	1.30	1.70	3.80
International	8	1.50	1.40	1.80	4.20
GRAND PRIX	9	1.60	1.45	2.00	4.50

* Percentage of maximum height obstacles dependent on the importance of the class by show image and prize-money
** Except no. 1 and natural obstacles
*** Triple bar + 20 cm

- limiting the number of competitions per year;

- increasing the challenges very carefully;

are particularly important when training young horses.

While young horses (five to six years old) should at first enter only Table A competitions, not against the clock, or occasionally with a jump-off, the number of different types of classes for older jumping horses has increased considerably to give organisers the opportunity to create variety in their show programmes (table 7.2).

Table 7.2 also shows, however, that individual competitions are judged differently and attract different amounts of prize money, and also vary widely in terms of their sports appeal. This should be clearly stated in all tournament publications (announcements, programme, the media), as any kind of false impression has a counter-productive effect on show-jumping.

Table 7.2: *Structure and challenge of various jumping courses*

Importance/ category	Type of competition	Rules	Speed m/min.	Remarks
A Main Competitions	1 GRAND PRIX	1.60 m, 2 diff. rounds, j/o	400	Olympic Format (Individual)
	2 NATIONS CUP	2 identical rounds, 1.60 m	400	Olympic Format (Team)
	3 GRAND DERBY	1 round, 1.60 m, table A, j/o more than 1,000 m	400	e.g. Hamburg, Hickstead, La Baule
B Second Competitions	4 Final Competition	1.50 m, 1 or 2 rounds, j/o	375/400	
	5 Friendly Derby	1 round, Table A or C more than 700 m	375/400	e.g. Aachen, La Bagnia Monterrey, Valkenswaard, Wiesbaden
	6 Team Classes	various modi,	375/400	instead of Nations Cup
	7 Big Table A	with or without j/o	375/400	Classical Qualifier
	8 Change of Horses	1.50 m, 8 obstacles 4 riders/horses	350/375	modus of World Championships Final, attraction dependent on class of riders/horses, prize-money
C Third Competitions	9 Stallion Classes	1.40/1.50 m	350/375	
	10 Young Horses	1.35/1.45 m	350/375	
	11 Young Riders /Jun.	min. 1.40 m	350/375	
	12 Puissance	max. 4 j/o	300	very rare today
D Fourth Competitions	13 Table C	1.40/1.45 m	375/400	
	14 Relay Competition	1.40/1.45 m	350/375	
	15 Joker	1.40/1.45 m	350/375	
	16 Six-bar		350/375	
Entertainment	17 Jump and Drive			mostly indoors or small arenas
	18 Fancy Dress/ Wearing Costume			
	19 Pairs Competition Senior/Junior			
Boring	20 Two Phases			not really attractive
	21 Two Jump-offs			

8 SCHEDULES, TIMETABLES AND THE ORGANISATION OF JUMPING TOURNAMENTS

The competition schedule defines the competition framework of a planned tournament and is very important in terms of the overall organisation. Normally, one or several other tournaments will already have been held in the same location, so the following important aspects should be considered when preparing the schedule for the next tournament.

1   How were the major jumping competitions conceived in terms of the sequence of events? In the case of the 2002 CHIO Aachen, these were (table 8.1):

- GRAND PRIX (Sunday);

- Nations Cup (Friday);

- Preis von Europa (Wednesday);

  all ranking as very important GRAND PRIX.

2   What are the secondary major competitions. At 2002 CHIO Aachen they were:

- First GRAND PRIX qualifying competition (Tuesday);

- Nordrhein-Westfalen-Preis (Thursday);

- GRAND PRIX second-string horses (Saturday);
  Best of champions (Saturday);
  Friendly Derby-type competition (Saturday).

3   The secondary jumping competitions are intended for second- and third-string horses.

The following aspects are important for planning the next tournament.

1   Thorough analysis of the previous year's jumping competitions (see chapter 22);

  - jumping class/speed/max. height;

  - number of starters, eliminated, withdrawn;

  - clear rounds, jump-off;

  - double clear rounds;

  - the proportion of rounds with eight or fewer penalties.

2   Time that was required for the preliminary round, jump-off/first round, second round, jump-off, etc. is important for the timing of subsequent classes.

3   Special incidents, such as horses falling, unexpected weather conditions, excessive number of faults at water jumps, etc.

4   Other observations; as, for example, 'the competition is boring; spectators are leaving'.

The following experiences, questions and ideas help in further planning.

1   For an important GRAND PRIX, the best should qualify.

2   Forty starters (from among the world's top combinations) is a good number for the first round in big and important outdoor tournaments.

3   The most important outdoor tournaments – GRAND PRIX – are contested according to the Olympic format:

Table 8.1: *Tentative programme CHIO Aachen 2002*

Day	N° Competition	Competition	FEI-Rules Table	Money EURO	j/o	obstacles	speed	height	rider	class
Dienstag 11.00 h	S 1	accom-Preis	A 238. 2A2	11,000	-	11	375	1.45	2	40
	S 2	Qualification GP	A 238. 2A2	30,800	-	14	400	1.50	1	70
		Eröffnungsfeier		3,300						
Mittwoch	S 3	Sparkasse Youngster Cup	A 238.2A2	55,000	-	11	350	1.40	2	29
	S 5	Preis von Europa Warsteiner	A 238. 3AM5	16,500	1	14	400	1.50	1	60
	S 4	Preis des Kreises Aachen	10 in Siegerrunde	50,600	1		375	1.45	1	50
Donnerstag	S 8	NRW 1. Umlauf	A 266.5.2+283.3.1	11,000	1	13	400	1.50	1	60
	S 7	Preis des Handwerks (Joker)	C 239, 268, 274		-	10	375	1.50	1	50
	S 8	NRW 2. Umlauf		4,400	-		400	1.50	1	15
	S 6	Sparkasse Youngster Cup	A 238.2A2	11,000	-	14	350	1.40	2	29
Freitag	S 10	Preis d. Tuchfabrik Becker	C. 239+268	138,000	-	12	375	1.45	1	27
	S 11	NC 1. Uml. Mercedes Preis	A. 269.1.2		1	12	400	1.60	1	40
	S 11	NC 2. Uml. Mercedes Preis		8,800						24
	S 9	Youngster Cup Final	A 238.3AM5	11,000	1	14	350	1.45	2	20
Samstag	S 12	Ericsson Trophy 1. round	A PJA-Modus	50,600	1	12	400	1.50	1	32
	S 12	Ericsson Trophy 2. round			1	12	400	1.50	1	16+
	S 13	Rolex Best of Champions	Pferdewechsel	49,500	1	8	375	1.50	1	8
	S 14	Gräben und Wälle Sparkasse	C 239+268	28,600	-	10	375	1.45	-	4 x 4
										28
Sonntag	S 15	Zentis Preis	Siegerrunde	25,300	-	11	375	1.45	1	30
	S 16	Großer Preis AM	A 266.5.2+283.3.1	253,000		15	400	1.60	1	40
		2. Umlauf				10	400	1.60		40
		Stechen			1		400	1.70		4
				747,400						

- two rounds over different courses;

- 1.60 m/400 m/min.;

- grass surface with natural obstacles.

Prominent examples are the CHIO Aachen, CSIO Spruce Meadows, Calgary, CSIO Rome and CSI Valkenswaard, the Netherlands – with appropriate prize-money.

4   These competitions place Olympic demands on the best horse/rider combinations. They are no walkover, and certainly not an opportunity to experiment with primitive penalty-production methods and manipulations that allow a standard well below the Olympic requirements! Olympic standards and top performances are not negotiable in top-level sport!

5   Real latent risks for the horse and rider in show-jumping have been largely eliminated over the last 25 years or so, due to the work of leading course designers and other experts. (There have been a variety of technical safety improvements in obstacle construction, safety cups, modern jumping surfaces and the more thorough and improved training of course designers, judges and other competition experts.) However, one should only expect a top horse to face the challenges of a CSIO Aachen or Calgary very few times each year.

Irrespective of whether tournaments are big or small, the most important rules for good tournaments are the same.

1   Consistent quality of the programme, including a first-class field of competitors, jumping stadium, surface, course, decoration, professionalism and friendliness of all staff, the stable area, the treatment of grooms, catering, treatment of sponsors, spectators and guests of honour, as well as short distances to walk and good parking facilities (as far as the author is concerned, every visitor to a tournament has VIP status).

2   Programme planning based on the laws of dramatic production:

- excitement and tension right to the end;

- the best horse/rider combinations start last;

- the main events happen at the end of the tournament.

3   Spectators are the greatest asset of a good tournament because they demonstrate public interest in the event and have a major influence on the atmosphere and mood.

4   The officials (judges, course designers, stewards, etc.) of a tournament should be chosen on the basis of their professional expertise and ability to work as a team. In this role, they should act unconditionally as advocates for the sport rather than as 'sticklers for the rules'!

5   Young tournament organisers, in particular, can systematically and quickly increase the quality and importance of their tournament if they integrate a decent, team-oriented, well-respected adviser with significant international experience into their organisation in an appropriate way.

Apart from the competition schedule itself, timing is an important element in a well-functioning competition (avoid delays and/or boring, unplanned breaks in the proceedings. The essential ingredients for a good timetable are:

1   a fairly accurate estimate of the actual number of starters (compare previous years' figures);

2   the average time requirement per starter is

$$T = n_p \cdot t_p \, [\, min. \,]$$

The data in table 8.2 could be used as an initial guide for a realistic timetable.

Table 8.2: *Average time needed per participant*

Length of the course m	Speed m/min.	Time allowed sec.	Average time per participant min./participant	Number of participants /h
300	350	51	1.5	40
400	350	69	2.0	30
500	350	86	2.4	25
	400	75	2.2	27
600	400	90	2.8	21
800	400	120	3.5	17

9 REMARKS ON OBSTACLE DESIGN

GENERAL ASPECTS AND TYPES OF OBSTACLE

As jumping is a 'nature-based sport', the course has its roots in the natural landscape which is characterised by:

● variety and change;

● variation of the track;

● nature, aesthetics and culture in any form.

The main materials for obstacles and arenas are therefore taken from nature (figure 9.1).

Other materials, such as plastic or rubber, are accessory materials which, although important, are generally of secondary significance where design is concerned.

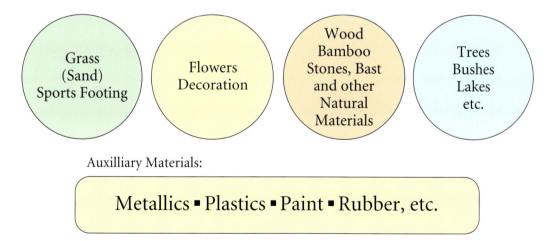

Figure 9.1: *Basic materials used in course design – all nature-based.*

In practice, we differentiate between:

- a variety of permanent natural obstacles, such as water jump, bank, wall, lake, devil's dyke, dry ditch (Trakehner), etc.;

- and an equally varied range of moveable obstacles.

On the course, we differentiate between various obstacle types as shown below, both in diagrams and in photographs to give a clearer understanding:

1   vertical obstacles (figures 9.2 and 9.3);

Flower and other natural decoration
is welcome and not forbidden!

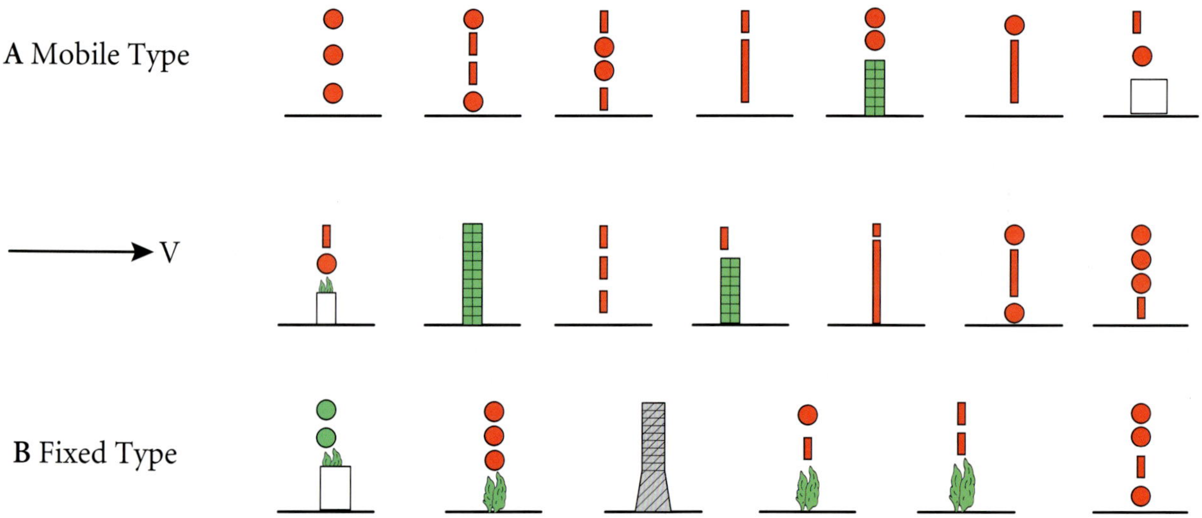

A Mobile Type

⟶ **V**

B Fixed Type

Figure 9.2: *Some examples of vertical obstacles.*

2   spread obstacles (figures 9.4 and 9.5);

3   intermediate obstacles (figures 9.6 and 9.7);

4   no. 1 obstacles (figures 9.8 and 9.9) are predominantly a mixture of the first three types of obstacle mentioned above. These should always be friendly and inviting (*'ouverture'*), and not at all difficult!

Figure 9.3: *Examples of vertical obstacles. Photos by Christa Heibach.*

Flower and other natural decoration
is welcome and not forbidden!

A Mobile Type
1.50/2.00 m

⟶ V

Gate

B Fixed Type
1.50/2.00 m

| Bush | Water | Water | Dry Ditch | Dry Ditch |

Figure 9.4: *(Above and below) Some examples of spread obstacles.*

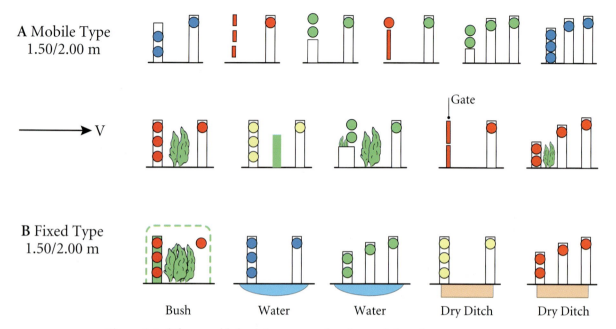

Figure 9.5: (Above and below) *Examples of spread obstacles. Photos by Christa Heibach.*

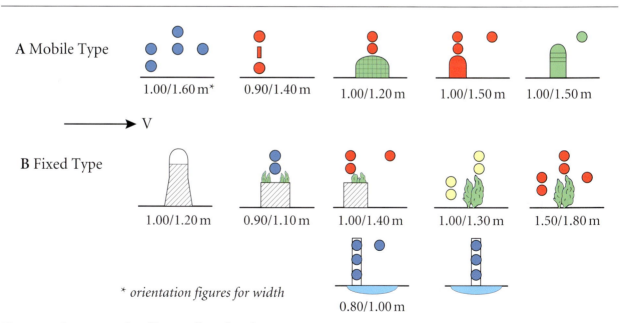

Figure 9.6: *Some examples of intermediate obstacles.*

Figure 9.7: *More examples of intermediate obstacles. Photos by Christa Heibach.*

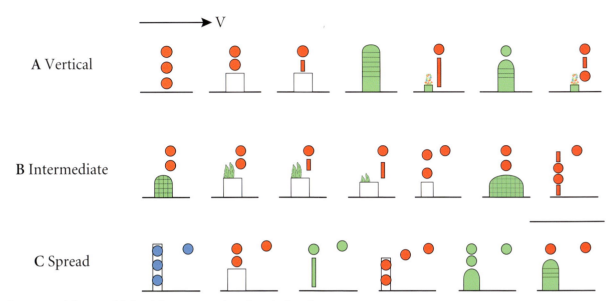

Figure 9.8: *(Above and below) Some examples of no. 1 obstacles.*

Figure 9.9: *More examples of no. 1 obstacles. Photos by Christa Heibach.*

5   walls, which can be part of all the obstacle types described above, are dealt with separately (see p. 145).

A frequent criticism of courses today is that they have little variety and rarely make full use of the broad range of available types of obstacle. Frequent mistakes, for example, include:

- an excessive use of poles;

- not having a wall;

- a lack of variety in design;

- the absence of a water obstacle (e.g. a water ditch/Liverpool);

- many course designers almost completely ignore triple bars or a large number of mixed types which help to create variety;

- existing natural obstacles often fail to be included in the course;

- not all sponsor obstacles conform to the higher standards expected in terms of design and taste.

PERMANENT NATURAL OBSTACLES

Natural obstacles originate from cross-country riding, as encountered by horse and rider while out in the open countryside, for example during fox-hunting or in military operations. These include:

- paddock fences

- gates

- walls

- small or wider streams

- lakes

- earth mounds

- hedges and bushes

of various different shapes and sizes.

Cross-country riding and fox-hunting come closest to preserving the experience of natural obstacles.

Permanent natural obstacles are a fundamental and characteristic part of major international GRAND PRIX or Derby stadiums with a grass surface; examples have already been given.

Natural obstacles contribute greatly to the charm and identity of these and other important GRAND PRIX arenas. As equestrian sport is a 'nature-based sport', natural obstacles form an obvious part of it.

The purpose of natural obstacles is:

1 To present as a design feature to make GRAND PRIX-level arenas attractive and unique.

2   Water jumps and Liverpools (water ditches), in particular, are traditionally part of jumping at Olympic level.

3   Medium water jumps, water ditches, drop jumps (devil's dyke), small/medium banks, dry ditches, obstacles with tree trunks, etc. are interesting features of:

    - smaller jumping competitions (with one or two natural obstacles);

    - competitions against the clock;

    - 'friendly' Derbys (for example, CSI La Bagnia, Italy, CSI Monterrey, Mexico, CSI Valkenswaard, the Netherlands).

4   A good principle to adhere to is that an arena should not have more natural obstacles, even when carefully and expertly placed, than is appropriate for its size. The principle of 'better one too few than one too many' should be observed.

5   A major exception is a type of grand Derby of the kind held in Hamburg since 1920, which, without doubt, has a justified place in the future.

The claim that natural obstacles are out of fashion [106] is diametrically opposed to the view of leading competition organisers, many leading international course designers, judges and other tournament experts and cannot be accepted here.

It is also untrue that natural obstacles create a higher risk of injuries, provided that they are designed in an inviting way and are maintained in good condition.

As far as I can judge, looking at the tournaments in Aachen, Calgary, Hickstead, La Baule, Monterrey and Valkenswaard as prominent examples over the last five years, there has not been a serious accident at any of them.

The most spectacular case of serious falls occurred in 1998 at the Hamburg Jumping Derby [130], when seven horse/rider combinations, among them Nelson Pessoa and Hugo Simon, had serious falls at one single obstacle, a non-solid bush oxer, no. 11.

The simple reason for these falls was an oxer planted with too much greenery, which the horses repeatedly tried to bank (see also figure 9.24).

When building this oxer, the people responsible clearly failed to recognise, or overlooked, this well-known risk. It may be of interest to learn that there were 21 falls in a medium-size jumping class (approx. 1.35 m) over a similarly over-planted bush oxer at the 1961 CHIO Aachen. There are also other well-known examples from the 1960s.

The published view of one course designer [106] that 'natural obstacles are a hindrance, ... [which] establish many tracks in advance and thus prevent modern lines' must be clearly contradicted here.

1   Anyone who studies the course lines of great natural arenas will be amazed at how much variety is possible, even over a period of decades.

2   The area of the jumping arena of the CHIO Aachen, which has no permanent obstacles, is larger than 90 per cent of all other arenas in Germany.

3   On the question of 'so-called modern lines', I agree with Leonard Bernstein who, when asked about the difference between classical and so-called 'modern' music, answered: 'There is only good or bad music.' The same applies to track designs.

4   Arenas with their own distinctive shape and permanent features make it easier to create different lines and much greater track variety than can be seen on smaller sand arenas without natural obstacles, which are often characterised by track repetition and limited attractiveness.

GOD IS IN DETAIL!

(Ludwig Mies van der Rohe, 1886–1969, one of the most important architects of the twentieth century)

The directors of the Metropolitan Opera in New York or La Scala in Milan cannot demand a new opera building if they think that their 'creativity' needs a different structure in order to implement so-called 'modern ideas'. The structure of traditional, major jumping stadiums, with their natural obstacles, is usually modified only in small, well thought-out stages, without changing the basic appearance, just like golf courses.

The following aspects should especially be borne in mind when designing permanent obstacles.

1   An open water jump is the first permanent obstacle that should be built before all others, because the water jump is a fixed part of GRAND PRIX-level competitions. No outdoor GRAND PRIX should take place without a water jump.

2   There should be one or two water ditches (Liverpool, normally 1.2–2.0 up to 2.5 m wide).

3   Other types of permanent obstacles include a devil's dyke, various single-step or multiple-step banks, dry ditches, natural stone walls, bush oxers, etc.

4   The number and size of permanent obstacles should be proportionate to the size of the arena.

5   Building permanent obstacles demands careful planning by an experienced course designer.

6   Permanent obstacles require regular care and maintenance.

7   Permanent obstacles should only be built on the outer track if they will neither obstruct the view nor impair the flexibility of the track.

A few rules need to be observed when designing an open water jump.

1   The size of the open water jump should be commensurate with the importance of the competition and the size of the arena (3.00–3.8 m).

2   The length of the front should be 50 per cent greater than the width of the jump.

3   The deepest point in the middle should be approximately 15 cm if the water jump can be approached from both directions, which is preferable.

4   Dyeing the water azure (a mixture of green and blue, comparable to the Caribbean or Mediterranean Sea) gives the water jump a more serious and friendly look. (It should not be a dark inky blue.)

5   A rubber or woven mat with a rough surface, in a light green-blue colour, should be glued to the base because it will provide a soft landing for the horse's legs and thus prevent quite a few accidents.

6   One possible design is shown in figures 9.10–9.12.

7   The final width of the water jump is determined by the take-off element (hurdle, small wall, etc.). The water jump always remains filled with water to the same level.

8   There are a number of different designs for take-off elements.

9   A vertical take-off element with a maximum height of 50 cm results in a better jump than low take-off elements.

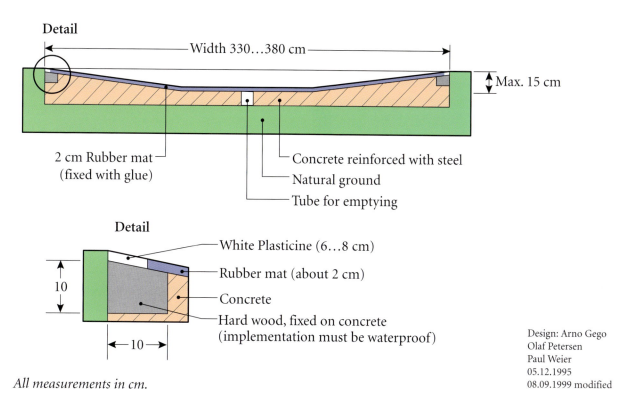

Detail

Width 330...380 cm

Max. 15 cm

2 cm Rubber mat
(fixed with glue)

Concrete reinforced with steel

Natural ground

Tube for emptying

Detail

White Plasticine (6...8 cm)

Rubber mat (about 2 cm)

Concrete

Hard wood, fixed on concrete
(implementation must be waterproof)

10

10

Design: Arno Gego
Olaf Petersen
Paul Weier
05.12.1995
08.09.1999 modified

All measurements in cm.

Figure 9.10: *Water jump design I.*

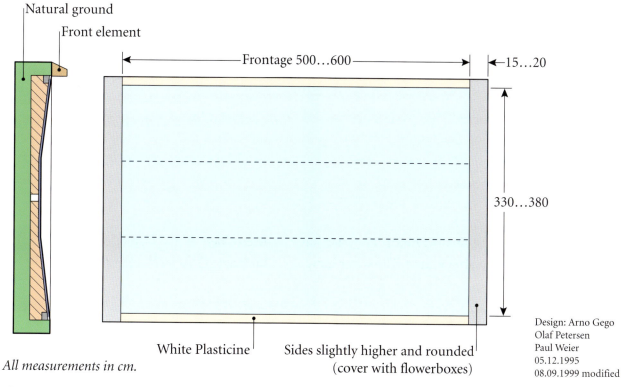

Natural ground

Front element

Frontage 500...600

15...20

330...380

White Plasticine

Sides slightly higher and rounded
(cover with flowerboxes)

Design: Arno Gego
Olaf Petersen
Paul Weier
05.12.1995
08.09.1999 modified

All measurements in cm.

Figure 9.11: *Water jump design II.*

Figure 9.12 *Some examples of water jumps. Photos by Christa Heibach.*

10 The water jump should allow an obstacle in the middle; for example, for use at the start of the event. This will normally produce a higher trajectory which, in turn, motivates the horse. However, a 4.50-m wide trajectory will result in a parabolic height of 1.50 m – not 1.10 m.

11 A white strip made of Plasticine is currently the best option for accurate judging of the water jump.

12 Water jumps that are filled to slightly lower than the ground surface are easier to jump than those with a high water level because of the mirror effect.

13 Water jumps, as well as other permanent natural obstacles, should be surrounded by natural borders such as shrubs, flowers, large boulders, etc. If the sides are raised

higher, with decorations towards the middle of the water jump, it makes the jump easier for the horse to negotiate, as Frédéric Cottier of France has rightly commented.

Water ditches (English: Liverpool, French: *bidet*) can be of great help in making arenas and jumping tracks more interesting and varied.

- On the one hand, they are a valuable means of encouraging young horses and riders in competitions;

- but they are also a classic obstacle in GRAND PRIX-level competitions.

When designing Liverpools (figures 9.13 and 9.14), a few rules need to be observed during construction.

1 Permanent Liverpools should be embedded in cement below ground level.

2 They should have round edges, and be approximately 15 cm deep at the centre.

3 As with the water jump, the bed should be covered with a rubber mat or woven matting (approx. 2 cm thick, with a rough surface to provide grip) and glued down.

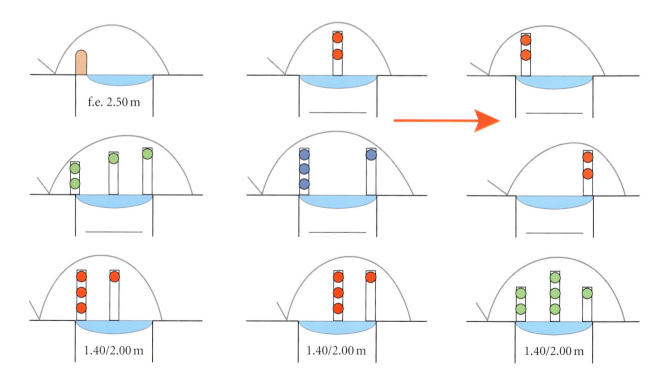

Figure 9.13: *A variety of Liverpools (obstacles upon water).*

Figure 9.14: *Examples of Liverpools. Photos by Christa Heibach.*

4   On each side three posts made of hardwood, with a 12 x 12-cm cross-section and metal tracks with holes, should be inserted into suitable square pipes which are set in the cement on the sides; these pipes should have a water outlet below to prevent the post from standing in water.

5   The sides should be planted with bushes and/or flowers, or decorated with moveable features.

6   The spread of the Liverpool depends on the size of the arena and is normally fixed between 1.40 and 1.80 m.

7   If a permanent Liverpool is lacking, a rubber or plastic tub or pond liner makes a good substitute. The water should be dyed – just like the water jump – and the tub or liner should be decorated with greenery and flowers to create as much of a natural environment as possible.

Apart from the classical permanent natural obstacles described here, such as the:

- water jump; and

- water ditch (Liverpool),

a large number of other permanent natural obstacles (figure 9.15) continue to form part of a main arena – with or without a Derby. Some are outlined briefly below.

1 The devil's dyke (figure 9.16) continues to be an interesting natural obstacle that rewards the well-schooled jumping horse. It is quite amazing, if not frustrating in terms of classical equitation, to see how many horses today are not prepared to jump such a simple and natural obstacle. Where does that leave 'natural schooling'?

2 A large number of single-step or multiple-step banks (figure 9.17) can often be approached from several directions, which increases their attraction. The side slopes can either be completely covered with grass (the maximum gradient of the slopes is 60–65 degrees), or cemented in with rubble or other materials (gradient up to 90 degrees).

It is, of course, important to make sure that an expert with sufficient experience is consulted when designing natural obstacles.
   Unfortunately, bush oxers and other spread obstacles filled carefully with small shrubs and flowers are used increasingly

Figure 9.15: *Some examples of natural fixed obstacles (banks and devil's dykes). (Top) photo by Susanne Gossen. (Centre) photo by Rolf Peter. (Bottom) photo by Rolf Peter.*

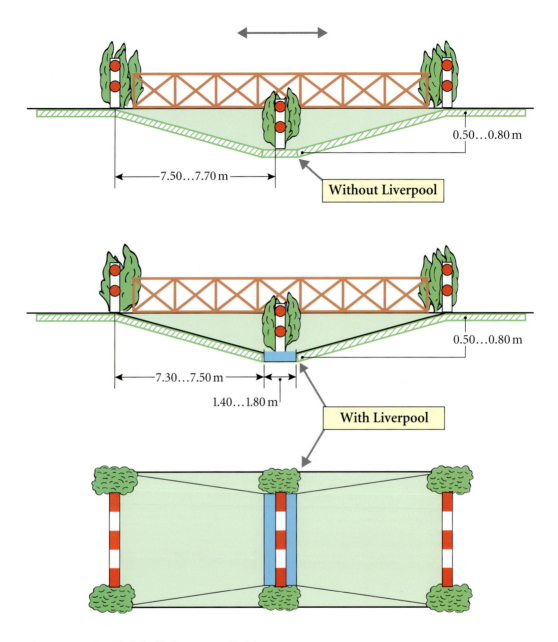

Figure 9.16: *Devil's dyke (Pulvermanns Grab)*.

rarely, even though they are part of a list of possible options to introduce variety. The reasons for this may be:

- a lack of creativity;

- laziness;

- lack of experience in dealing with this type of obstacle.

Bank

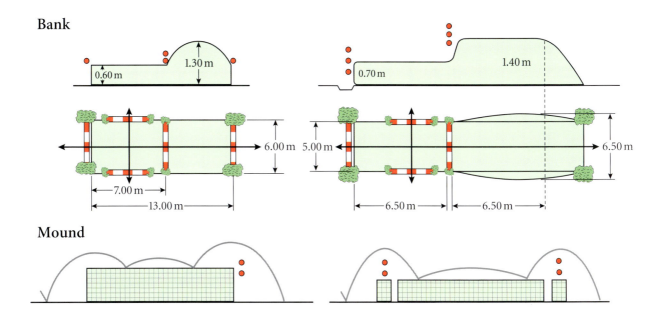

Mound

Figure 9.17: *Natural fixed fences (banks and mounds).*

Figure 9.18: *Further examples of natural fixed obstacles (banks and devil's dykes). (Top left) photo by Christa Heibach. (Top right) photo by Rolf Peter. (Bottom) photo by Susanne Gossen.*

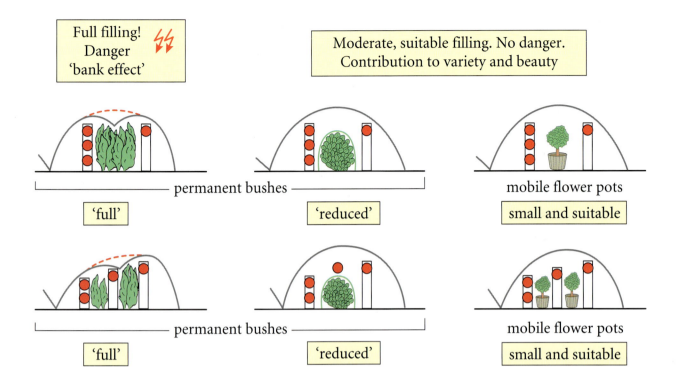

Figure 9.19: *Bush oxer and triple bar.*

Like other natural obstacles, bush oxers have a long tradition and are part of the development of show-jumping and course design.

As a rule, the only obstacles which should be omitted, or expertly adapted, from the traditional obstacle repertoire are those which:

- involve objective risks that cannot be remedied; for example, a 6-m high, steep slope, a devil's dyke with a high ground-water level which cannot be drained, excessively huge Irish or English banks where there is a danger of the horse 'banking';

- are temporarily not jumpable because of bad weather conditions.

Natural arenas and natural obstacles obey their own laws and cannot be mastered through indoor or sand arena practice, however extensive. They demand a high degree of experience which many course designers lack.

The examples in figure 9.19 show that spread obstacles that are stuffed too full and grass banks with obstacles carry a clear risk of the horses 'banking' and thus of accidents or falls.

MOVEABLE OBSTACLES AND ELEMENTS

The available obstacle material consists of a large number of different components which should allow the very varied and flexible composition of obstacles of different character. Courses have a tendency to become boring if individual obstacle components belong exclusively to a specific obstacle which, day after day, and year after year, has exactly the same appearance and composition.

Good obstacle material must meet some basic requirements.

- All parts must be easy to transport. Heavy components should have a sufficient number of well-placed carrying handles.

- Despite being low in weight, all parts subject to impact should have sufficient rigidity and solidity.

- The obstacle material should allow varied compositions of material and colours. Standard lengths of hanging and standing elements are helpful.

- To ensure solid stability, load-bearing parts should have a low centre of gravity.

- The obstacle material should allow gradual changes in height and width to be made.

- Changes in dimensions should be easy to carry out, quickly, and without the need for tools or another person's help.

- The front length of the obstacles should be in appropriate relationship to the width of the arena. In small jumping arenas, such as indoor arenas, the front length should, at most, be roughly 20–25 per cent of the width of the jumping area.

KNOCK-DOWN ELEMENTS, STANDS, WINGS AND CUPS

Wings, standards or stands, cups and knock-down elements are the main components of an obstacle. The following recommendations are worth considering.

- The height of the stands and wings should normally not exceed the maximum height of the obstacle by more than 30 to 50 cm (figure 9.20).

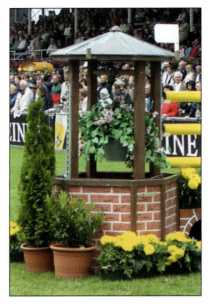

Figure 9.20: *Examples of different wings. Photos by Christa Heibach.*

- The diameter of the cross foot of upright stands should be around 80 x 80 cm. The cross foot should bear the weight on the outside.

- The foot of the stand (for example, with the profile dimension 16 x 16 cm) in upright stands should be noticeably heavier than the post (for example, 10 x 10 cm), so that the centre of gravity is low.

- The distance between the holes for inserting the cups should be a maximum of 5 cm, or, alternatively, it should be smoothly adjustable (as, for example, at the 1955 Olympic Games in Stockholm). It should be possible to adjust it over the entire standard height.

- The cups should be narrow and allow the intended spacing of knock-down elements.

- In bigger tournaments, it is a good idea to have available cups of different depths, often 18 and 20 mm (figures 9.22–9.24), that are, for example, easy to identify by their different colours, to achieve proper knock-down behaviour with different hanging elements (according to weight, diameter and shape), and obstacle height.

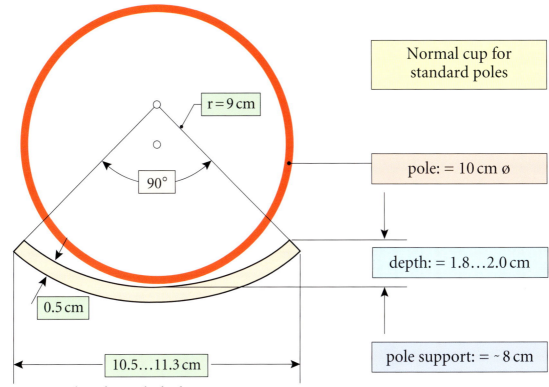

Figure 9.21: *Normal cup for standard poles.*

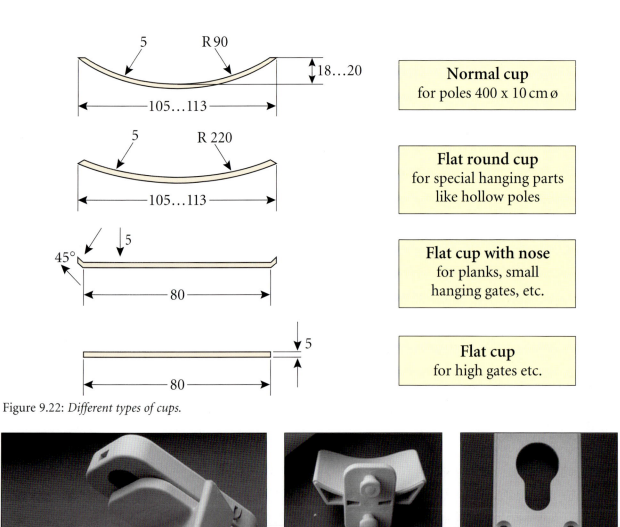

5 R 90 18...20 105...113	**Normal cup** for poles 400 x 10 cm ø
5 R 220 105...113	**Flat round cup** for special hanging parts like hollow poles
45° 5 80	**Flat cup with nose** for planks, small hanging gates, etc.
5 80	**Flat cup** for high gates etc.

Figure 9.22: *Different types of cups.*

Figure 9.23: *Safety cups (Olaf Petersen system)*

- The length of the cups in the direction of the knock-down elements should be sufficient (for example, between 8 and 10 cm) to ensure that even with stands whose position is not exactly vertical, the cups are long enough for the top and bottom hanging elements to be securely fixed.

- The shape of the cups must be so stable that, even with heavy impact, no deformation will occur. False economy will quickly show in poor results.

- The diameter of the cup should be clearly bigger than the pole diameter so that the pole is able to roll.

Recent developments in cups have resulted in considerable advances.

- Safety cups [031] have now become an FEI standard and have significantly improved safety in jumping spread obstacles (figure 9.24). To prevent proliferation, all safety cups must be tested before they get an FEI certificate.

- Many cups are now made of plastic, making them light and corrosion-proof.

KNOCK-DOWN UPPER ELEMENTS

The judging of most jumping competitions is based exclusively on measurable criteria. An exception would be when judging is based on penalties and style. It is important that the knock-down elements of the individual obstacles (poles, planks, gates, wall bricks, etc.) exhibit an appropriate and consistently reproducible drop-down behaviour.

The drop-down behaviour must be thoroughly checked before each competition and for each obstacle. The following aspects should be taken into account.

1   The upper hanging elements should remain in place if they are just touched, but should fall down if they are clearly knocked against. The clean-jumping horse should be rewarded.

2   The drop-down behaviour must not change during the competition (for example, through deformation of the cup, a change in the position of the upper pole, replacing the upper pole, plank, etc., or wedging in of the knock-down elements etc.), in order to ensure a fair ranking.

3   It should be possible to have a combination of various hanging elements (for example, poles, planks, gates, etc.). Here, it is advantageous to have the smallest possible number of different lengths for the hanging elements (with the exception of narrow obstacles) to allow for different combinations.

4   In spread jumps, the rear hanging elements should fall particularly easily (use a flatter cup). Except for natural poles, turned poles are the standard, as they have a

constant diameter across the entire length and can be easily replaced because they are all the same.

The standard Olympic measurement (with the exception of narrow obstacles) for poles of middle-level and top-level tournaments is:

- 4.00 m length and 10 cm in diameter

for dry spruce with a density of $\gamma = 500$ kg/m³. The weight (mass) of poles depends on the dimensions (l, d) and density γ.

$$ m = \frac{\pi \cdot d^2}{4} \; l \cdot \gamma \quad [kg] $$

For commonly used pole dimensions, the associated weights are shown in table 9.1.

Table 9.1: *Weight of poles with different dimensions*

Length of pole	Weight m (kg) (density 500 kg/m³) Diameter of poles					
l (m)	d = 9	10	10.5	11	11.5	12 cm ø
2.00	--	--	--	--	10.4	11.3
2.50	--	--	10.8	11.9	13.0	14.1
3.00	--	11.8	13.0	14.2	15.6	--
3.50	11.1	13.7	15.2	--	--	--
4.00	12.7	15.7	--	--	--	--

In tropical and subtropical regions in particular, the density is clearly above 500 kg/m3, so that the diameter and/or the pole length must be correspondingly adjusted.

In practice, pole weights should be in the range of 10 to 15 kg.

As a matter of principle, the rule applies that:

- the heavier the pole, the flatter the cup.

Table 9.2 *Diameter of poles and cross-section area*

Diameter (cm)	Cross-section Area absolute (cm²)	relative (%)
9	63.6	81
9.5	70.9	90.3
10	78.5	100
10.5	86.6	110.3
11	95	121
11.5	103.9	132.3
12	113.1	144

In order to compensate for the reduced weight of shorter poles, it is necessary to increase the diameter of the poles.

Table 9.2 can be used as an aid. Proportional increase in the diameter does not achieve the desired aim because the cross-section area of the pole increases in line with the squaring of the diameter.

At the same density a 3-m pole would need a 33 per cent larger cross-section area than a 4-m pole if the same weight is wanted. Unfortunately, in practice one can note an increasing trend towards obstacles made up of ever-smaller top elements – which is clearly detrimental to the development of the sport.

This trend is not new. At the end of the 1950s, for example, there were obstacles at the CSIO in New York's Madison Square Garden where a light lath (a thin strip of wood) lay on the top pole, which, when knocked down, resulted in a penalty fault even if the pole itself remained in place. However, this subtle practice was soon stopped because it is contrary to the principles of the sport (*anti-sportif*).

WALLS

There are a large number of different wall designs and constructions (figure 9.25) which I will not describe in detail here. My purpose here is merely to give some generally valid information.

Figure 9.24: *Examples of various different types and designs of walls. Photos by Christa Heibach.*

1 Walls today are only interesting if they are light and flexible in design.

2 A wall thickness of approximately 20–30 cm has proved successful in the sport at international level (with the exception of puissance).

3 Normally, walls only need bases added if they are less than 30 cm thick.

4 Standing elements (for example, one to four parts) should be no higher than 100 cm.

5 All sections are designed to be vertical.

6 Light-weight upper sections should be available in a mixture of:

   ● 20 cm

   ● 15 cm

   ● 10 cm.

   This allows the height of the wall to be varied by 5 cm. Whether there is still a need for 5-cm capping bricks (the effect of ever-smaller top elements) is questionable and depends on the thickness of the wall.

7 A wall should also allow for the possibility of:

   ● poles

   ● planks

   ● hanging gates, etc.

   to be added, in order to increase the variety of the design.

8 If the base of the wall consists of several standing elements, it can be used in a variety of ways, both as a:

   ● narrow obstacle;

   and as

- an obstacle with an open design of the base.

9   Walls should have two to three different upper sections with a view to visual variety and different uses:

- obstacle no. 1;

- with upper sections;

- classical use as a wall.

10 The design of wall bricks should ensure that no nails can stick out to cause a risk.

OTHER OBSTACLE MATERIALS AND AIDS

Other important obstacle parts include:

- standing elements used as fillers;

- extras;

- numbers;

- flags;

- accessories for decoration;

which I will not consider in detail here because a description of obstacle material is not the prime task of this book. It could, perhaps, be the valid subject-matter of another publication.

However, it is worth mentioning some small aids which are of greater importance than they sometimes seem.

1   Knock-down elements (especially poles) can be clearly identified with coloured sticky tape. For example,

- a piece of tape can be fixed to the right end of the front pole at the top, in the jumping direction;

- a piece of tape can be fixed to the right end of the back pole at the top, at a right angle to the jumping direction.

This means that the upper poles can be replaced correctly when putting them back after a knock-down. The same applies for planks, gates, elephant poles, etc.

2   One can make small height corrections or stabilise the position of wobbly upright parts using small wooden boards (0.5; 1.0; 2.0; 3.0 cm thick).

3   A toolbox containing a hammer, pliers, saw, electric drill, screws, nails, etc. is an essential piece of equipment in an arena.

4   A basket with greenery (fir branches, ivy or similar) often proves a useful accessory to make small visual improvements, as, for example:

- surrounding a Liverpool;

- woven through fence railings;

- for closing a hole in a defective part of a wall (for example, caused by a refusal).

THE INFLUENCE OF POOR WEATHER CONDITIONS

There have been several occasions over the last 50 years when thunderstorms were so strong that no obstacle could be put up firmly enough to prevent it from being knocked over by hurricane-force winds. Tournaments or jumping classes either had to be stopped or interrupted.

In regions where frequent hurricane-force winds or extreme storms have to be anticipated, special attention should be paid to ensuring the stability of obstacles by:

- using wings with a low centre of gravity;

- limiting the area of the wings that is exposed to wind;

- not using planks, gates or similar for upper parts;

- using deeper cups for planks, gates, etc. below the top pole;

- using stable and wind-resistant start and finish equipment;

- using small sandbags to weigh down wings, support parts and many other bases.

This was my own experience as a technical designer (TD) at the 2000 Olympic Games in Sydney, Australia. Although I had previously visited Australia over a period of 15 years at different seasons, I was taken by surprise by the 90 km/h storms at the individual final on the last day of the games when poles dropped from the cups as a result of the wind.

This sort of occurrence is a good reason for including this phenomenon in planning, especially for GRAND PRIX-level tournaments.

FALLING TIME OF KNOCK-DOWN ELEMENTS

As the finishing line has come ever closer to the last obstacle (6 m) in the FEI rules since the beginning of 2003, the observer may be interested, even if only tangentially, in the following questions.

1   How much time does it take a knock-down element (for example, a pole or wall bricks) to hit the ground?

2   How far does the horse move forward in this time?

A small physical observation (tables 9.3 and 9.4) shows that, during jump-off for example, the horse can move 4 m or more forward before the knock-down element touches the ground.

It is well known that a fallen pole always incurs 4 penalties – even if the finishing line has been crossed. Nevertheless, this brief diversion may help to pose the right questions in future decision-making.

SPONSOR OBSTACLES

Sponsor obstacles (figure 9.25) should be positive advertising for the respective sponsor. The higher the quality and prestige of the particular tournament, the more important is the advertising for the sponsor.

There are some rules, based on experience, for designing sponsors' obstacles at leading tournaments.

Table 9.2 *Normal falling time of 'faultable' parts (poles, planks, etc.)*

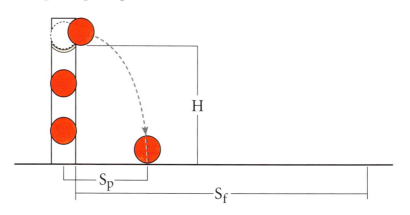

Newton's equation

$$H = g \cdot \frac{t_f^2}{2} \ (m)$$

Falling time

$$t_f = \sqrt{\frac{2.H}{g}} \ (sec)$$

Horse moving forward during fall of pole

$$S_f = \frac{v.t_f}{60} \ (m)$$

H = falling height (m)
g = earth acceleration = 9.81 (m/sec.)
t_f = falling time to ground (sec.)
V = speed of horse (m/min.)
S_f = forward movement of horse (m)
S_p = path of pole falling (m)

Table 9.4 *Calculating the forward movement of the horse during the fall of the 'faultable' part*

Height of Fall (m)	Required Time of Fall (sec.)	Forward Movement of Horse (Sf) (m) during the Fall of the Faulting Part Speed (m/min.)		
		350	400	450
1.40	0.534	3.116	3.562	4.007
1.50	0.553	3.226	3.687	4.148
1.60	0.571	3.332	3.808	4.254
2.00	0.639	3.725	4.257	4.789

- Sponsor obstacles must integrate in the most effective way with the quality of the existing obstacles and become part of the overall presentation in the stadium.

- They must comply with the current regulations of television stations.

- They should be pleasing and promote equestrian sport.

- It should be possible to vary their design. Obstacles that keep an identical image day after day become boring.

- They should have so much charm and meaning that they can be easily identified after several presentations even without the company logo.

- Clever organisers or course designers will be able to convince sponsors of the qualitative superiority of the above rules, and will not accept inferior proposals — not least to protect top companies who are already well placed.

DESIGN OF FLOWER ISLANDS AND DECORATION

Reference has already been made on p. 119 to basic materials that are essential when designing obstacles (figure 9.8).

Particularly where arenas have no permanent obstacles or other fixed points, and especially on sand arenas, colour, flowers and decoration play an important role.

Specially designed flower islands are particularly suitable for enhancing the overall presentation (figure 9.26). There is no limit to the imagination. Many different parts, such as:

- filling material in stands and other standing elements;

- wall bricks;

- low-platform wagons;

- old horse carriages;

- small Liverpools;

Figure 9.25 *Examples of sponsor obstacles. Wölffer Estate photo by Steve Stephens. All other photos by Christa Heibach.*

Figure 9.26: *Examples of islands. Photos by Christa Heibach.*

- stones, flowers, etc.;

are all suitable.

The examples of various different arenas (shown in figure 9.26) give an idea of the great variety of design possibilities using flower islands and decoration.

COLOURS ARE THE JOY OF LIFE!

*(Ernst-Ludwig Kirchner, 1880–1938,
architect, designer, engineer, painter)*

10 TRAJECTORIES OVER OBSTACLES, TAKE-OFF AND LANDING DISTANCE

A horse's jump over an obstacle conforms to the physical law of a thrown ball following a parabolic path. This applies strictly only to the horse's centre of gravity, or the joint centre of gravity of the rider and horse.

We can, however, more or less assume that the form which the movement of the horse's lower limbs (hooves, legs, rarely the stomach) takes will be a parabolic curve such as can be observed, for example, in video-recorded 2-D movement analyses [101].

If we start with the simplest case of a vertical obstacle, then the quasi-parabolic arc will run approximately symmetrically to the obstacle. This means that the take-off and landing distances are approximately equal.

In practice, for naturally schooled jumping horses, the landing distance (L) is, in the case described above, slightly greater than the take-off distance (A) (figure 10.1) when taking an average of natural jumps. This is connected, among other things, with factors such as:

- the movement of the rider's centre of gravity in a perfectly light seat;

- shifting of the centre of gravity of the naturally forward-jumping horse (head/neck/legs).

Of course, the take-off and landing distances also depend on the forward speed, the ground conditions, the horse's jumping ability, visual effects and many other aspects.

If we stay with the simple example of the upright obstacle, then the following laws also apply (figure 10.2).

- Take-off and landing distances increase with the height of the obstacle and forward speed.
- The possible area of the take-off and landing zone decreases with the dimension of the obstacle.

The first comment relates to vertical obstacles, but applies equally to other types of obstacle. It clearly shows that the demands on the rider's and horse's ability, harmony and skill increase disproportionately with the increase in the obstacle size and minimum speed:

- 350 m/min. for standard competitions;

- 375 m/min. for international jumping competitions;

- 400 m/min. for GRAND PRIX, Nations Cup and Grand Derby.

If we broaden the investigation to a few other important and different obstacle types such as:

- upright (as the starting scenario)

- oxer/parallel

- triple bar

- water jump

then additional laws pertain that are not devoid of logic (figure 10.3).

- The take-off distance decreases accordingly.

- The parabolic curve and the landing distance shift accordingly backward.

- As long as the culmination point (maximum) of the parabolic curve remains the same, the distance of the curve hardly changes (at constant forward speed).

For the trajectories of the most important obstacle types, approximate laws still apply (figures 10.4–10.6), as can be seen when consulting various references in the literature [048/056/166].

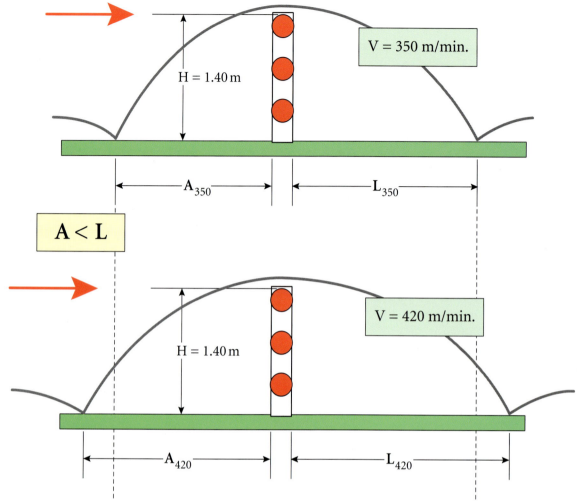

Figure 10.1: *Quasi-parabolic trajectory over a vertical obstacle at different speeds.*

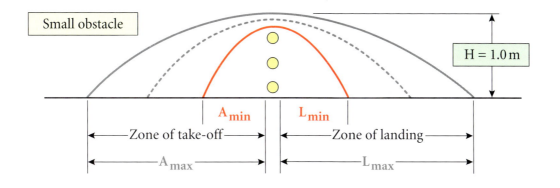

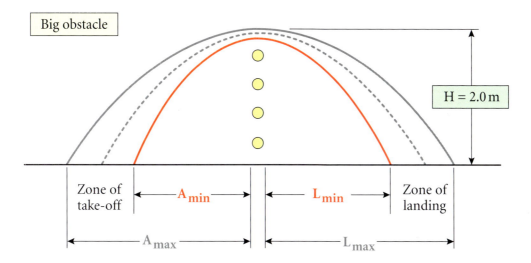

General observations:

1. Take-off and landing distances are growing with speed and/or height.
2. Take-off and landing distances are relatively decreasing with spread width.
3. Zones of take-off and landing are relatively decreasing with the dimension of the obstacle.

Figure 10.2: *Analysis of take-off and landing distances for a vertical at different heights.*

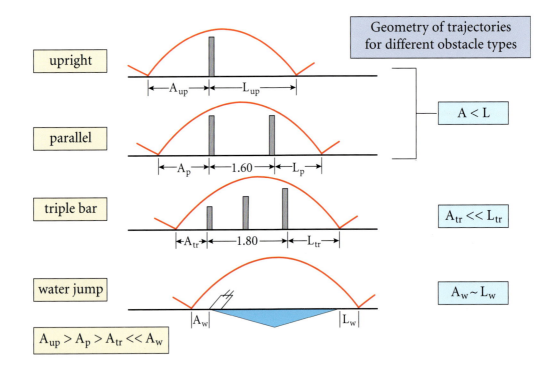

Figure 10.3: *Take-off and landing distances of different types of obstacle (concept of Olaf Petersen).*

Take-off distance

$$A = (A_o + \frac{H}{2}) \cdot x \ [m]$$

Landing distance

$$L = (L_o + \frac{H}{2}) \cdot x \ [m]$$

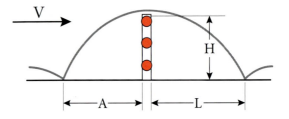

Correcting factor:

$$X = 0.9 \ldots 1.5 \ [-]$$

dependent on speed, footing conditions, jumping ability of the horse, optical effects of obstacle and background and many other influences.

H [m]	A (A_o = 1.10)	L (L_o = 1.40)
1.00	1.55	1.85
1.20	1.70	2.00
1.40	1.80	2.10
1.60	1.90	2.20

Figure 10.4: *Trajectory over vertical obstacles.*

Take-off distance

$$A = (A_o + \frac{H}{2}) \cdot x \; [m]$$

Landing distance

$$L = (L_o + \frac{H}{2}) \cdot x \; [m]$$

H [m]	A (A_o = 1.10)	L (L_o = 1.40)
1.20	1.60	1.90
1.30	1.65	1.95
1.40	1.70	2.00
1.50	1.75	2.05

Correcting factor:

$$X = 0.9...1.5 \; [-]$$

dependent on speed, width/spread, footing conditions, jumping ability of the horse, optical effects of obstacle and background and many other influences.

Figure 10.5: *Trajectory over parallels.*

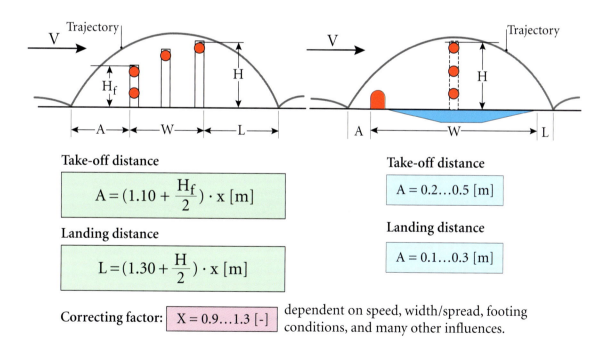

Take-off distance

$$A = (1.10 + \frac{H_f}{2}) \cdot x \; [m]$$

Landing distance

$$L = (1.30 + \frac{H}{2}) \cdot x \; [m]$$

Correcting factor: $\quad X = 0.9...1.3 \; [-]$

Take-off distance

$$A = 0.2...0.5 \; [m]$$

Landing distance

$$A = 0.1...0.3 \; [m]$$

dependent on speed, width/spread, footing conditions, and many other influences.

Figure 10.6: *Trajectory over triple bars and open water jumps.*

Take-off distances initially correspond to normal observation, but also conform to other criteria that are explained in table 10.1. It can be seen that:

1   the dimensions (height, spread) of the obstacle;

2   the forward speed;

3   the particular abilities of the horse;

are significant.

Table 10.1 *Criteria for the take-off distance*

Minimum take-off distance	Maximum take-off distance
1 Height of the obstacle	1 Width of the obstacle
2 Speed	2 Speed
3 Skill of the horse	3 Jumping capacity of the horse

It should be made clear at this point that the entire observation relates to the case of naturally schooled jumping horses. The connections described here do not apply if jumping horses are rapped or otherwise maltreated. Such cases are undoubtedly the exception but they do occur repeatedly and can be recognised by the expert at a competition.

●   Rapped horses jump more steeply (earlier take off point).

●   This changes the parabolic curve.

●   The early curve is often not sufficient for real oxers (for example, 1.70 to 2.00 m).

●   For some riders (usually those involved) the behaviour of obviously rapped horses is an argument against large-spread obstacles *per se*. But deep oxers are not the main problem, rather it is the maltreatment of the horses. Unfortunately, too little attention is paid to this in public discussion. This judgement should not be seen as a general plea in favour of the exclusive use of spread obstacles of Olympic dimensions, but rather for their measured use in suitable jumping competitions.

Each 1.60-m vertical in a major GRAND PRIX should correspond to an approximately 1.50 x 1.80/1.90-m oxer or a 1.60 x 2.00/2.10-m triple bar.

The slow-motion illustration in the Russian book, *The Sound of the Horse's Hooves* [021], shows the natural movements of a horse jumping over an upright obstacle (figure 10.7) very impressively.

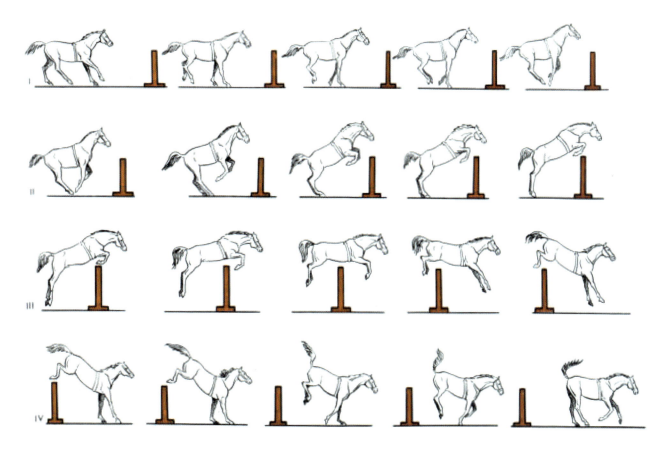

Figure 10.7: *Slow-motion study of a horse jumping a vertical obstacle (parabolic trajectory).*

11 MINIMUM SPEED AND TIME ALLOWED

Alongside dimensions, distances, visual aspects, tracks and many other competition criteria, the complexity of the task of completing a course with a clear round is very much determined by the minimum speed (obstacle no. 15!) (table 11.1).

1   The faster the minimum speed ...

2   ... the shorter the permitted time.

Table 11.1 *Minimum speed for jumping competitions*

Type of competition	Max. height (m)	Speed m/min.	km/h	m/s	%	Type of Event
1 GRAND PRIX	1.60	400	24	6.67	114	Outdoor
2 NATIONS CUP	1.60	400	24	6.67	114	
3 International	1.40/1.50	375	22.5	6.25	107	
4 Standard	1.20/1.30	350	21	5.83	100	Indoor
5 Special cases	-	325	19.5	5.42	93	

The minimum speed is thus an important and frequently decisive competition criterion.

Such famous Olympic individual and team riders as:

- Fritz Thiedemann at the first show-jumping world championships in 1953 in Paris;

- the US team at the 1972 Olympic Games in Munich;

- Hartwig Steenken at the 1972 Olympic Games in Munich;

- Eddy Macken at the World Championships at Hickstead in 1974 and at Aachen in 1978;

- David Broome at the GRAND PRIX Aachen 1992;

all lost their chance of victory because of 0.25 time faults (this corresponds to less than one second).

Figure 11.1: *Arno Gego and friends. (Top left) Arno Gego and his sons Roman and Marlon, CHIO Aachen 1988. Photo by Aachener Zeitung.(Right) Michael Gockel (left) and Harry Cornford CHIO Aachen. Photo by Arno Gego.(Bottom left) Harry Cornford, Arno Gego and Christa Jung, CHIO Aachen. Photo by Gloria Transparente International.*

On the other hand:

- Ulrich Kirchhoff won the individual show-jumping final at the 1996 Olympics in Atlanta because he was the only one to complete two rounds without a knock-down, kept his nerve and permitted himself a time fault.

Rodrigo Pessoa and John Whitaker missed the chance of a jump-off for the silver medal in the same competition because of time faults.

All these examples show the extreme importance of a precisely determined course length and minimum speed and time allowed in GRAND PRIX-level sport.

They also demonstrate, however, how a course designer can suppress an important competition criterion – consciously or unconsciously – through the incorrect specification of the course length.

Here, it becomes clear that the function of the technical delegate, a skilled, autonomous and sovereign international personality, is absolutely vital, especially for all important jumping competitions not just the Olympic Games and major championships, in which the FEI position of TD already exists in any case.

12 THEORY OF STRIDE LENGTH AND DISTANCES

The canter is the pace in which jumping horses move forward on the course. The length and frequency of the canter stride determines the forward speed:

$$V = L_s \times f \times 60 \quad [\text{m/min.}]$$

The Hungarian Nations Cup rider d'Endrödy [048], who was head of the Royal Hungarian Cavalry School between the two world wars as well as the teacher of de Némethy, found out early on that the horse's stride length (L_S) in free, dynamic forward movement (he speaks of 'liveliness') increases roughly in proportion to the forward speed (V) (table 12.1). This means that if we measure the speed in metres per minute [m/min.], as is normal in show-jumping, then the speed must be divided by 100 in order to get a rough measurement of stride length. This observation corresponds to the theoretical concept set out in table 12.2.

The measured values published by d'Endrödy confirm the proportionality of stride and speed.

D'Endrödy's V ~ Ls rule also shows that the frequency of the strides, irrespective of the speed, stays roughly constant, and that this is also true of the rhythm of the strides and thus the forward impulsion.

Therefore, the frequency of the strides of well-trained horses lies roughly between 1.6 and 1.7 strides/second, which corresponds to approximately 0.59–0.62 seconds/stride. So the following rule of thumb applies.

- Well-trained, active horses with good scope will make about 100 strides per minute on a good, flat and even footing!

Table 12.1 *Length of strides, frequence and speed on the flat for horses with good, average action*

Speed V (m/min.)	Competition type	Length of stride Ls (m)	Time per stride t_s (sec.)	Frequence of stride f (strides/sec.)
380	International jumping	3.90	0.616	1.62
400	and GRAND PRIX	4.10	0.615	1.63
450	Fast parcours and	4.50	0.6	1.67
500	Cross-country	4.95	0.595	1.68
600	Steeple-chase	5.90	0.59	1.69
650	Flat racing	6.50	0.6	1.67
700		7.20	0.617	1.62

Table 12.2 *Length of strides, speed and frequence of strides for normal competion galloping*

Length of a normal stride

$$L_s \sim \frac{V}{100} \ [m]$$

L_s = length of stride [m]
V = speed [m/min.]
t_s = average time per stride [sec.]
f = frequence of stride [1 sec.]

Average time per stride

$$t_s \sim \frac{L_s}{V} \ 60 \ [sec.]$$

in practice

$$t_s \sim 0.6 \ [sec/stride]$$

Frequence of strides

$$f \sim \frac{1}{t_s} \ [strides/sec.]$$

(biological rhythm)

$$f \approx \frac{1}{0.6} \approx 1.67 \ [strides/sec.]$$

- The biological rhythm of the canter of well-trained horses is approximately 0.6 sec/stride or 1.67 strides/sec.

  In practice, however, my own approximate investigations show that in 1.40–1.50 m jumping competitions, the frequency of strides varies much more than d'Endrödy indicated, depending on the type of horse and the type of race, and can be around 1.6–2 strides/second. This corresponds to a time of approximately 0.5–0.62 seconds/stride.

- D'Endrödy further noted that, after landing, a certain shortening in the length of strides happens which must be taken into account in distance analyses [048].

According to d'Endrödy, what is required to measure the speed and the stride length of a sports horse is:

- a suitable, flat, straight track with good surface conditions;

- a measuring distance of roughly 200 m in length plus run-up and slow-down;

- a stop watch and stride counter;

- regular, active riding over the distance to be measured;

- a suitable climate.

Poor ground and/or weather conditions will lead to falsified results.

Recent publications [208], however, report that the frequence of strides is not constant, but slowly growing with the speed (about 4% per 100m/min. of increase of speed).

In sport at the grass-roots level, however, it would be fine to work roughly on the basis of a mean stride length of around 3.50 m–3.60 m.

At a high-level FEI seminar on course design [190] for leading international course designers and jumping judges in November 1989 in Utrecht, the Netherlands, a table was drawn up with guideline data for normal distances between obstacles of 1.20 to 1.40 m in basic-level competitions (table 12.3). This guideline data assumes the horses will be forward ridden.

The reason for the 'from ... to' distance ranges for different numbers of strides is that the quality of a distance (the actual effect, such as short, normal, long or slightly short, slightly long, etc.) depends on many different factors. Some of these are outlined below.

Table 12.3 *Orientation figures for normal distances between obstacles for basic competitions*

Number of strides between obstacles	Normal distances D (m) from.....to	Application
3	14.30....15.00	primarily indoor distances
4	17.90....18.60	
5	21.50....22.50	
6	25.00....26.00	primarily outdoor distances
7	28.50....29.50	

1   The following situations have the effect of shortening the quality of distance:

- downward gradient of the land;

- footing that has elasticity and grip;

- riding in the direction of the exit;

- after a spread obstacle or ditch;

- meeting a vertical obstacle after a spread obstacle.

2   The following situations have the effect of lengthening the quality of distance:

- upward gradient of the land;

- footing that is deep and slippery;

- riding away from the entrance/exit;

- coming to the end of a long course;

- narrow obstacles;

- meeting a spread obstacle after a vertical obstacle.

A distance between two obstacles can be analysed according to the diagram shown in figure 12.1, whereby the 'shortening' and 'lengthening' effects must be taken into account in order to estimate a 'distance quality'.

A normal distance between obstacles in medium competitions (1.30/1.40 m) means a calculation for a rhythmical forward movement of well-developed and trained horses.

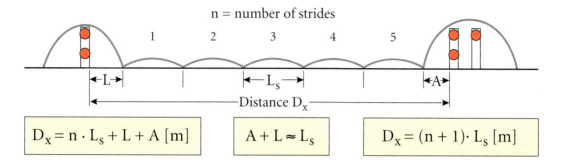

$$D_x = n \cdot L_s + L + A \ [m]$$

$$A + L \approx L_s$$

$$D_x = (n + 1) \cdot L_s \ [m]$$

Figure 12.1: *Distances between obstacles.*

'A DISTANCE IS NOT A DISTANCE ...'!

A so-called 'normal distance' of, for example, 22 m, can in some cases appear either very short or very long. In addition to all the theoretical considerations, there is another important aspect to take into consideration. The way in which a rider approaches a distance task is also of considerable significance in affecting a given distance calculation. To quote Emile Hendrix, the Olympic rider from the Netherlands, during a discussion at the 2003 World Cup tournament in Palm Beach, Florida: 'In the end, each rider creates his or her own distance'!

OBSTACLE COMBINATIONS

Combinations are a series of two, three or more individual obstacles placed in sequence, with the intervening distances reduced to one or two strides. The maximum distance in combinations is fixed in the FEI rules for jumping events at 12 m.

Combinations can be either open or closed. Closed combinations are most characteristic of natural combinations such as a bank, devil's dyke or mound. It seems sensible, in a closed combination, to make it possible to jump out without external help after a refusal so that the course can be completed. Furthermore, it is important that the closed nature of the combination is unambiguous. If necessary, standing gates, post and rail or similar material should be used to demark the closed area clearly.

Together with the type and dimension of the individual obstacles and their sequence, the distance of a combination is of particular significance because it has a major influence on the degree of difficulty.

It is important to remember that, after landing (having jumped an obstacle), the length of the stride shortens because the trajectory of the jump affects the forward movement. The shortening of the stride length increases as the size of the obstacle increases. It can be approximately 10 per cent of the stride length in high-level competitions, and must be compensated for with a more resolute forward impulsion. A stride length of, say, 3.80 m being required in the combination clearly marks it out as 'long distance'.

The quality of distances in obstacle sequences and combinations is determined by many different variables:

- the quality of the competitors;

- the condition of the footing (deep, firm, slippery, good grip, elastic, etc.);

- the slope of the land (horizontal, upward, downward, steep or less steep, etc.);

- types and dimensions of distance-related obstacles;

- obstacles before and after the particular distance-related task;

- length and minimum speed of the course;

- position of the task during the course (early, middle, late);

- visual aspect and construction/design of the obstacles;

- direction towards the entrance/exit or away from it;

- measured distances.

This means that the quality of distance from A to B or from B to C can only be determined from the many pieces of information listed above.

In our fast-moving and sometimes superficial world, many riders, judges, course designers and others are ready, when the subject of distance comes up, to go quickly back to 'just numbers/metres', but that is wrong, as the remarks below will demonstrate.

First it must be noted that: 'The distance is measured on the ground, from the base of the first obstacle on the landing side to the base of the next obstacle on the take-off side' (FEI art. 212.1). This is particularly important where obstacles are preceded by structures (for example, small walls, brushes, flowers, etc.) but is also true for ditches and water jumps. Some combinations are outlined in figure 12.2 which give indications on the correct measuring of distances in combinations.

Although the rule outlined above concerning the measuring of distances, which is also laid down in the FEI 'Rules for Jumping Events', applies, this does not release the course designer from fixing appropriate distances and calculating, or estimating, in advance the expected effect of the distance.

If open ditches or obstacles with ditches are included, it should be noted that distances are always measured as far as the start of the ditch, or from the end of the ditch. It goes without saying that the effect of a given distance can change significantly with the ditch width. One should therefore be extremely careful when setting distances.

If one consults FEI article 212.1 (figure 12.2) referred to earlier, it can easily be seen that assessing a distance in combinations can be much more complicated if poles are not the only materials used.

'The distance is measured from the base of the obstacle on the landing side to the base of the next obstacle on the take-off side'

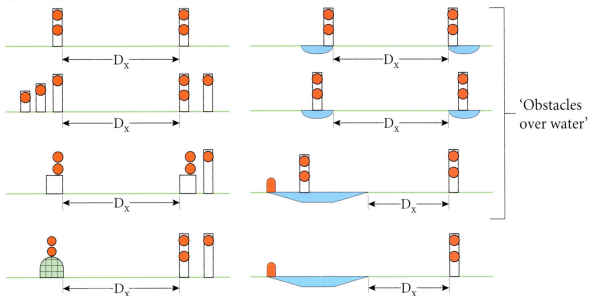

But: 1 Distances need accurate analysis of speed, distribution of strides, trajectories, etc.
   2 Only the measured distance in metres together with the obstacle types in sequence and their dimensions, footing, slope, position, speed, etc., give a distance quality (a little long, short, normal, etc.)
   3 The figure in metres alone means NOTHING!

Figure 12.2: *Distances (FEI Article 212.1).*

Great tournaments with equally great stadiums demonstrate very quickly that 'pole to pole distances' are not the only option, but that high-level sport offers, or should offer, much greater quality and variety.

At the FEI Seminar in Utrecht, the Netherlands, referred to above, a table of 'normal distances' in combinations for simple vertical obstacles, oxers and triple bars was recommended and agreed (table 12.4). Its purpose was to provide the basic sport with important guidance. 'Simple' in this context means moveable obstacles on a horizontally flat surface and not in combination with natural obstacles. This FEI recommendation, based on the experience of leading course designers, makes a good guideline for less experienced colleagues.

Table 12.4 *True/fair distances between elements of a combination under normal conditions*

Type of fence	A Vertical	B Parallel oxer	C Triple bar
A VERTICAL	7.60 ... 8.00 10.60 ... 11.00	7.50 ... 7.80 10.50 ... 10.80	7.10 ... 7.40 **
B PARALLEL OXER	7.60 ... 7.80 10.60 ... 11.00	7.40 ... 7.70 10.40 ... 10.70	7.10 ... 7.40 **
C TRIPLE BAR	7.70 ... 8.00 10.70 ... 11.00	7.60 ... 7.80 10.50 ... 10.80	** **

** Not recommended

Note: The course designer may alter these distances according to:
- class of horses, type of competition
- sloping ground, deep going, sharp turns
- ascending ground, construction of fence (solid, filling, etc.)

A few other aspects or rules are important in relation to distances.

1   According to the FEI rules, combinations are limited, as already mentioned, to distances up to a maximum of 12 m. Greater distances are numbered as individual obstacles.

2   This rule does not apply to natural obstacles. Here, the course designer can decide

whether, for example, he numbers a 15-m-long bank in sequence or declares it to be a combination. At a corresponding height, this bank must be declared as a 'closed combination' in accordance with FEI article 214. Exiting the bank by the side will result in exclusion.

3 Walls have the effect of shortening the length of the stride, and tend to act as a slight brake. That is why the normal distance in a wall to wall double is somewhat shorter than in a pole to pole double.

4 In GRAND PRIX-level competitions, the first combination should be placed no earlier than no. 4 or 5.

5 Where there are several combinations in a jumping competition, the first element of the combination should vary.

6 The rhythm of one- or two-stride distances should also vary.

Without going into the question of whether triple bars within combinations (with the exception of the first/A-element) are currently excluded in the FEI rules, it is worth pointing out the risk of the 'triple bar effect' (figure 12.3).

● In combinations that lead to a triple bar in two strides, some horses tend to jump off after only one first, long stride. This quickly leads to falls and less pleasing images.

● This problem does not occur where distances are measured for one stride.

Similar risks can also occur with natural obstacles, as shown in the case of the bank or mound in figure 12.3.

LIVERPOOLS

A Liverpool is a water ditch. It can be either moveable or permanent.

A double Liverpool is particularly suitable for a discussion about distances and their quality. Moreover, a double Liverpool has a special charm as a distinctive water obstacle. The basic dimensions given in table 12.5 would be suitable for different types of competition.

Particularly with permanent double Liverpools, the two-stride distance should be preferred because:

- it allows the variety of design to be better exploited, without risk;

- in critical situations, horse and rider have more opportunity for making corrections ('*corriger la fortune*');

- the condition of the footing is easier to check between the obstacles.

Figure 12.4 compares four different types of combination, all with the same basic data.

- The distance is always 10.50 m.

- The Liverpools both have a spread of 1.80 m.

Table 12.5 *Recommendation for double Liverpools (approximate)*

Size of event	Width of first Liverpool m	Distance m	Width of second Liverpool m
• small	1.30	10.50	1.30
• medium	1.60	10.50	1.60
• big	1.80	10.50	1.80
for comparison			
• CHIO Aachen	2.00	10.80	2.00
		11.00 (until 1995)	2.00

The comparison is interesting. Depending on how the Liverpools have been constructed, distance qualities range from 'very short' to 'very long'. This does not take into account other, more subtle, aspects of differentiation (for example, 'shortening/lengthening effects', see above).

This example confirms in particular that:

- 'A distance is not a distance'!

- A 'measured distance' in metres does not necessarily mean anything!

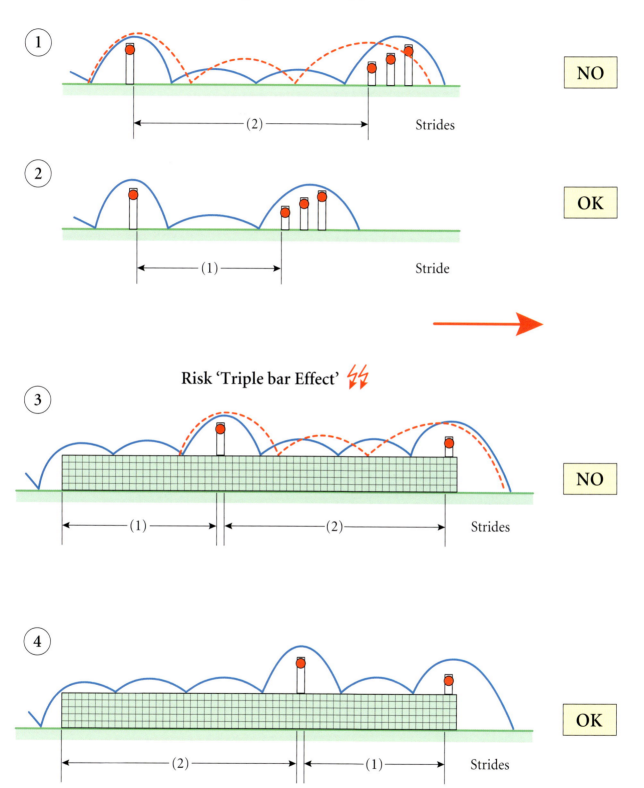

Risk 'Triple bar Effect' ⚡⚡

(1) NO

(2) — Strides

2 OK

(1) — Stride

Risk 'Triple bar Effect' ⚡⚡

3 NO

(1) — (2) — Strides

4 OK

(2) — (1) — Strides

Figure 12.3: *How to avoid the 'triple bar effect'.*

The course designer carries great responsibility, particularly in determining and choosing combinations and distances. Here, it is particularly important that:

1   The talented, but not yet very experienced course designer will show his greatness by starting off with fairly normal types of combination – there are many promising singers who, despite great talent, had to end prematurely what might have been a great career because they took on difficult parts much too early and were unable to cope with them due to lack of experience.

2   A responsible course designer will never set tasks on the course that are beyond his experience and thus his skills. This applies not only to combinations but in general, as the difference between a demanding but solvable test and overtaxing rider and horse is often very small.

3   If the preceding statements are correct, there should be no outstanding course designers without formative training. Only the greatest geniuses of the century should remain excluded from this dictum, but even Leonardo da Vinci (1452–1519) started as a pupil of Antonio del Verrocchio in Florence.

4   The training of piano players does not begin by tackling Chopin! And even the greatest painter, sculptor and graphic designer of the century, Picasso (1882–1973), invented Cubism jointly with Braque.

5   A 'school' does not mean simply going along with an idea or being a mere follower.

6   A training that sets standards is tough and demands serious commitment, staying power, loyalty and also, very frequently, unpleasant subordination over a lengthy period (that is, accepting the position of being second).

Combinations are usually outstanding tasks in the exciting progress of a GRAND PRIX-level jumping competition.

Figures 12.5–12.9 depict 25 different types of treble combinations. I have built almost all of these types over the years or have been, in the case of combination no. 17, responsible as the Technical Delegate (1984 Olympic Games, Los Angeles). It should be explained that:

1   For reasons of clarity, the combinations have predominantly been drawn with poles, but any other materials, such as planks, gates, walls, palisades, etc. are possible.

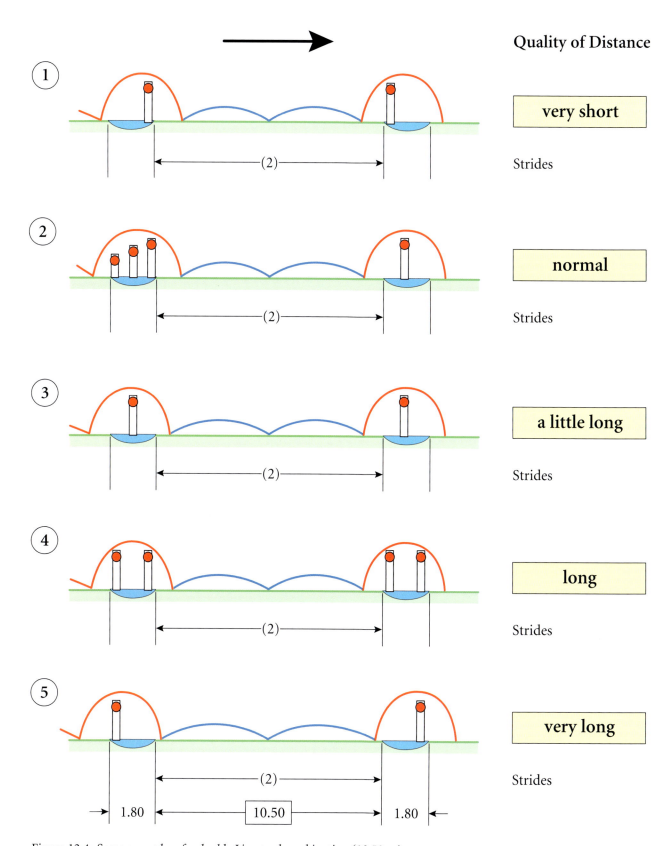

1 very short

Strides

2 normal

Strides

3 a little long

Strides

4 long

Strides

5 very long

Strides

1.80 10.50 1.80

Figure 12.4: *Some examples of a double Liverpool combination (10.50 m).*

2   Indications are also given as to what number of strides would be possible or sensible to avoid risks.

3   The comparison from a to b indicates how the distances a and b should relate to each other (see the explanation of the symbols in table 12.6), if the combinations are to be jumped in a steady, forward-oriented rhythm. Optimum ground surface conditions, horizontally flat and on grass, are assumed, with inviting obstacles. If one also takes the recommended mean values in the distance table (table 12.4) as the base values, one comes close to the desired aim of a combination that is consistently smooth to ride. Other influences on the quality of distances have been discussed above. A genuinely independent, experienced course designer must be in a position first to set a 'normal task' in the sense of 'free forward movement' before he gets into the intricacies of further task differentiation.

4   These illustrated examples are discussed from a professional point of view and do not take account of recent rule restrictions by the FEI:

   ●   no triple bar in combinations;

   ●   water jumps only with an upright, with one or several poles placed no further than 2 m from the front of the obstacle. Neither restriction applies in Germany.

5   The cases shown for the sake of completeness are:

   ●   triple bar in combinations;

   ●   obstacles over water in combinations;

   ●   in any case, three spread obstacles only form part of high-level international sport and do not figure in normal jumping competitions up to 1.50 m.

6   Prohibitions, however well meaning, clearly reduce the variety of the sport. It would be better to intensify the training of course designers, particularly of those who are already on the FEI list, or to remove those course designers from the FEI list who have demonstrably failed repeatedly, rather than to try and protect the sport through bans (as, for example, on water jumps in indoor arenas). What objection can be made against a well-designed and attractively decorated, 3.00 or 3.50-m wide water jump in a large indoor arena?

A – For basic sport 1.20/1.30 m classes and upwards
B – For international level of 1.40/1.50 m classes and upwards
C – For Olympic level 1.50/1.60 m classes

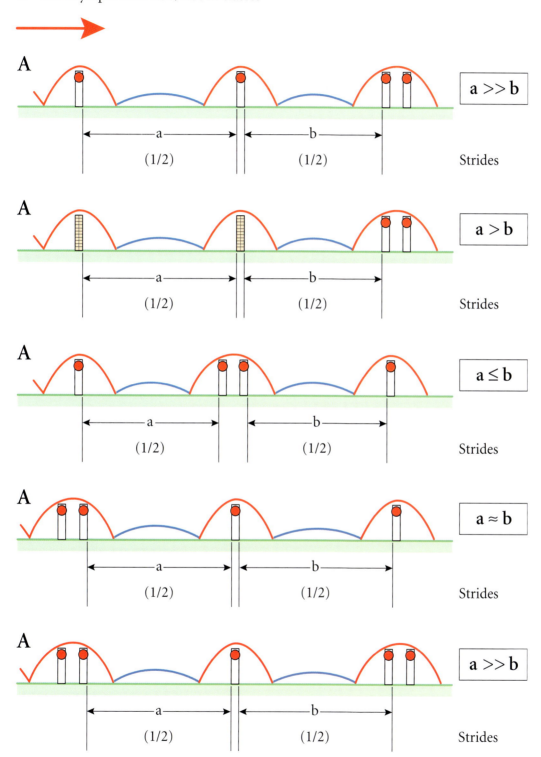

Figure 12.5: *Examples of triple combinations.*

A – For basic sport 1.20/1.30 m classes and upwards
B – For international level of 1.40/1.50 m classes and upwards
C – For Olympic level 1.50/1.60 m classes

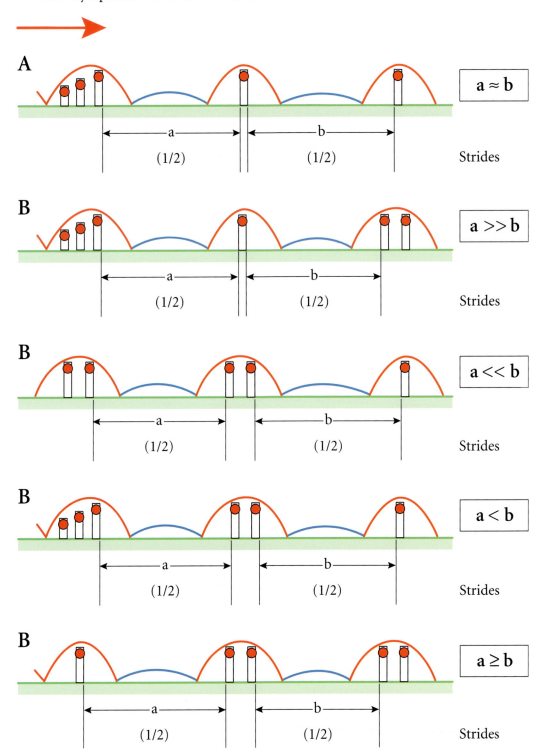

Figure 12.6: *Examples of triple combinations.*

A – For basic sport 1.20/1.30 m classes and upwards
B – For international level of 1.40/1.50 m classes and upwards
C – For Olympic level 1.50/1.60 m classes

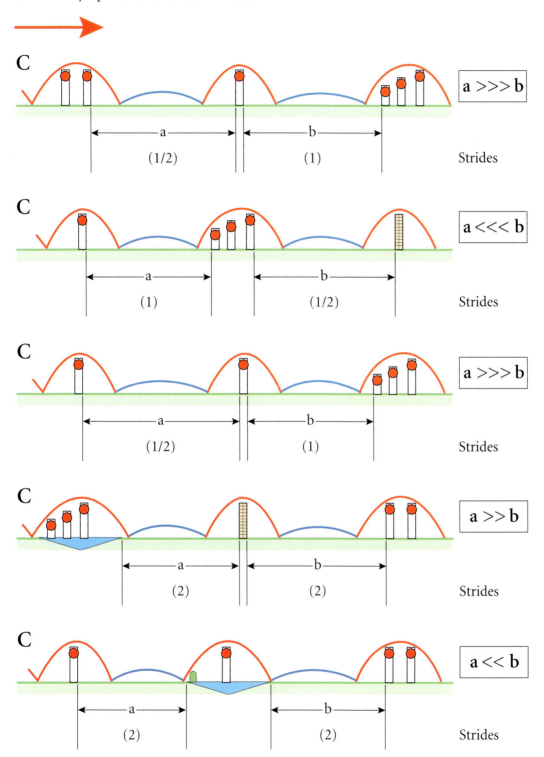

Figure 12.7: *Examples of triple combinations.*

A – For basic sport 1.20/1.30 m classes and upwards
B – For international level of 1.40/1.50 m classes and upwards
C – For Olympic level 1.50/1.60 m classes

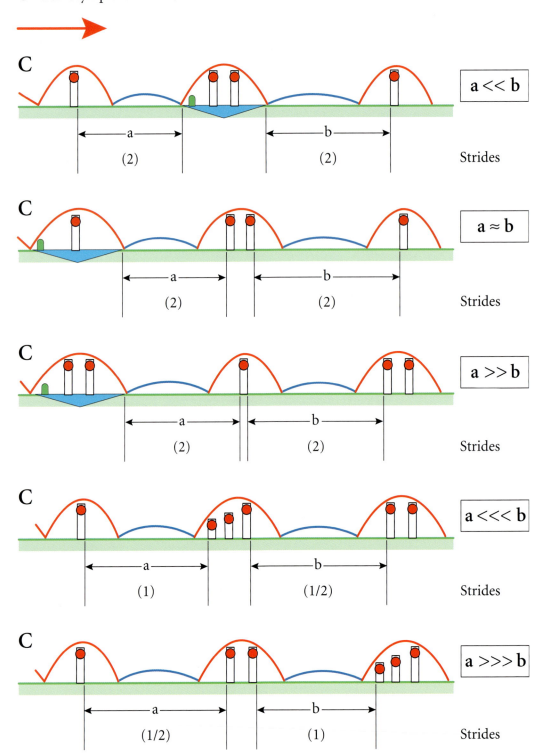

Figure 12.8: *Examples of triple combinations.*

A – For basic sport 1.20/1.30 m classes and upwards
B – For international level of 1.40/1.50 m classes and upwards
C – For Olympic level 1.50/1.60 m classes

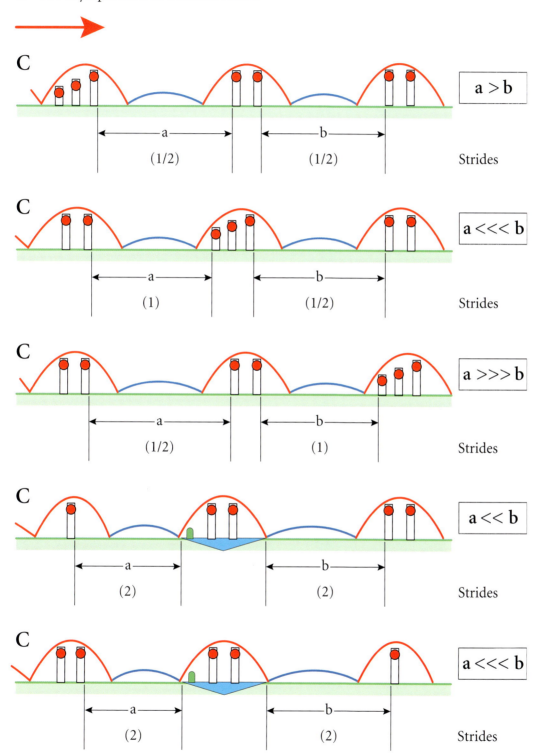

Figure 12.9: *Examples of triple combinations.*

Table 12.6 *Explanation of distances or distance relations in combinations*

Comparison of distances: mathematical	verbal	Difference between a and b
$a \approx b$	approximately equal	Δ a/b $\approx$ 0 cm
$a \geq b$ $a \leq b$	longer or equal shorter or equal	Δ a/b $\approx$ 0...10 cm
$a > b$	a little longer a little shorter	Δ a/b $\approx$ 10...15 cm
$a \gg b$ $a \ll b$	clearly longer clearly shorter	Δ a/b $\approx$ 15...30 cm
$a \ggg b$ $a \lll b$	much longer much shorter	Δ a/b $\approx$ 30...50 cm

In figure 12.10, another teaching example is displayed to help explain the issue of combinations and distances:

- double of oxers (1.40 x 1.80 m);

- double of verticals (1.40 m);

- distances (7.50 and 10.50 m).

The examples shown are analysed for normal cases and in approximation.

For the double oxer, the significant spread of 1.80 m was deliberately chosen to make the effects more evident; a double consisting of double *staccionatas* (1.40 x 1.40 m) would not be very different from the double of verticals.

Comparing this example again demonstrates that:

- At a constant distance, significantly different effects and qualities occur.

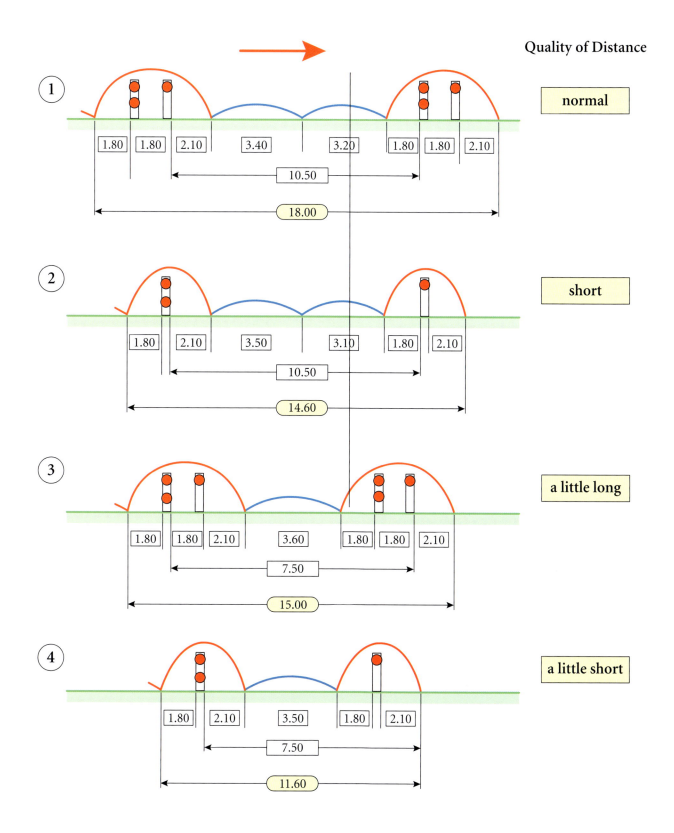

Figure 12.10: *A comparison of some double vertical (1.40 m) and double oxer (1.40 x 1.80 m) combinations with one (7.50 m) and two strides (10.50 m) (approx.).*

- The total distance from take-off at A to landing at B varies considerably, and thus clearly shows the different overall dynamic.

- A two-stride distance at a double oxer offers the rider and horse considerably more opportunities for correction in the event of problems.

- A double vertical is rather more delicate.

- A double oxer demands courage, energy and impulsion.

In figures 12.11 and 12.12, a few exceptional GRAND PRIX combinations are shown that are reserved exclusively for high-level tournaments or championships at Olympic level. All the combinations shown here were built in GRAND PRIX and have caused faults and brought the best to the front, but have not led to any problems.

Basic aspects of planning, designing and building combinations:

1 Prepare a combinations plan long before the tournament and use it as a basis for drafting MASTERPLANS.

2 The best footing should be reserved for combinations.

3 The position of combinations on the course and on the arena should vary.

4 Vary the:

- type of combination;

- type of first element;

- distribution of 1- and 2-stride distances;

- distance.

5 Take account of visual effects such as:

- colour;

- the sun;

- lightness/solidity of obstacles.

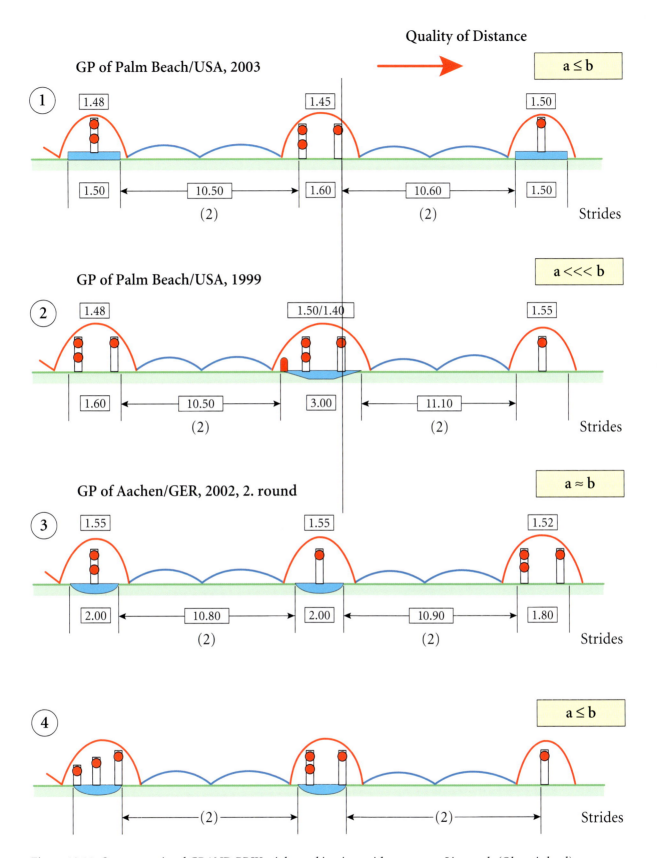

Quality of Distance

GP of Palm Beach/USA, 2003 $\quad a \leq b$

GP of Palm Beach/USA, 1999 $\quad a <<< b$

GP of Aachen/GER, 2002, 2. round $\quad a \approx b$

$a \leq b$

Figure 12.11: *Some exceptional GRAND PRIX triple combinations with one or two Liverpools (Olympic level).*

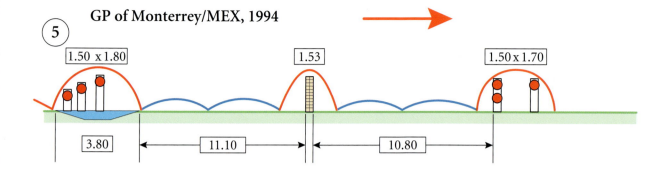

5 GP of Monterrey/MEX, 1994

1.50 x 1.80   1.53   1.50 x 1.70

3.80   11.10   10.80

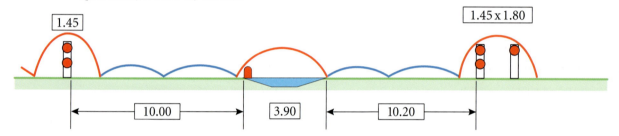

6 World Jumping Championships, Aachen, 1986
1. Qualifier, Table C, 1.50 m

1.45   1.45 x 1.80

10.00   3.90   10.20

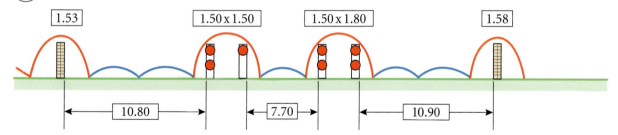

7 GP of Aachen/GER, 1992, 1. round

1.53   1.50 x 1.50   1.50 x 1.80   1.58

10.80   7.70   10.90

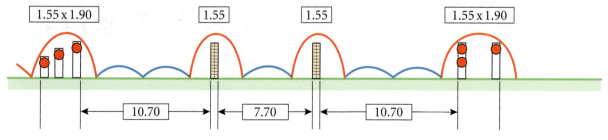

8 GP of Aachen/GER, 1998, 1. round

1.55 x 1.90   1.55   1.55   1.55 x 1.90

10.70   7.70   10.70

Figure 12.12: *More examples of GRAND PRIX combinations at Olympic level.*

6   A combination should be visually recognisable as a 'unit' and be a particularly difficult feature on the course.

When choosing distances in obstacle sequences – especially when there are three or more obstacles in a series – it becomes clear that so-called 'true distances' are, as a rule, more difficult to ride than optional distances, as, for example, 4/5, 5/6 or 6/7 strides.

● In true distances, the rider is forced to adhere to a prescribed rhythm (for example, six strides for the triple combination in the 2002 Aachen GRAND PRIX). Any deviation inevitably leads to faults.

● In optional distances, the rider can still change his or her strategy on the course within the distance.

Thus, for example, Franke Sloothaak missed a certain medal at the 1984 Olympic Games in Los Angeles in the individual jumping final because he checked the horse once too often in the pre-specified five-stride distance from the wall to the water jump.

Some practical examples for combinations in high-level jumping competitions are shown in figures 12.13–12.18.

Aachen 2002

Aachen 2002

Valkenswaard 2003

Palm Beach 2004

Figure 12.13: *Various examples of double combinations. Photos by Christa Heibach.*

Palm Beach 2003

Aachen 2002

Aachen 2001

Aachen 2002

Figure 12.14: *Examples of double combinations. Photos by Christa Heibach.*

Aachen 1995

Monterrey 1996

Monterrey 1996

Aachen 2001

Figure 12.15: *Examples of double and triple combinations. Photos by Christa Heibach.*

Monterrey 1996   *Aachen 2002*

Monterrey 1994   *Aachen 2002*

Figure 12.16: *Examples of combinations. Photos by Christa Heibach.*

Aachen 1998 (quadruple)   *Aachen 1998*

Aachen 2001   *Aachen 2001*

Figure 12.17: *Examples of combinations. Photos by Christa Heibach.*

Aachen 2003

Monterrey 1996

Palm Beach 1996

Aachen 2002

Figure 12.18: *Examples of combinations. Photos by Christa Heibach.*

13 THE MASTERPLAN

Designing a course is a creative act that is based on experience, consideration, imagination and intuition.

The MASTERPLAN is the graphic design for a course, drawn and designed freehand, which contains a maximum of information to allow the draft and design of the course to be implemented as a real, competitive jumping course, with:

- the track/line;

- the position of obstacles and combinations;

- the types of obstacles;

- distances;

- dimensions of obstacles;

- obstacle materials;

- colours;

- decoration;

- natural islands, etc.;

on an existing showground with its own particular characteristics.

A well-prepared MASTERPLAN that is worthy of the name should at least meet a certain artistic standard!

Before the course designer becomes involved in the MASTERPLAN of, for example, a GRAND PRIX, Nations Cup or Derby, he will first consider the realities of the planned tournament.

A course designer who takes responsibility for the first time at a tournament that is new to him must spend a lot of time in order to inwardly digest, sufficiently understand and get to know the core and periphery of the new task.

For example, I have never yet responded to the demands from organisers to send preliminary course sketches – whether in Europe, North/South America, Africa, Asia or Oceania – if I was not able first to familiarise myself with the conditions on site. Nevertheless, I prepared thoroughly and arrived at the first tournament with 20 or more design sketches, even if at the end I needed only ten MASTERPLANS. No prior information can be as good as a first on-site inspection. At the first visit, physical or technical conditions are not the only important aspects to consider: equally, and perhaps even more important, are discussions with the people on the spot, and the usually overwhelming overall impression gained of the host country, the host organisers and the showground (figure 13.1).

Figure 13.1: *Inspection of a new tournament site. Photos by Christa Heibach.*

REALITIES BEFORE THE START OF THE TOURNAMENT

In addition to personal basic equipment, ranging from a tape measure to a laptop computer, prior to the tournament the course designer should also be equipped with other information on which he will base his design work:

1   the status of the tournament, the locality, layout, the showground as a whole, the jumping arena/stadium, the infrastructure;

2   the jumping stadium with all the important details such as shape, size, permanent/natural obstacles, entrance/exit, judges' box, distribution of spectators and stands, prize-giving position and formation, etc.;

3   this also includes such important details about the jumping stadium as:

   • the gradient (slope) of the stadium area, degree of gradient and direction;

   • minor surface undulations noticed by the responsible course designer;

4   tournament organisation, officials, media, the entire team, especially the course helpers;

5   the team responsible for tending the ground, sprinkling, repair and general maintenance, with a ground supervisor in charge;

6   schedule and prize-money, quality of the competitors;

7   obstacles, obstacle area, decoration; position, size and distance of the storage area for the obstacle material. The approach and entrance to the stadium should preferably be separate from the entrance and exit for the riders, and from the roads used by the spectators;

8   office and team premises for course designers, assistants and course helpers;

9   means of transport, such as flatbed wagons pulled by smallish tractors with low-pressure tyres for use on grass surfaces;

10 progress of the day in relation to the sun's path (that is the arena's position on a south-north axis);

11 workshop with carpenter, tools, spare materials and equipment;

12 sprinkler system;

13 stands, number of visitors;

14 sponsor concept, distribution plan of sponsored obstacles;

15 media and infrastructure, position of TV cameras;

16 production and distribution of course plans, including publication on the internet, etc.

In all of the course designer's preparation, the image and international standing of the tournament and the quality of the competitors, the prizes and the image of the sponsors play a vital role.

Some important aspects concerning the necessary technical infrastructure for course designers and their teams are summarised in table 13.1.

Table 13.1 *Necessary infrastructure*

Office for course designers and assistants	Covered place for ring crew/ arena party	Stock for obstacles	Maintenance, carpenter, painter
• at least 4 x 4 m	• at least 5 x 5 m	• as close as possible to main stadium	• small tractors/ 1-axle-platform-wagons, twin tyres, turf tyres
• light, electricity	• light, electricity	• possibly independent traffic from horses	
• bathroom	• bathroom		• leveller, roller and other equipment
• tables, chairs	• tables, chairs	• fenced and lockable to protect flowers, cups, flags etc. from being stolen	
• lockers	• lockers		• green sand to repair grass footings
• room, closed and lockable	• room, closed and lockable	• firm ground	• irrigation

The basis for the course designer's work is a scale drawing of the arena with all details in place such as:

a. entrances/exit;

b. position of the judges' box and north-south axis;

c. position of the practice arena;

d. position of permanent natural obstacles such as water jumps, Liverpools, dry ditch, bank, bush oxer, permanent walls, etc.;

e. position of stands, standing places and other areas for visitors;

f. main visitor flows;

g. commercial area.

SOME ASPECTS CONCERNING THE DESIGN OF TRACKS

Before the course designer thinks about developing a MASTERPLAN, he must consider some general aspects concerning track design that have emerged as the shared views of leading course designers over the last 50 years.

1   The line of the course forms the basis for developing the tasks, rhythm and aesthetic design of a course. And one should not forget that the:

●   free forward movement and

●   the flow or 'musicality' of the lines ('*musicalité des lignes*') are vital elements in the courses of GRAND PRIX-level jumping competitions.

2   The track should make use of all parts of the arena. On large arenas, the outer tracks in particular must be properly used. Nevertheless, a few metres of the outer track normally remain empty!

3   Particularly for main events, such as GRAND PRIX or the Nations Cup, the obstacles

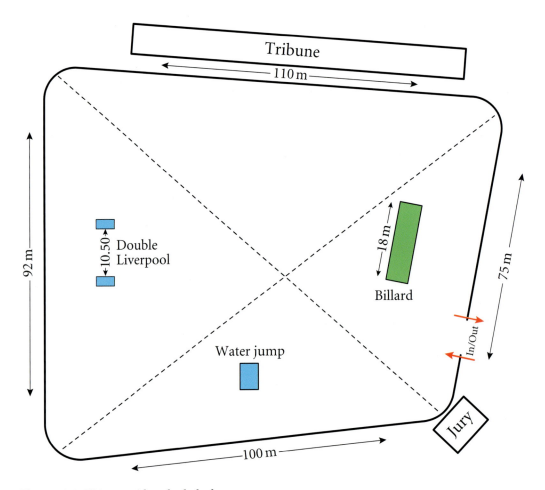

Figure 13.2: *Using a grid to check the layout.*

should be distributed evenly across the whole arena. This is verified by using a grid (figure 13.2) which is a tool also used in art, particularly by painters [153].

4   In tournaments with several jumping competitions – which is the norm – the position of the:

●   start/obstacle 1

and

●   finish/last obstacle

should vary, as should the question of approach on the left and/or right rein.

5   The sequence of the obstacle types of the first and last line of obstacles should also vary.

6   Moreover, the obstacle types of the first and last obstacle should change (upright, oxer, intermediate type, triple bar, etc.).

7   The line of a course should lead naturally from one obstacle to the next. It is important that obstacles that follow each other are always in a logical sequence.

8   Three-quarter circles (270-degree curves) should be the exception, unless the track goes around a natural fixed point such as a permanent natural obstacle, a group of trees, a small lake or similar. Otherwise, the arbitrary three-quarter circle is often just a stopgap used by the course designer when he lacks imagination (as commented on by a leading rider from South America in 2003).

9   The much more difficult quarter-circle segments (90-degree curves) should be carefully adapted, in terms of their radius and therefore the number of strides required between obstacles (x and x+1 [table 13.2]), to the quality of the competitors and the importance of the competition.

Table 13.2 *Considerations about 90-degree line/sequence*

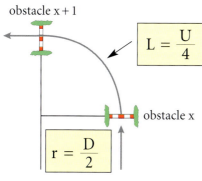

$$L = \frac{U}{4}$$

$$r = \frac{D}{2}$$

U = periphery of circle [m]
n = amount of strides

Path of quarter circle

$$L = \frac{U}{4} = \frac{\pi \cdot D}{4} = \frac{\pi \cdot r}{2} \; [m]$$

Practical examples (all lengths in m)

r	D	L	n	Comment
15	30	23.56	5/6	very difficult
16	32	25.13	6	only for top riders/ horses
17	34	26.70	6/7	still difficult
18	36	28.27	7/8	

10   The lines of major tracks should be varied, and should, in addition to the criteria mentioned above, be characterised by:

- sufficient movement of the lines (changes of rein) and free forward movement ('*sempre avanti*');

- variation between single obstacles, obstacle sequences on a straight or curved line, and combinations within or outside of obstacle sequences (table 13.3);

- galloping passages;

- variation of obstacle types, obstacle material, colours and decoration.

Table 13.3 *Analysis of line elements in courses*

Types	Differentiation	Further explanation
1. Single obstacle	• individual fence • unrelated combination	• free approach • not related to the next obstacle
2. Sequence of obstacles	• two or more obstacles • in a straight line or • in a curve	• individual and/or combination • ≤ 25 ... 30 m
3. Combination	• 2, 3 or more efforts • individual obstacle or • in line	• distance ≤ 12 m * • a combination can be understood as a sequence with distances ≤ 12 m

* except natural obstacles

11 There should be variation of the number of strides between obstacles and of the distances in combinations.

12 The initial line should be inviting, generous and forward-oriented (so no three- or four-stride distances in outdoor tournaments). The course should give the horses and riders a chance to get naturally into their stride.

13 The final line of a major course should stand out as of special importance. The final

obstacle should be imposing (a final 'chord') and not a tricky lightweight fence. The final line is of dramatically important significance and should not lead into just any corner. It should not look like a stopgap solution.

14 The law of variety and change applies to a special degree.

ON DEVELOPING A MASTERPLAN FOR A GRAND PRIX

As already explained in chapter 2, the criteria of vital creative potential for a MASTER-PLAN are:

- the track;

- the architecture of the obstacles, including colour, decoration and visual details;

- dimensions and distances;

- the overall dramatic setting.

The MASTERPLAN is the result of a developmental process involving many small, logical, emotional and creative steps (figure 13.3), in roughly the following sequence:

1   selection of permanent obstacles to be used (as, for example, water jump, permanent wall, permanent bush oxer, Liverpool, etc.) and possibly the direction of jumping;

2   position of the main combination and jumping direction;

3   position of one or (much more difficult) several main lines of obstacles;

4   position/area/part of the arena where the start and finish are to be located.

The experienced course designer will note that it gets very difficult to find a course track if more than two or three of the above criteria cannot be changed. So it is also a question of sufficient flexibility in the creative design of a new, important track.

One of my working principles is first to design the track, including across planned permanent obstacles, such as the water jump, and only then deal with moveable obstacles and their position.

5 Some initial ideas about the lines now start to emerge.

6 The developmental process of the MASTERPLAN is accompanied by minor or major corrections (an eraser is essential equipment).

7 The idea of an overall line 'grows' slowly before an overall line design emerges.

8 This line is then gradually filled in in a sensible and logical sequence with further obstacles – using a continuous strong line for easier identification.

9 This leads to the creation of an internally consistent and varied track which undergoes minor or major corrections in the process,

10 Only then does the course designer gradually get involved in more details, such as:

- distances

- types of obstacle

- dimensions

- colours/decoration

- obstacle material.

11 With important jumping tournaments such as the Nations Cup and GRAND PRIX, the course designer must also be careful to ensure that he does not repeat the prominent parts and combinations used in previous years, or perhaps anticipates the main focal points intended for a centenary celebration two years later on (CHIO Aachen).

12 Not every important GRAND PRIX is designed in a day. Often, I take many evenings to complete an overall design.

THE STRAIGHT LINE IS HUMAN, THE CURVED LINE IS DIVINE!

(Antoni Gaudi, Barcelona, 1852–1926, architect)

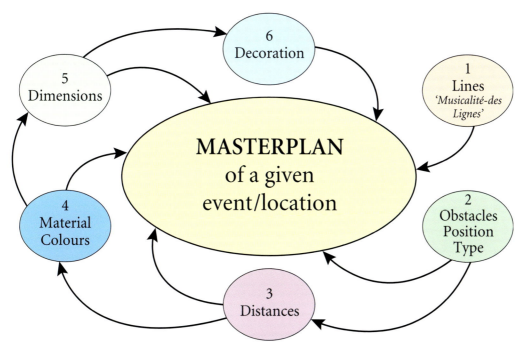

Figure 13.3: *The main creative steps of a MASTERPLAN.*

And by the way, a freehand MASTERPLAN for a major jumping competition is a unique piece of work that cannot be produced twice. The course designer would rather keep on rubbing it out and changing it until he thinks he has achieved his goal, or else – often after leaving it for some time – he will start a completely new design idea (and that is very rare).

The course designer plans variety through variation. To achieve this, he uses the following planning instruments so as to leave nothing to chance.

- A plan of combinations for all the classes in the tournament (figure 13.4) – I have decided on great combinations for major tournaments months, sometimes years, in advance.

- Position and type of the first and last obstacle.

- Rein (left/right) option for start and finishing line.

- Position of combinations and main lines of obstacles for the main competitions.

- Material and colours, particularly for main competitions.

- Distribution of the sponsor obstacles.

Another important rule in drafting track designs is the principle of planning from 'big to small'. This means that I would first draft:

- the MASTERPLAN for a GRAND PRIX;

- then a Nations Cup;

- and then further jumping classes in diminishing importance.

In this way, one avoids using important parts of the GRAND PRIX-level competitions in earlier, minor competitions.

ON DEVELOPING THE TRACK

Alongside all the aspects referred to and the systematic rules, the creative design of the track is of particular significance.

A French article about landscape architecture, published a few years ago, discussed, in a different connection, the '*musicalité des lignes*' ('musicality' of the lines). This is precisely the term that best describes the demands placed on the course line:

- movement of the line;

- free forward movement;

- change of rein;

- distribution of space;

- accentuation;

- rhythm;

- overall musicality;

- general dramatic content;

and other aspects of a 'rhythmical composition'.

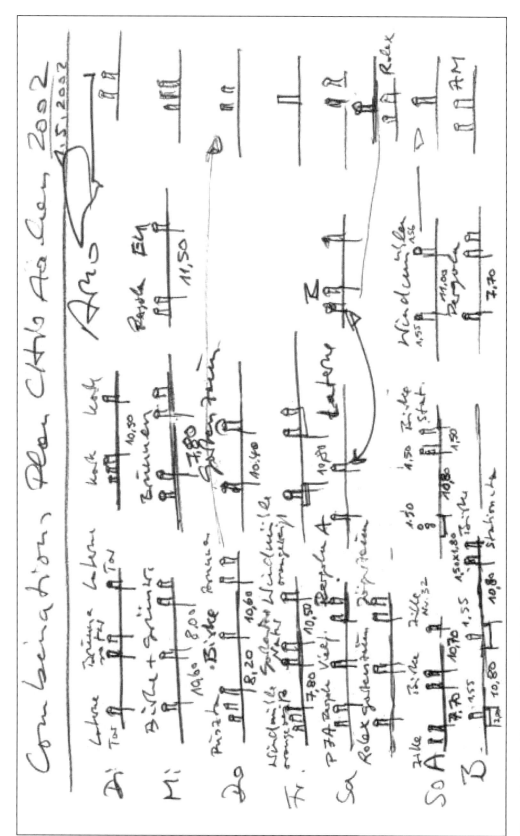

Figure 13.4: *Combination plan, CHIO Aachen 2002.*

In practice, one can often observe that the design of curved lines leads to faults. These are due to difficult-to-ride tracks on a curved line from one obstacle to the next. Here, track analysis through observation of the intersection of the middle lines (figure 13.5) of the two consecutive obstacles is helpful. When judging the degree of difficulty of a curved line, the condition of the footing, topography, etc. are important, in addition to the distance of the consecutive obstacle types.

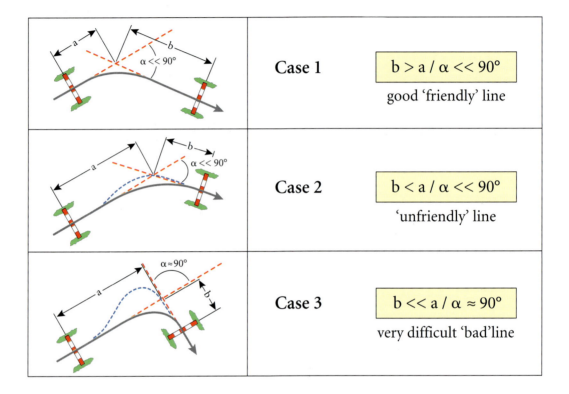

Figure 13.5: *Case study of bent lines (theory of secants).*

FREEHAND DRAWING IS THE MOTHER OF ARTS!

(Leonardo da Vinci, 1452–1511)

One might compare a good MASTERPLAN (figures 13.6 and 13.7) for a major jumping competition to a musical score.

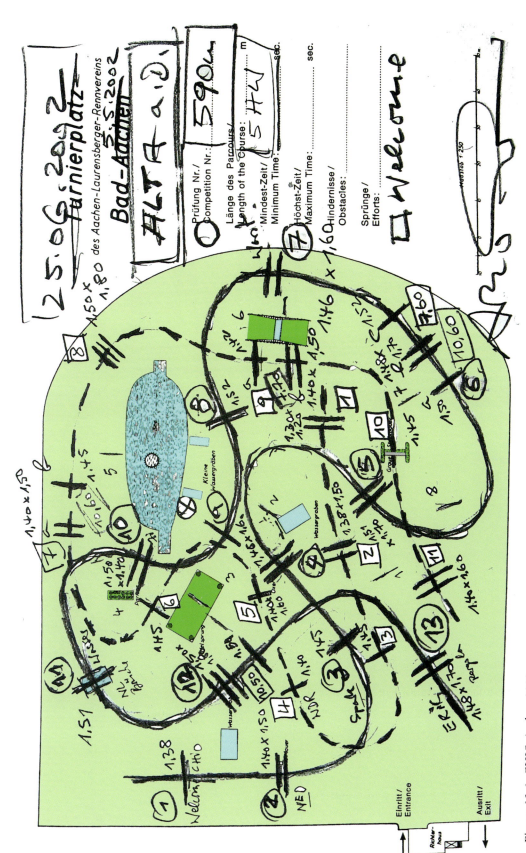

Figure 13.6 *CHIO Aachen 2002.*

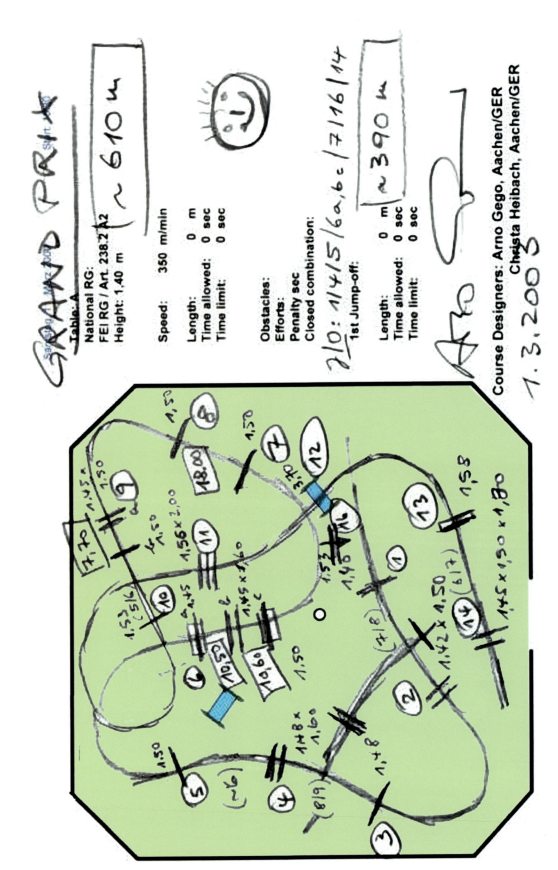

Figure 13.7: *Winter Equestrian Festival, West Palm Beach 2003.*

FURTHER ASPECTS OF VARIATION

The design and creation of courses demand variety and conceptual creativity to make them interesting and attractive.

This is particularly important for outstanding, high-level events. The courses of GRAND PRIX-level competitions should distinguish themselves by the fact that they are visually instantly recognisable as the main event and stand out clearly from lesser competitions. The track on important arenas can be identified, at least by experts, long before it is finished, even without numbering.

However, in other jumping competitions, too, the law of variety should apply.

1   A classical course should consist of:

- upright obstacles;

- spread obstacles;

- natural obstacles and intermediate types;

and also contain varied elements, as for example:

- a wall;

- a plank as a knock-down element;

- narrow obstacle;

- triple bar;

- Liverpool;

- paddock fence, gate or similar.

2   The individual types of obstacle should change along the course in a lively rhythm.

3   Sometimes, the same obstacle types can be repeated once or, at most, twice in the sequence.

4   The placement of colour in the overall arrangement in the arena also contributes considerably, from the point of view of the spectators and television, to the uniqueness of the overall presentation.

5   Finally, the course of a major tournament that is ready for inspection should be a composition which can claim to be a unique piece of work.

A checklist (table 13.4) can help the course designer to make sure that he has not forgotten or overlooked important parts of this great composition.

Table 13.4 *Potential for variety of obstacle types in classical courses – outdoors/indoors*

No.	Minimum requirements/criteria	
1	one maximum height obstacle	is a MUST
2	one maximum spread obstacle	not negotiable
3	one wall	
4	one triple bar	
5	one obstacle over water (Liverpool or open water jump)	} at least 4 items
6	one plank on top	are mandatory
7	one faultable gate	
8	one narrow obstacle	
9	one open water jump (3.00…4.50 m) – outdoors	a MUST for main
10	one fixed natural obstacle	competitions at
		major outdoor eventsd any
11	and any other special obstacle, if applicable	

14 ON THE QUESTION OF SO-CALLED 'TECHNICAL' COURSES

There is a lot of talk nowadays about 'technically demanding' courses, and some course designers claim that they alone have invented the perfect course design. However, this is not the case. It should be recalled that at the second high-level FEI Seminar in Warendorf, Germany 1978, presided over by:

- H.-H. Brinckmann

- Pamela Carruthers and

- Bertalan de Némethy,

on the initiative of the then general secretary, Fritz Widmer, who was present at the seminar, the FEI discussed the question of the future development of show-jumping and course design.

Under the strong influence of recent developments in course design, and particularly of the huge dimensions of the obstacles in the individual jumping final at the 1976 Olympic Games in Montreal, Canada, after intensive discussions at the seminar the FEI decided to recommend, in addition to the already agreed and clearly implemented requirements such as:

- dimensions (height and spread);

- visual aspect, sun, colour;

- position of the task on the course;

THE RULER IS A TOOL OF THE DEVIL!

(Friedensreich Hundertwasser, 1928–2000)

- narrow obstacles ;

- distances in lines of obstacles and combinations;

the more rigorous inclusion of further technical requirements on courses – especially in high-level competitions. This included, and still does include, aspects such as:

1   reducing the standard length of hanging/knock-down elements to 4.00 m in outdoor competitions (until then the height was often 5.00 m) and to 3.00 to 3.50 m in indoor arenas;

2   the standard diameter of poles to be 10 cm (dried and machine-turned);

3   the use of flatter and open cups which ensures that a turned pole can roll in the cup (principle: touching the pole does not count as a knock-down and thus as a fault, while knocking it down does);

4   lighter, less solid walls, with easier to knock down upper parts;

5   lighter, less solid construction overall, which does not, however, mean that bush oxers or wall oxers should disappear completely;

6   lighter planks with flat cups (plus a lip on each side);

to mention just a few important examples.

This meant that the trend towards much lighter knock-down behaviour of:

- poles (round, rolling, lighter);

- planks;

- parts of walls;

Figure 14.1: *Arno Gego with HRH Prince Philip and Fritz O. Widmer, Olympic Games, Los Angeles 1984. Photo: private collection.*

Figure 14.2: *Arno Gego, Luciano Pavarotti and Alfonso Romo, Pavarotti International, CSIO Modena 1991. Photo by Pulsar.*

- gates, etc.;

was formally adopted.

For example: at the CHIO Aachen, the whole system was radically changed after the 1978 World Championship by using:

- open, more shallow cups;

- 4-m turned poles;

- lighter walls.

In addition, leading course designers constantly tried to improve the quality of the riding surfaces by using:

- grass for GRAND PRIX-level outdoor tournaments – grass is the queen of surfaces;

- sand for smaller outdoor arenas and indoor arenas;

while paying particular attention to ecological criteria such as:

- reduced dust creation;

- avoiding, in particular, the creation of fine-haired fabric dust harmful to health;

- moderate watering requirement.

Moreover, from around 1980, leading course designers also started to get together at national and international level to increase professional co-operation and to ensure that show-jumping would continue to develop.

This did not in any way mean that the beauty of arenas and jumping courses, particularly their variety and uniqueness, notably in connection with great, important arenas, was to be called into question.

Nor was the beauty-enhancing and enriching presence of permanent natural obstacles as a firm fixture in international sport ever called into question.

The recommendation to integrate technical requirements more clearly into GRAND PRIX-level sport was therefore not intended either to:

- fundamentally call into question the existing foundations of show-jumping;

- or prevent further development (as, for example, safety cups).

The development of the safety cups, based on a patent registered by a southern German engineer and inventor, Kurt Bender, has been closely monitored and supported by Olaf Petersen and me, from initial trials at tournaments in Germany to the FEI rules and standard tests at the RWTH Aachen.

This development offers:

- a lighter construction method, with lighter knock-down behaviour;

- a way of preserving the variety of requirements and design of jumping courses and arenas;

- better sports surfaces;

- better training of course designers;

and has had a lasting influence on the progress of course design in the last 25 years.

In this respect (Warendorf, 1978) the following events:

- OS Los Angeles, USA 1984 (Berthalan de Némethy);

- WC Aachen, Germany 1986 (Arno Gego);

- OS Seoul, Korea 1988 (Olaf Petersen);

- OS Atlanta, USA 1996 (Linda Allen);

- OS Sydney, Australia 2000 (Leopoldo Palacios);

- and also, from 1979, world-class tournaments in Aachen, Calgary and Monterrey

can be seen as positive examples of this new development.

Show-jumping is proud of the fact that falls of horses are now the exception. However, today the term 'technical' or 'technical course' often means simply:

1   small-minded course design;

2   impoverishment of the 'tournament landscape'; for example, only 'ground-floor acrobatics' and the use of lots of poles;

3   also, due to simple hired courses, one often no longer sees walls, Liverpools or planks;

4   lack of variety in every respect;

Figure 14.3: *Arno Gego, Pilar Cepeda and Alfonso Romo, CHIO Aachen 1993. Photo by CHIO Aachen.*

Figure 14.4: (*From left*) *Ron Southern, Pamela Carruthers and Alfonso Romo, CSI Monterrey 1994. Photo by Tish Quirk.*

5   excessively difficult distances of between 13 and 18 m in the sport at the grass-roots level (a deliberate disturbance of the horse's natural rhythm which is ultimately detrimental to encouraging young horses in particular, to encouraging riders and to the beauty of the sport.) Even in sport at the top level, such extremes are not necessary in order to set challenging tasks;

6   the neglect of large spread obstacles and free forward movement;

7   a manipulation of information; for example, on the official course drawing:

- an indication of greater obstacle height, greater oxer spread or greater water-jump width than actually measured;
- an indication of the wrong track length and thus manipulation of the time allowed;

8   so many different types of misleading labels (for example, unjustified superlatives).

Show-jumping should reject this type of 'technical course' for the sake of maintaining its classical principles and safeguarding its future interests!

A few representatives of our profession reduce their supposedly high standard to adopt slogans such as:

- so-called 'modern and technical courses';

- a 'leap into the modern age';

- so-called 'modern lines';

in order to dazzle and mislead both organisers and the media alike.

If, one day, the CHIO Aachen and the CSIO Calgary were no longer to be considered the most difficult competitions in the world, then great harm would have been done to these tournaments and to show-jumping as a sport.

15 PLANNING THE USE OF OBSTACLE MATERIAL FOR MAJOR TOURNAMENTS

A piano has only 52 white and 36 black keys, yet they can be used to create any number of musical compositions, not least because it is possible to vary the:

- key

- loudness

- tone colour

- sequence of notes

- rhythm.

Even when the piece of music, the hall and the orchestra are identical, it is often possible to identify the conductor purely by listening.

Equally, the available obstacle material is the starting point for:

- the overall visual presentation of obstacles in the stadium or arena;

- creating variations to achieve a new overall image every day;

- helping to determine the degree of difficulty beyond pure measurements (colours, visual aspect, positioning, choice of material, decoration of the sides, etc.).

Important showgrounds have their own obstacle material which contributes greatly to the uniqueness, identity and recognition of the respective tournament.

The amount of available obstacle material depends on the significance of the tournament. In order to ensure variety, more obstacle material should always be available than is needed, even for the greatest jumping competition:

- approximately 50 per cent more in small to medium-sized tournaments;

- in major international tournaments, about three to four times as many obstacles as are required in the GRAND PRIX.

This applies to the main stadium or arena, although separate material is also required for second or third jumping arenas.

The size, importance and impressive nature of the obstacle material should reflect the importance of the arena and of the class of the jumping competition. That is why lighter and simpler material should be used on second or third arenas.

Another important aspect is the maintenance, development and continuous part-replacement of the obstacle material to keep it smart (table 15.1, particularly point 3). This aspect is not always relevant for the Olympic Games or international championships because all or some of the obstacle material will be new.

In addition to major event organisers, with their own obstacle material, there are other types of organisers who mix their own and hired obstacle material.

- This represents a compromise which allows the tournament to have some autonomy in its presentation.

- There is also exclusive use of hired obstacle material.

At present, this second example is leading to a significant impoverishment of the tournament scene. Every weekend, one can see the same, basic, hired obstacles, even at competitions shown on television:

- no wall;

- no water ditch;

- often little or almost no decoration;

- no prominent wings;

Table 15.1 *Planning obstacle stocks for major world events*

Type of event	Stadium/arena	Obstacle stock
1 Olympic Games	mostly new	totally new 1 new motives (related to host city/country) 2 modernised known motives 3 others
2 World/continental championships	mostly given place of regular events	mixture of existing and new obstacles

3 Regular CSI/CSIO	given place and facilities	1 existing obstacle stock, permanently maintained, repaired and painted
		
		2 keeps overall image young by
		  • two/three new obstacles/motives per year
		  • permanent improvement of colours, details and decoration
		  • occasionally improving/ renewing of fixed natural obstacles
		
		3 regular elimination of outdated material

- no varied standing elements;

- often only poles as knock-down elements;

- often not very attractive sponsor obstacles.

Praise must go to the tournament organiser and course designer Steve Stephens, a former
rider in the US team, who is a passionate obstacle designer and has by now created such

an extensive and varied range of obstacle materials that he can put together a completely different mix of obstacles for various different tournaments. This mix also takes account of the size of the individual stadium and the importance of the event.

This obstacle material meets the highest international standards. Stephens is able simultaneously to:

- provide a small tournament with a variety of more simple obstacle materials; and, at the same time, to furnish completely different, constantly changing material of the highest standard for the main arena over a period of several weeks.

He is an obstacle designer who works out of conviction, and an FEI-approved Official International Course Designer. For him, the financial aspect takes second place. He is an exception and is not one of those who seek to gain at the expense, and above all to the detriment, of the sport.

To illustrate the spectrum between a medium-range three-day tournament and a GRAND PRIX-level event, the obstacle inventory of the CHIO Aachen is briefly listed below, in simplified form:

1   125 pairs of wings (figure 15.1);

2   5 walls (see also figure 9.25);

Figure 15.1: *(Left and above) Some examples of different wings. Photos by Christa Heibach.*

3　8 moveable Liverpools (different shapes and sizes);

4　500 poles, with approximately 45 different colour compositions and different lengths (table 15.2);

5　100 planks, small hanging gates and similar items in different colours and lengths (table 15.3);

6　60 palisades, standing gates, *stationata* and other standing elements used as fillers;

7　small elements (cups, flags, etc.);

8　3 sets of obstacle numbers (different colours);

9　small tractors with a single-axle (as well as a tandem-axle) platform wagon with tyres suitable for grass.

This list does not include important items such as:

- decoration;

- ground maintenance equipment;

- small pieces of wood (1, 2, 3 cm);

- different coloured sticky tape;

- indoor arena material, practice arena material, etc.

My aim here is to show what a world of difference there is between a medium-level tournament and a GRAND-PRIX event.

The value of the two comparative tournaments, without vehicles, permanent natural obstacles and decoration, can range between:

- approx. 30,000 Euro for the normal three-day tournament;

- up to approx. 500,000 Euro for GRAND PRIX-level tournaments such as Aachen.

Table 15.2 *Part of the plan of poles (4.00 m long)*

No.

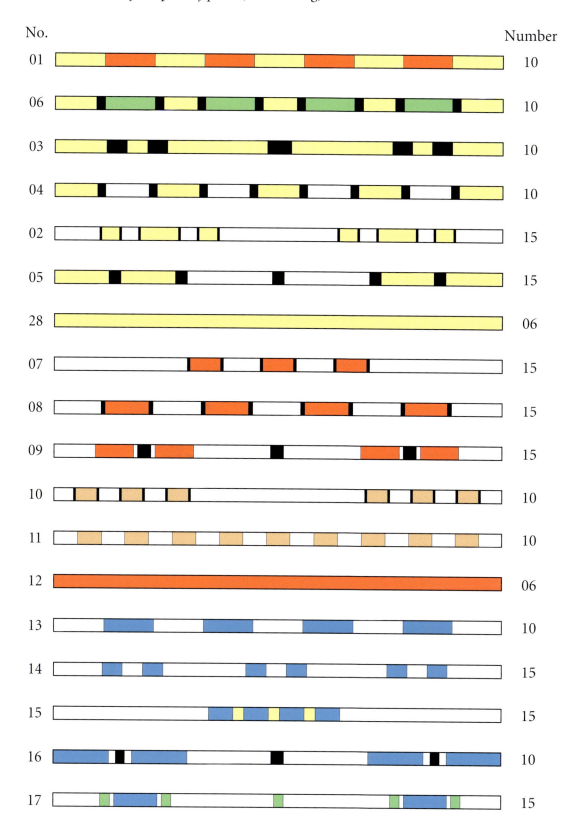

Number

No.	Number
01	10
06	10
03	10
04	10
02	15
05	15
28	06
07	15
08	15
09	15
10	10
11	10
12	06
13	10
14	15
15	15
16	10
17	15

Table 15.3 *Part of the plan of planks (4.00 m long)*

Number

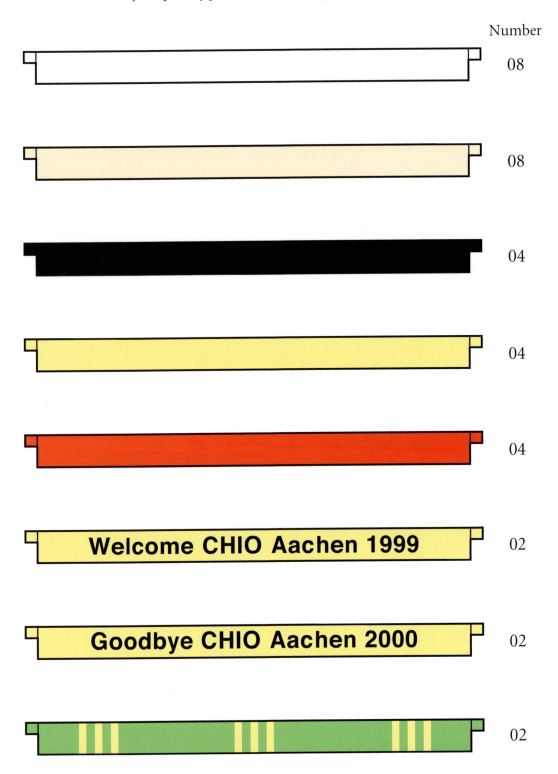

08

08

04

04

04

Welcome CHIO Aachen 1999   02

Goodbye CHIO Aachen 2000   02

02

It is up to the responsible course designer to secure obstacle material for his tournament which:

- is in line with the quality of the tournament;

- is as cost-effective as possible;

- nevertheless, can be developed and renewed.

It is recommended that all the obstacle material should be recorded in an 'obstacle material book'.

Where course designers change constantly, a qualified first assistant, or better still a permanent co-course designer, can perform the above task on site.

It is not the intention of this book to take away the course designer's personal responsibility for the obstacle material for his tournament by providing detailed tables and recommendations. Course design is a highly creative responsibility in this area, which, in an ideal situation, can be a creative art.

16 THE ORGANISATION OF COURSE BUILDING

For major tournaments, the practical implementation of a MASTERPLAN is characterised by tight time schedules and considerable complexity. It requires:

1   the most efficient organisation of the available team (course designers, assistants, construction team);

2   the setting up of working groups, each with one person in charge (usually an assistant);

3   ideally, a transport vehicle for each working group (figure 16.1);

4   a detailed obstacle material plan in addition to the MASTERPLAN (figure 16.2 and table 16.1);

5   appointing a responsible material manager who organises and checks the proper order, receipt and delivery of the obstacle material;

6   the appointment of an assistant to provide:

  ● a course plan, including all information demanded by the FEI rules;

  ● dissemination of information (to the ground jury and on various notice boards serving the entrance, practice arena, media, spectators, etc.);

  ● internet connection.

7   the appointment of a working group to deal with:

Figure 16.1: *Some useful tools: platform wagon; cups, flags, numbers; mobile phone (communication with jury and organisation); tractor with turf wheels. Photos by Christa Heibach.*

- decoration;

- numbering;

- placing flags;

- placing of start and finish;

- repair of damages in the stadium and in the obstacle storage area;

8 a working group for ground maintenance (rolling, raking, sprinkling, stamping, etc.). This should be given to a professional groundsman or another co-operative expert. In each case, the course designer makes the decisions and has the last word. Some so-called 'ground experts' tend to misuse their service function for media-effective self-promotion. This is, of course, not acceptable.

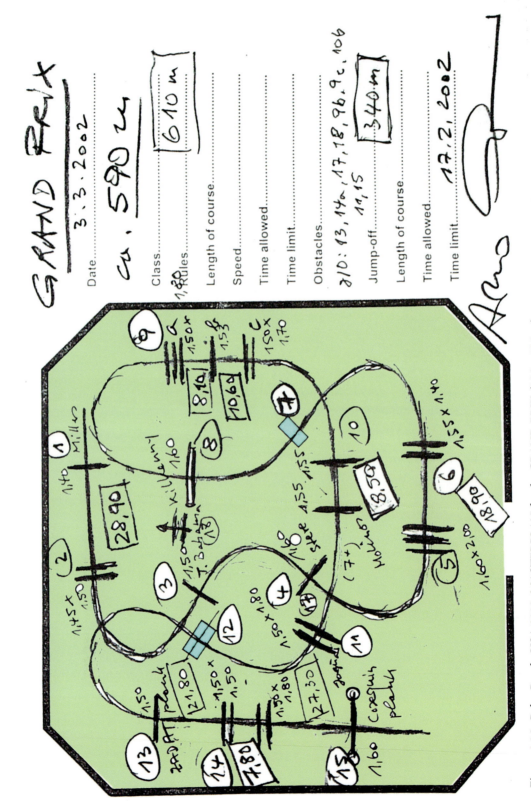

Figure 16.2: *Palm Beach, USA 2002, MASTERPLAN for the GRAND PRIX (120 x 120 m).*

Table 16.1 *Sample material list*

Competition   GRAND PRIX Palm Beach   Date 03.03.2002

No	Wings	Gates and Planks	Poles	Type
1	2 Octogon	4 Boxes 2 Standings	maroon, white	
2	2 Bevel 2 Uprights	Bevel Gate	Bevel	
3	4 White Pillars 2 RV		orange, white, yellow	
4	Steve Bridge 2 Iron			
5	2 Cathedral + 2 PVC 2 Uprights	1 Paris Gate	orange, white, yellow	
6	4 Brown Stone 2 Molinos	Land Rover	green, white	
7	2 Lighthouses	Water Jump		
8		Wall		
9a	2 Judge Towers 2 Giraffe	1 Judge Gate	Judge	
9b	2 Tommy Bahama	1 Tommy Gate	Tommy Bahama	
9c		3 Hurdles Bamboo	Bamboo	
10a	2 Grey Houses 2 Horse Show	1 Plank red	red, white	
10b	2 Grey Houses 2 Horse Show	1 Plank red	red, white	
11	2 Jaguar	1 Jaguar Gate	blue, white	
12	2 PCV	Water Jump	light blue, white	
13	2 Zada	1 Zada Plank	black, gold, white	
14a	2 Towers + 2 Molinos 2 Uprights	1 Box	yellow, black, white	
14b	2 Towers + 2 Molinos 2 Uprights	1 Box	yellow, black, white	
15	1 Cosequin + 2 PVC	4 Planks Aqua	aqua blue, white	

The requirements for such organisation demand:

- considerable management experience;

- continuity of the entire course team (as little change as possible from year to year);

- the ability to work as a team, especially of the management team (the foot soldiers are only as good as their officers);

- excellent communication and total discipline;

- the experienced course designer will organise and motivate his team so well that he can remain largely in the background during the construction process;

- thanks to mobile phones, two-way radio and telephone communication, many things have become much easier in recent years – especially over large arenas.

The better and more efficient a building organisation is, the more time the course designer has left to deal with the really important remaining issues, namely:

- track length;

- degree of difficulty;

- overall visual presentation.

17 THE PHILOSOPHY AND RULES OF MEASURING

USING A METRE RULE AND TAPE MEASURE

The MASTERPLAN for the course shows the main details involved in its construction (see also chapter 13). These include:

- tracks (for example, first and second round, jump-off);

- position of the obstacles;

- obstacle material;

- colour and decorative design;

- dimensions (height, spread, width) and distances in combinations and obstacle sequences.

When building a course based on a MASTERPLAN, an experienced course designer who is building the course alone or with only inexperienced helpers will be forced to rely largely on his own 'eye' and his own 'pace'.

But of course he will also measure the:

- obstacle height in the middle of the obstacle;

- obstacle spread on both sides;

- distances in combinations on both sides;

Figure 17.1 (Above): *(From left) Leopoldo Palacios, Christa Jung and Mehves Trak checking the Derby course at Valkenswaard. Photo by Rolf Peter.*

Figure 17.2 (Right): *A course designer from earlier times. Photo: private collection.*

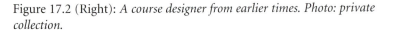

- distances between obstacles, at least in the middle;

to confirm that he has implemented the MASTERPLAN correctly and to satisfy himself that his visual judgement was accurate.

Normally, however, the course designer will work with a team of experienced assistants and helpers when preparing for a major tournament. In such cases it is important to build quickly and safely and to be aware of a few rules concerning precise measurement using a metre rule and tape measure.

1   The level of difficulty of a jumping class, a line of obstacles or a combination cannot be measured; it can only be judged on the basis of experience (figures 17.1 and 17.2). One can only measure dimensions and distances.

2   The metre rule is used to 'check the intention' (Brinckmann). A very experienced, focused course designer is largely able to make a visual judgement about the height of the obstacles in high-level competitions.

3   Obstacle heights are normally only measured in the middle (generally not on the left or right, which is a matter for the eye).

4   The ground of fairly large arenas often slopes or is uneven because of minor surface undulations. In all such cases, the course designer has to judge by eye whether the top line of the obstacle should follow the gradient of the terrain or whether horizontal vision would be preferable (this also depends a lot on the track). The overall visual appearance of an obstacle certainly cannot just be 'nicely measured'!

5   The spread of spread obstacles and the width of the water jump are always measured on both the left- and right-hand side.

6   Distances in combinations and outside of combinations, up to roughly 20 m, are always measured with the tape measure. Combinations are measured on both sides. Nevertheless, a combination can be placed on a curved line if the track and the natural conditions of the terrain allow this; for example, in a speed class (table C) or a Derby.

7   In its rules (art. 212.2), the FEI has specified how distances should be measured. This is particularly important in combinations. This article seems to be unknown to some course designers who are clearly not aware that permanent (natural) obstacles also obey their own laws (figure 17.3).

8   The 'cross measuring' of distances is an interesting method of measuring, but one which can, however:

  - lead to errors where the ground is quite uneven, and which, in the end, cannot absolve the course designer from the responsibility of checking by eye and taking responsibility for the final decision;

  - lead some course builders to overestimate the role of the metre rule and tape measure, measure till the cows come home, and still nothing is right at the end!

  - it is therefore important that assistants or course designers are able to stand back from their task to gain a better perspective and judgement.

9   It happens repeatedly that distances in combinations or short distances (up to approximately 20 m) are changed by accident, wrongly implemented or even manipulated.
     It is therefore important that, during his last round, the course designer, usually with the ground jury, checks all strategically important distances with a tape measure. It is sufficient to re-measure only the distances on the centre line.

'The distance is measured from the base of the obstacle on the landing side to the base of the next obstacle on the take-off side'

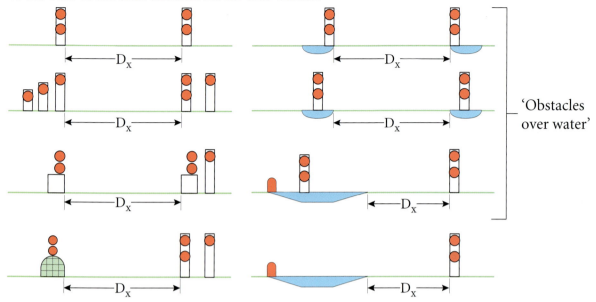

'Obstacles over water'

But: 1 Distances need accurate analysis of speed, distribution of strides, trajectories, etc.

2 Only the measured distance in metres together with the obstacle types in sequence and their dimensions, footing, slope, position, speed, etc., give a distance quality (a little long, short, normal, etc.)

3 The figure in metres alone means NOTHING!

Figure 17.3: *Distances (FEI art. 212.1)*

Figure 17.4: *Arno Gego and HRH Prince Tsunekazu Takeda of Japan at the final check before the GRAND PRIX, CHIO Aachen 1991. Photo by Findlay Davidson.*

10 It has been found repeatedly that obstacles and/or distances have been changed overnight by unknown persons (even at the Olympic Games!). At the Luxembourg CSIO in the early 1990s, it even happened that a vital upright obstacle at the Nations Cup was reduced in height from 1.60 m to 1.55 m during the course inspection when no one was looking.

(It is therefore a good idea to check the course one last time after the course inspection (figure 17.4).

11 At indoor tournaments, and where a course is being built in a very short time, obstacle distances should always be measured on both sides with the tape measure so as to avoid mistakes occurring due to pressure of time during construction, as frequently happens when using assistants and/or helpers who have little experience.

In conclusion, it is necessary to define the spread of spread obstacles.

1   Following FEI article 212.1, the spread of obstacles is measured from the base of the obstacle on the take-off side to the base of the obstacle on the landing side (figure 17.5).

2   Therefore the width/spread of the entire obstacle must always be taken into account.

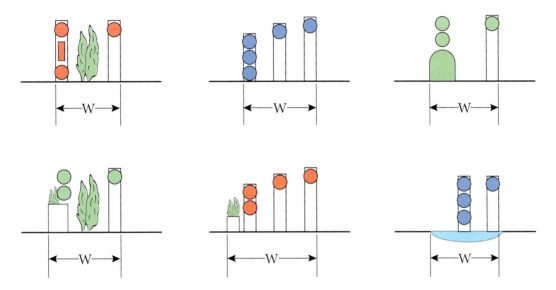

Figure 17.5: *Measuring the width of spread fences.*

The discussion that follows below deals in detail with the measurement of track lengths.

MEASUREMENT OF TRACK LENGTHS

As the required speed is an important part of the test in a jumping class (obstacle no. 15), skilled and serious measuring of the track length is particularly important. The time allowed (T) (sec.) depends on the length of the track (l) (m) and the minimum speed (v) (m/min.) required according to the schedule, based on the following formula:

$$T = \frac{L}{V} \times 60 \; [sec.]$$

Of all the measurements, such as height, spread, width, distance, etc., measuring the track length is the most important by far!

This is because athletes and trainers will undoubtedly note any faults, irregularities, etc. when walking or inspecting the course before the competition, yet none of them measures the length of the course. It will only be possible to identify grave errors in the course length after ten or 20 riders have competed.

So we continue to need the good old measuring wheel that is still used by construction engineers and landscape architects in serious measuring work.

Measuring wheels should have a circumference of at least 1 m.

$$U = \prod \circ d = 1.00\,m$$

This results in a wheel diameter of:

$$d = 0.3183\,m$$

Measuring wheels with a larger diameter are also used successfully but they are less practical if they have to be transported.

When measuring the length of the course using a measuring wheel, there are some practical points to remember.

1 Each measuring wheel must be checked for slippage, based on the existing condition of the footing.

2 To do this, place a tape measure of at least 20 m length on the ground.

3 Follow the length of the tape measure with the measuring wheel and identify any slippage.

- On a well-maintained grass surface this may be between 0 and 1.5 per cent; and

- can vary between 1.5 and 10 per cent on sand surfaces.

Measuring the track length accurately (table 17.1) is a skill that comes with experience and it must be taken very seriously.

Table 17.1 *Methods of defining the length of the course*

	Method	Explanation	Final practical use
1	Walking	Walking the real course	No further application
2	Cartographical wheel	Measuring the MASTERPLAN	Good for approximate orientation, not acceptable for 'final length'
3	Computer calculation	Based on computer drawing	Good for orientation, not acceptable for 'final length'
4	Landscaper's wheel	Measuring the reality	Is an absolute must to get accurate results!

1   The track length must be measured with a measuring wheel on an actual footing (figure 17.6).

2   A cartographic wheel on paper or computerised measurements are fine to get a preliminary idea, but are not acceptable for a final determination of the track length because they are not sufficiently precise (often erring by up to 5 per cent or more!).

3   Measuring course lengths requires a great deal of experience.

4   In major tournaments, two to three course designers measure independently of each other (figure 17.7).

5   Where measurements vary by more than 10 to 15 m, the measurement is repeated.

6   A final measurement when walking the course with the ground jury makes sense. An assistant should guide the measuring wheel.

(Left) Figure 17.6: *Arno Gego measuring the length of the course at CHIO Aachen. Photo by CHIO Aachen.*

(Right) Figure 17.7: *Olaf Petersen (right) checking Arno Gego's 'creation'. Photo by Deutsche Meisterschaft.*

7   If the course designer determines the track length on his own (without a TD or ground jury) he leaves himself open to accusations of manipulation.

- If a certain course designer is worried that there will be too many clear rounds, he may reduce the track length and the time allowed (which means increasing the speed from, for example, 400 to 430m/min.). This changes the nature of the competition considerably.

- If the same course designer is worried that there won't be a jump-off, he may add 30 or 40 m to the measured track length and thus reduce the speed from, for example, 400 to 375 m/min.).

Both instances demonstrate the huge importance of correct track length and time allowed. Both examples would be cases of unauthorised manipulation. In both cases the schedule will not have been adhered to and the character of the respective class will have been changed.

I have experienced both of the above-cited cases at two high-level outdoor tournaments with the same course designer.

Here are some rules on measuring the course length.

1   The final measurement of the track length takes place when the course has been largely built.

2   The basic principle is that the normal route is measured from one obstacle to the next in a particular jumping class: the same applies to the jump-off course.

3   Curved lines, approach and finish depend on the importance, class and degree of difficulty of the jumping competition (a 1.10-m class is shorter than a 1.60-m GRAND PRIX) with the same obstacle positions and track.

4   For a specific jumping competition (dimensions, condition of the footing, importance, etc.), there can only be one course length. The track length is never in doubt.

5   Proper measuring of the track length of a course is only possible if the person using the measuring wheel has previously studied the course in detail. Measuring the course length is not just a case of simply following the obstacle numbers.

6   A course length that has not been measured correctly, or manipulation of the course length, destroys the character of the competition and is thus neither in conformity with the rules nor fair, but, rather, *anti-sportif*.

7   For example, a 270-degree curve should be measured in such a way that the prescribed minimum speed can be ridden, even if many riders will still ride a smaller curve, over a shorter length at slower speed (see also tables 17.2 and 17.3).

8   Distances to be ridden in jumping competitions are always the links between straight and more or less curved lines. Curved lines, whether over a narrow or a wide curve, are always round. There are no sharp corners in the theory of dynamics.

The measurement of 270-degree curves continues to be rather an open question.

● What diameter should be assumed for which height of jumping class as the basis for measuring the curve?

Figure 17.8 and tables 17.4 and 17.5 show the results of research carried out for two different curves, A and B, in the first round of a 1.50-m GRAND PRIX. As can be seen on the course drawing, curve B was influenced by a sponsor vehicle.

Table 17.2 *Theoretical considerations about 270–370-degree turns*

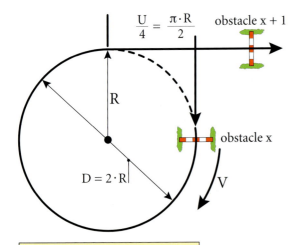

$$\frac{U}{4} = \frac{\pi \cdot R}{2} \quad \text{obstacle } x + 1$$

Distance from x to x (360°)

$$U = S_{x/x} = (n+1) \cdot L_s \ [m]$$

$$U = \pi \cdot D = 2 \cdot \pi \cdot R$$
$$\frac{U}{4} = \frac{\pi \cdot R}{2} = 1.57 \cdot R$$
$$\frac{U}{4} = \frac{\pi \cdot D}{4} = 0.785 \cdot D$$

Distance from x to x + 1 (270°)

$$S_{x/x+1} \approx S_{x/x} = U$$
$$S_{x/x+1} \approx (U+1) \cdot L_s \ [m]$$

$$D = \frac{U}{\pi} = \frac{(n+1) \cdot L_s}{\pi} \ [m]$$

Table 17.3 *270–370-degree turns*

Strides	Length of stride (estd.)	Diameter	Periphery	Quarters	Time (360°)	Speed
n	L_s	$D = 2 \cdot R$	$U = ? \cdot D$ $U = (n+1) \cdot L_s$	$\dfrac{U}{4}$	$t_{360°} = (n+1) \cdot t_s^{*}$	$V = \dfrac{U}{t_{360°}} \cdot 60$
-	m	m	m	m	sec.	m/min.
13	3.60	16.04	50.4	12.6	8.4	360
15	3.70	18.84	59.2	14.8	9.6	370
17	3.80	21.77	68.4	17.1	10.8	380
19	3.90	24.83	78	19.5	12	390
21	4.00	28.01	88	22	13.2	400

* t_s = 0.6 sec/stride

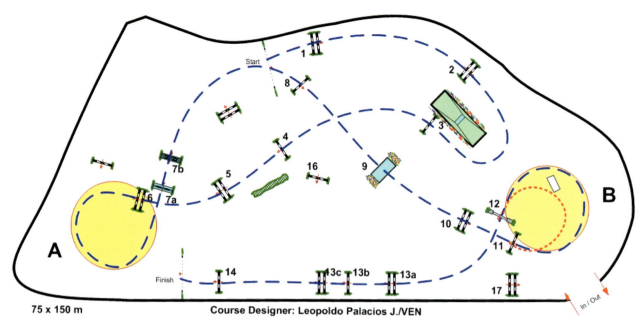

Figure 17.8: *CSI Monterrey 2003, GRAND PRIX 1.50 m/555min.*

A

75 x 150 m

Course Designer: Leopoldo Palacios J./VEN

Table 17.4 *The riding distance of 270-degree turns from obstacle to obstacle*

1. Average number of strides

$$\bar{n} = \frac{\sum_{i=1}^{n} n_i \cdot x_i}{m} + 1 \ [\text{number of strides}]$$

2. Average distance between following obstacles

$$D_{a/b} = \bar{n} \cdot l_s \ [\text{m}]$$

l_s = estimated length of stride [m]

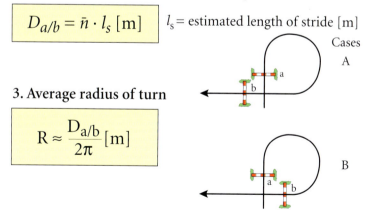

Cases

A

B

3. Average radius of turn

$$R \approx \frac{D_{a/b}}{2\pi} \ [\text{m}]$$

Srides per turn $n_i[-]$	Statistical Distribution x_i = amount occurrance at $n_i[-]$	
	1. turn	2. turn
10	-	1
11	-	1
12	1	1
13	1	ЖЖ
14	ЖЖ 1	1
15	ЖЖ 111	-
16	111	ЖЖ
17	11	ЖЖ 11
18	1	111
19	-	1
20	-	11
21	-	11
22	1	-
23	-	-
24	-	-
25	1	-
Number of Starters m	24	26
Total Number of Strides $\sum_{i=10}^{25} n_i \cdot x_i$	376	408

The average number of canter strides for both curves was n = 16.7. This results in distances from obstacle a to b of between 58.5 and 63.5 m at an assumed stride length ls and thus radii R of between 9 and 10 m.

Finally, some suggestions on the placement of the start and finishing line (figure 17.9). Both lines are placed so that they are perpendicular to the approach that would normally be taken. They should be open, wide and generous (at least three times the width of the obstacle front).

Table 17.5 *The riding distance of 270-degree turns from obstacle to obstacle (Monterrey 2003)*

Length of stride (std.)	Distance between two 270°-turn obstacles	Corresponding radius R (m)
ls (m)	D a/b (m)	A or B
3.50	58.45	9.30
3.60	60.12	9.57
3.80	63.46	10.10

General recommendations for START/FINISH lines

- open and wide (generous)
- must clearly refer to first and last obstacle
- should not be source of surprises and faults
- line 90° to normal riding line

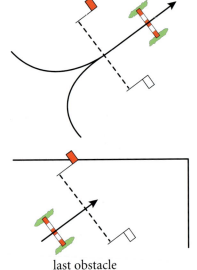

Examples

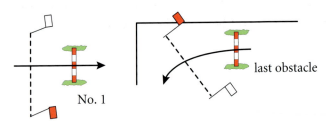

Figure 17.9: *General recommendations for start/finish lines.*

18 GRAND PRIX, NATIONS CUP AND DERBY COURSES

Alongside the great international championships and the Olympic Games, GRAND PRIX, the Nations Cup and great Derby competitions are the outstanding events in show-jumping.

The author's view, which may be contrary to that of some official representatives of equestrian sport, such as the federations or sponsors, is that the GRAND PRIX is the absolute pinnacle of a major international tournament.

- There is no Olympic sport with an individual and team ranking where the team final ranks above the individual final.

- It is therefore wrong to sacrifice the position of the GRAND PRIX at the end of the tournament (usually Sundays) in favour of the Nations Cup.

- Logically, one could then completely abolish the GRAND PRIX at CSIO tournaments because it is less important! That is theoretically conceivable, but it would considerably reduce the standard of the particular tournament.

In reality, the GRAND PRIX and the Nations Cup are at the same level in the sport, but the GRAND PRIX clearly has greater prestige – *primus inter pares* (first among equals)! This clearly answers the question of which competition is the highlight of the last show day.

- The main event comes at the end: the GRAND PRIX.

So the course designer plans the tournament by starting from the combinations plan and the MASTERPLAN of the GRAND PRIX (see figure 18.3). He gives it his utmost attention. Everything else must be subordinate.

Figure 18.1: *Christa Heibach and Arno Gego, course designers CSI Istanbul, Turkey 1996. Photo by Fatosh Istanbul.*

Figure 18.2: *Olaf Petersen, Technical Delegate WEG Jerez 2002 and his son, Olaf Petersen Jr. Photo by Christa Heibach.*

The GRAND PRIX is therefore marked out by specific distinguishing characteristics.

- At really outstanding tournaments, the GRAND PRIX is contested according to the Olympic format (two different rounds, one jump-off, 1.60 m, speed 400 m/min. water jump in the first round).

- Approximately 35 to 40 competitors take part in the first round, having already qualified for participation in earlier jumping classes (approx. 1.50 m).

- The number of competitors competing in the second round is restricted to approximately 50 per cent of the first round.

- The second round is shorter than the first.

- The starting order in the second round will be in reverse order of the total penalties in the first round (ranked according to penalties and time).

- The starting order in the jump-off is the same as in the second round.

- The GRAND PRIX is the most difficult competition of the tournament. Only the best horses and riders should be able to compete.

- The outcome of the most exciting GRAND PRIX is decided by the score of the last competitor after the last obstacle. This creates dramatic tension.

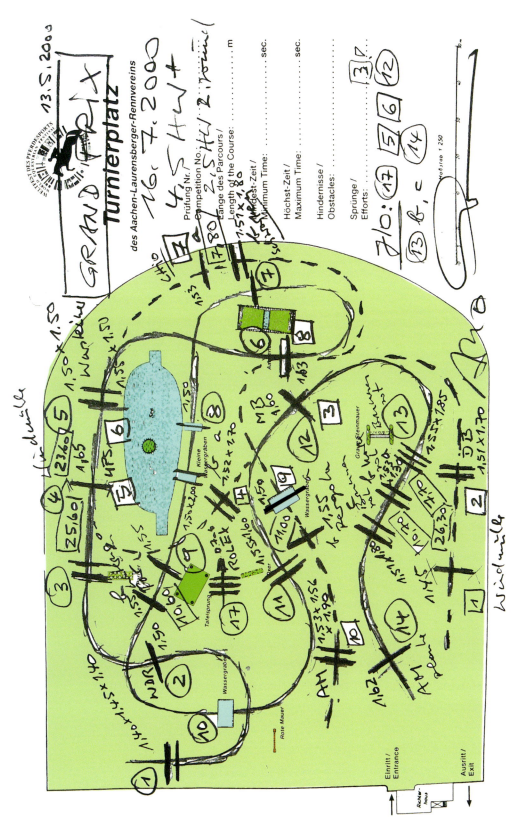

Figure 18.3: *CHIO Aachen 2000. MASTERPLAN for the GRAND PRIX (125 x 150 m).*

Some important design criteria contribute greatly to the presentation of a GRAND PRIX.

1   The track of the GRAND PRIX is characterised by:

  - the optimum use of space;

  - the even distribution of obstacles in order to create maximum involvement and interest for the spectators.

2   Combinations and other main challenges are placed in strategically important positions.

3   In its visual aspect alone, thanks to its more impressive obstacle material, colours and decoration, the GRAND PRIX distinguishes itself so clearly from other jumping competitions on the same day in the same stadium, that it can easily be identified from outside the showground and will never be confused with any of the secondary competitions.

4   Only GRAND PRIX that meet the criteria cited above have a chance of entering into the annals of the history of show-jumping as 'classic GRAND PRIX'!

5   The track of the jump-off must do justice to the size of the arena and should be visible to all spectators.

6   On arenas of approximately 10,000 m² or more, the construction of the courses for both rounds is completed before the first round starts. This allows the change from the first to the second round to take place without much delay.

THE NATIONS CUP

For the Nations Cup, a CSIO5, (see figure 18.6), there is another classical format.

1   two identical rounds;

2   max. height   1.60 m
    max. spread   2.00 m (triple bar 2.20 m)
                       4.50 m water jump (currently reduced)
    minimum speed   400 m/min.;

3 12 obstacles/15 efforts;

4 water jump obligatory.

Otherwise, the same general criteria apply as those for the GRAND PRIX. Here, the criterion of distributing the obstacles evenly, with only 12 obstacles on large arenas, is a particular challenge for the course designer.

The discussion so far leads to the following conclusions.

1 Large, important arenas need their own large stock of obstacle material with its own distinctive features. Even very small photographed sections of large arenas are easy to identify, while photographs of most indoor tournaments, with hired obstacles, are not.

Figure 18.4: *(Left) Steve Stephens of the USA and Michael Gockel of Germany, course designers CSI Valkenswaard 2003. Photo by Christa Heibach.*

Figure 18.5: *(Left) Luc Musette of Belgium and Mehves Trak of Turkey, both international course designers. Photo by Christa Heibach.*

2   Only outstanding individuality makes our sport important and attractive. This applies particularly when the arguments of:

- nature-based sport;

- aesthetics;

- ethics, animal protection and fair play;

are convincingly put into practice in a credible way.

In a few tournaments, for example Hamburg (figure 18.7), the Grand Jumping Derby replaces the GRAND PRIX discussed above. However, that is the exception.

This Derby is the main event of the tournament and usually takes place on Sunday afternoon. It has its own rules which have developed over time and are described in more detail in table 18.1.

In summary, it has:

- a very long track;

- predominantly natural obstacles;

- one round, one jump-off;

- 1.60 m/400 m/min.

Hamburg is the prototype of the jumping Derby, which was first designed by Eduard E. Pulvermann in 1920. This was an outstanding equestrian achievement – a 'once in a century' innovation in show-jumping that is not given the appreciation and importance it deserves. Hickstead, Dublin and La Baule are important, more recent successors of the Hamburg Derby idea.

However, more recent developments show that the Derby concept is clearly an attractive concept and, since around 1992, a limited number of tournament organisers have taken up the idea of the 'nature-based course' and imitated it as a sort of 'friendly' Derby. These include:

- La Bagnaia, Tuscany, Italy;

- Valkenswaard, the Netherlands;

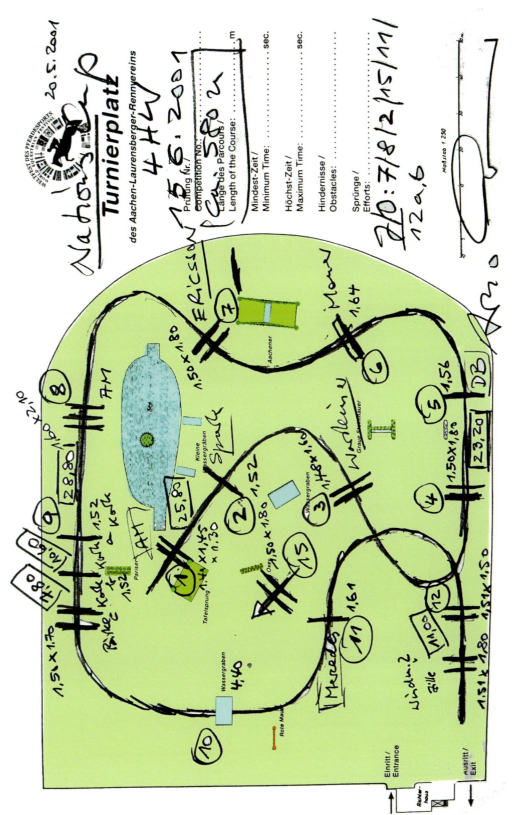

Figure 18.6: *CHIO Aachen 2000. MASTERPLAN for the Nations Cup (125 x 150 m).*

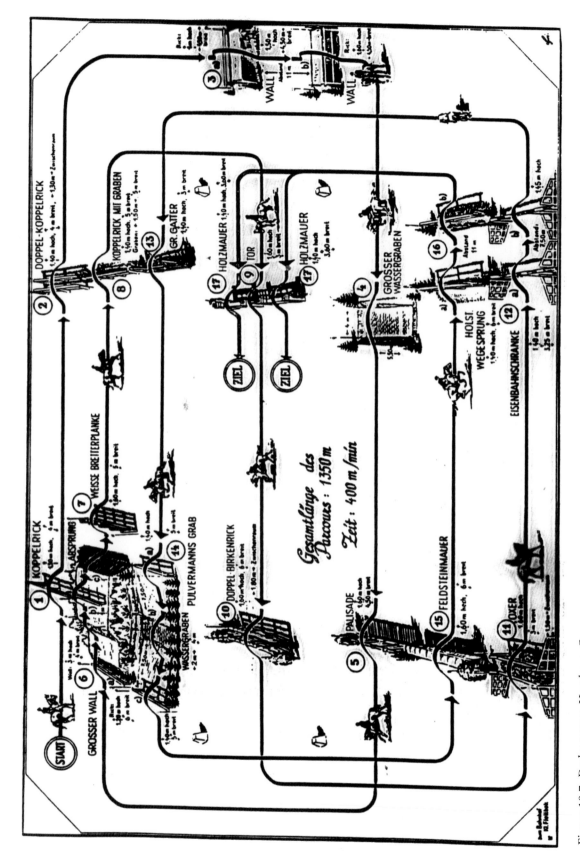

Figure 18.7: Derby course, Hamburg, Germany.

Table 18.1 *Specifications of Grand Derby courses*

Definition	a Derby is a special GRAND PRIX over a long course with mainly natural/rustic fences
Type of arena	outside, big, natural, grass, trees, flowers
Fixed natural fences	● open water jump (3.80/4.50 m) ● devil's dyke ● normal banks (various) ● obstacle over water (Liverpool) ● bush oxer ● dry ditch ('Trakehner') ● fences with hedges etc. ● big bank (various forms) ● etc.
Number of obstacles	16 .... 19 obstacles / 20 .... 25 efforts
Length of the course	more than 1,000 m
Further rules	● only 1 round ● speed: 400 m/min. ● maximum height: 1.60 m ● 1 jump-off if necessary

● Monterrey, Mexico;

● CSI Wiesbaden, Germany, with a so-called 'speed' Derby at around the same time.

A similar type of competition has existed at the CHIO Aachen for more than 30 years. This is the jumping class across ditches and banks, which was basically an early version of the 'friendly' Derby.

A 'friendly' Derby runs over a long natural course, up to a maximum height of 1.50 m, which can be tackled by any well-schooled, second-string horse as long as it will jump water, has been schooled over natural obstacles, is obedient and can gallop.

Structure:
● long course over a mixture of natural and mobile obstacles;

- no 'extreme' natural obstacles, such as super-high banks;

- no extreme dimensions (1.35–1.50 m maximum);

- length normally between 800 and 900 m;

- speed: 400 m/min.;

- rules: table A with or without jump-off.

Objectives:

- competition for normal (often second-string) international horses;

- forward-oriented, with exciting galloping stretches and enjoyable for spectators to watch.

Figure 18.8: *Arno Gego and friends.*

(Above left) With Leopoldo Palacios in Monterrey, Mexico. Photo by CSI Monterrey.

(Above) With John Madden and Leopoldo Palacios in Valkenswaard, the Netherlands. Photo by Christa Heibach.

(Left) Uliano Vezzani and Arno Gego during the first Pavarotti International, CS10 San Marino 1991. Photo: private collection.

19 SOME RULES FOR THE JUMP-OFF

The German word '*Stechen*' (jump-off) comes from the combat games played by knights in Europe in the Middle Ages, which included ring spearing and other forms of combat involving sabres [081].

The jump-off takes place when no clear winner has emerged after the normal round, or after two rounds in a jumping competition (for example, after several clear rounds).

1   A jump-off leads over a shortened and/or changed track of the preliminary round or of one or both rounds in jumping competitions with two different rounds.

2   The dimensions of some obstacles can be made slightly more difficult (for example, by 5 cm in height or 10-15 cm in the spread). The penalty requirement of the earlier round/rounds should be maintained.

3   The character of the obstacles should be preserved, so there should be no visual changes or changes in material or colours.

Figure 19.1: *With Wilhelm Stein (left) and Harry Cornford in Aachen. Photo by Franz Steindl.*

Figure 19.2: *With Christa Heibach and Joberto Pio da Fonseca in Rio de Janeiro, Brazil. Photo: private collection.*

4   At least two changes of rein should be the norm.

5   The track of the jump-off course should, if possible, use the entire arena and should offer appeal to the spectators. It should also include both:

  • galloping stretches; and the

  • possibilities of shortening or cutting out part of the track at the rider's risk.

6   The winner should be chosen on the basis of the horse's jumping ability, speed and skill, and the rider's ability, grasp of strategy and willingness to take risks.

7   The time needed should be minimised through galloping and risky turns.

8   Dispensing with one stride between a line of obstacles saves time. For example, at the 1984 Aachen GRAND PRIX, Paul Schockemöhle was the only one in the jump-off to master a 26-m distance (1.60 m vertical and 1.57 x 2 m oxer) in five strides, and thus won the competition.

9   The jump-off course should include a combination.

10 A water jump should not be part of the jump-off.

11 A maximum of two additional obstacles may be planned for the jump-off course, which can result in a more interesting track, particularly in a large arena.

Figure 19.3: *With Marcello Mastronardi in Monterrey, Mexico. Photo by CSI Monterrey.*

Figure 19.4: *With Linda Allen in Monterrey, Mexico. Photo by CSI Monterrey.*

Figure 19.5: *Arno Gego and friends. (Top left) With Harry Cornford and Christa Heibach, CSI Monterrey 1994. Photo by Tish Quirk. (Top right) (From left) Fritz Thiedemann, Christa Jung, Christa Heibach and Mehves Trak. Photo by Susanne Gossen. (Centre right) With Serge Houtmann, CSIO La Baule 2002. Photo by Christa Heibach. (Centre left) With Christa Heibach, CSI Monterrey 1994. Photo by Christa Heibach. (Bottom left) José Maria (Pepe) Gamarra and Wendy Chapot, CSIO Palm Beach 2004. Photo by Christa Heibach. (Bottom right) Christa Jung and Ferdi Rosellen, CHIO Aachen 2002. Photo by Susanne Gossen.*

12 The positions of the start and finish can be altered for the jump-off.

13 The changes to the course for the jump-off should be made in the shortest possible time to maintain tension and atmosphere and the attention of the spectators.

14 Watchable and exciting jumping competitions tend to have few clear rounds.

Major championships and the Olympic Games often have only one double clear round and no jump-off.

20 THE COURSE DESIGNER'S BASIC TECHNICAL EQUIPMENT FOR OUTDOOR TOURNAMENTS

In addition to his personal qualifications, a course designer needs to have the following tools in his basic equipment:

1   clothing suitable for all types of weather conditions, and subdued clothing appropriate for an FEI official (particularly for major events);

2   scale drawings of the arena on which to base his course sketches, which contain all the necessary details both inside and outside the stadium. With a modern photocopier, the desired format can easily be enlarged and reduced;

3   a metre rule and measuring wheel. Just as English and French are the FEI languages, so the ISO system (metric) is the only internationally recognised measuring system;

4   rulers (including curve templates) and cartographic wheels are additional tools for drafting a MASTERPLAN);

5   a soft pencil (4B) with an eraser as also used by architects;

6   coloured pens and markers in different colours;

7   sticky tape in different colours, to clearly mark the position of knock-down upper sections (especially poles);

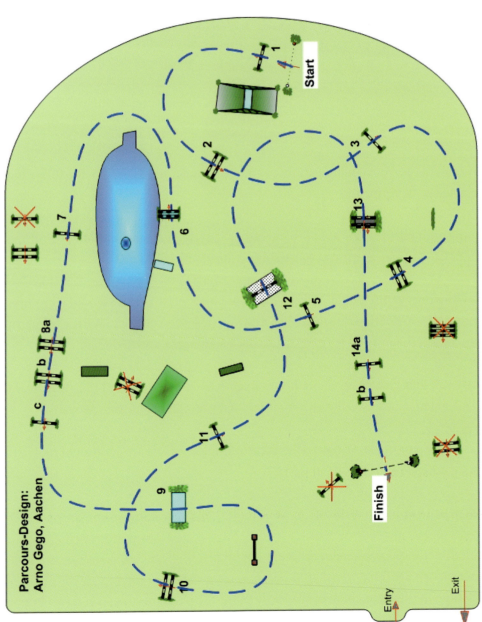

Parcours-Design:
Arno Gego, Aachen

Table A
FEI RG /Art. 266.5.2+283.3.1
height: 1.60 m

Speed: 400 m/min.

Length: 700 m
Time allowed: 105 sec.
Time limit: 210 sec.

Obstacles: 14
Efforts: 18

Size Main Stadium 125 x 150 m

Figure 20.1: *World Equestrian Festival, CHIO Aachen 2002, GRAND PRIX, first round, official course plan.*

8 naturally, the FEI 'Rules for Jumping Events' (or the rule book of the National Federation);

9 the competition schedule;

10 for larger tournaments, a laptop computer with a CAD course program and a printer to produce:

- drafts for the course (MASTERPLAN);

- official course sketches (for the ground jury, notices, the press etc.);

- if necessary, where the tournament is important enough, to provide information on the internet (figure 20.1).

This equipment is comparable to that of an architect or a landscape designer.

However, owning the perfect set of tools does not 'make' a course designer by a long shot.

LAPTOPS AND SOFTWARE

A computer is a useful tool for the course designer. Initially, stationary office PCs were used from the beginning of the 1990s for various types of coloured documents, such as:

- pole plan

- wings

- walls

- standing elements

- numbers, flags and other small parts

and also for producing scale plans of arenas. This technology, known as CAD, which had previously been used by mechanical and electrical engineers, car designers and architects, gained in importance as an aid for course designers at the end of the 1990s, when moderately priced laptops, digital cameras, colour printers and CAD programs adapted to the needs of course design became available on the market.

However, some representatives of the course design fraternity now present the PC as 'a revolution' in twenty-first century course design. That is nonsense.

1   The computer is not a substitute for a course designer's lack of creativity.

2   Its 'product' is the product of its user.

3   A bad MASTERPLAN will not get better no matter how precisely it is drawn on a PC.

4   The PC is simply a useful tool, just like the measuring wheel. In this context, the following analogies may help to gain a better understanding.

- Mozart would probably not have been an even more important composer if only he had had a computer!

- And Picasso would not have been an even more creative painter if only he had had access to computers.

Please also note here that dotted lines make the track on a course easier to see (figure 20.1).

Figure 20.2: *CHIO Aachen 1998. Photo: private collection.*

21 ON THE CO-OPERATION OF TOURNAMENT OFFICIALS

The smooth progress and successful implementation of a tournament depend, in addition to its proper preparation, particularly on the quality of the tournament officials (figures 21.1–21.6) and other collaborators involved in the organisation. Their effective co-operation is vitally important for the success of the tournament.

Despite their many different tasks and responsibilities, the co-operation of the:

- tournament director,

- course designer and

- president of the ground jury

is particularly important for the smooth running of the event in the arena. With the increased availability of mobile phones in recent years, co-operation is much easier today than was the case even ten years ago.

The tournament director is the friendly and yet resolute personality who:

1   is responsible for managing the tournament according to a previously fixed time schedule;

2   decides on necessary changes in the time schedule;

3   makes sure of effective communication inside and outside of the tournament organisation.

Figure 21.1: *Ethem Trak and Rolf Peter Fuß, jury. Photo by Christa Heibach.*

Figure 21.2: *Niko van Aken, master of ceremonies. Photo by Christa Heibach.*

The course designer is responsible for:

1   the planning and implementation of the course building and dismantling;

2   preparing the event's progress in such a way that the programme of events on the arena is only interrupted by a minimum of construction changes. On a large arena, both rounds of the GRAND PRIX will have been erected and be ready before the start of the first round, so that the change from the first to the second round can, if necessary, take place immediately; for example, to fit in with the transmission times of a television broadcast;

3   furthermore, the course designer is responsible for accurate information about obstacle dimensions, distances and track lengths and a maximum of well-performed, visually enjoyable sport.

Figure 21.3: *Course designer Olaf Petersen Jr and the team, CSI Valkenswaard 2002. Photo by Christa Heibach.*

Figure 21.4: *Course designer and jury at CSI Istanbul. Photo by Fatosh.*

The ground jury (president, foreign and other judges) is responsible in the arena for:

1 compliance with FEI rules and observance of the competition schedule;

2 ensuring the consistency of the class to be judged;

3 checking the correctness of the official course plan;

4 judging the competition.

The ground jury and the course designer co-operate closely on the shared tasks of:

1 walking the completed course together and formally accepting it (preferably with a course assistant who measures the course once more with the measuring wheel);

2 adhering to the approved time schedule as much as possible.

Occasionally, unnecessary tensions arise between the course designer and the ground jury, usually at smaller tournaments. Therefore, it is worth concluding with the following observations.

1 A professional course designer should be open to questions or constructive suggestions from the ground jury.

2 On the other hand, a qualified judge should act in a co-operative manner and avoid any categorical position.

3 Decisions required just before the start (for example, after a sudden thunderstorm) will be made jointly by the course designer and the judge in the shortest possible time, if necessary by telephone; for example, changing a dimension or leaving out an obstacle now standing in a pool of water.

4 Only weak course designers or judges are always right!

Figure 21.5: *Jury, course designer and technical delegate at the Olympic Games, Sydney 2000. Photo by Christa Heibach.*

Figure 21.6: *(From left) Niko van Aken, Rolf Peter Fuß, Francis Michielsens, Frans Terbeek and Dr Leo de Bakker during veterinary inspection, CSI Valkenswaard. Photo by Christa Heibach.*

5   A competent judge cannot replace a weak course designer or vice versa.

6   Nevertheless, a professional official who is diplomatic can support his weaker colleague without making a great fuss.

7   Instructions via a loudspeaker discredit the ground jury and are unacceptable (although they are a rare exception).

In order to avoid such problems, clever tournament organisers select their most important officials on the basis of professionalism and the ability to work in a team. Furthermore, in a successful organisation's team, only those employees who cannot work in the team get replaced.

At unique events, such as the Olympic Games or the World Equestrian Games, the aspect of team work is of particular importance.

22 ANALYSIS OF RESULTS

For the course designer, the tournament does not come to an end with the prize-giving ceremony at the GRAND PRIX or following the main competition in medium-sized and smaller tournaments. He still needs to complete the following pieces of work:

- carry out an analysis of the results of the individual jumping classes;

- prepare a report for the organiser, with practical suggestions for the future.

The basis for analysing the results of the jumping competitions is the list of all classes, compressed to fit on one page (figure 9.2) and already shown in chapter 9. The overview analysis of results is structured in the same way (table 22.1) and includes such important information as:

- competition and judging process;

- minimum speed, track length, height;

- number of participants and proportion of time faults;

- number of competitors who were eliminated or withdrew;

- number of clear rounds, double-clear rounds;

- number/proportion of 8 or fewer penalties.

Strictly speaking, the number of falls by horses should also be recorded. Fortunately, these have become a rarity in recent times when the course design has been good.

Table 22.1 *Analysis of the results of jumping competitions CHIO Aachen 2002*

No.	Class	Table FEI	Speed m/min.	Length of the course m	Height m	J/o	Particip.	Elem.	Ret.	Clear rounds A abs.	A %	Clear rounds B abs.	B %	Double clear abs.	Double clear %	Time faults %	8 faults and less abs.	8 faults and less %
1	Welc.	A	375	490	1.45	--	63	2	--	26	41					26	52	83
2	Elsa aD	A	400	570	1.50	--	62	1	1	17	27					23	49	79
3	YH	A	350	440	1.40	--	33	--	--	17	52					6	27	82
4	PJA	A	375	530	1.45	1	52	4	2	19	37					13	36	69
5	GP Eu	A	400	590	1.50	1	62	--	--	12	19					27	42	68
6	YH	A	350	490	1.40	--	33	--	--	9	27					0	30	91
7	AH	C	375	790	1.40	--	16	--	--									
8	NRW	A	400	540	1.50	1	58	3	2	9	16	8	53	6	10	46	27	47
	sec. round			430			18	--	--							0	14	93
9	YH	A	350	550	1.45	1	25	1	--	15	60					0	23	92
10	Beck.	C	375	500	1.45	--	40	1	1									
11	NC	A	400	610	1.60	1	40	--	3	14	35	13	50	8	20	3	34	85
				610			26	--	1							4	21	81
12	PJA	A	400	590	1.50	1	32	1	--	16	50	8	50	2	6	9	30	94
				390			16	--	--							0	14	88
13	Rolex	A	350	390	1.45	--	16	--	--	12	75					0	16	100
14	G+W	C	375	770	1.50	--	15	1	--									
15	Zentis	A	375	530	1.45	--	46	--	1	20	43					4	44	96
136	GP	A	400	700	1.60	1	40	3	2	12	30	6	33	2	5	7	33	83
				480			18	--	1							0	17	95

For important jumping competitions, such as the Olympic Selection Trials of groups F and G on 15 June 2003, immediately before the start of the CHIO Aachen 2003, tables 22.2 and 22.3 and figures 22.1 and 22.2 give examples on how to proceed in practice.

Table 22.2 *Tentative schedule for the Olympic trials*

Date	Competition	Rules	J/o	Horses per rider	Definite starters	Speed m/min.	Max. height m
Friday 13.06	Warm up		--	2		350	1.40
Saturday 14.06 No. T1	International competition	238.1.2	1	1	28	375	1.50
Sunday 15.06 No. T2	Olympic selection trials 1. round 2. round	273.3.2	1	1	38	375	1.60 1.60

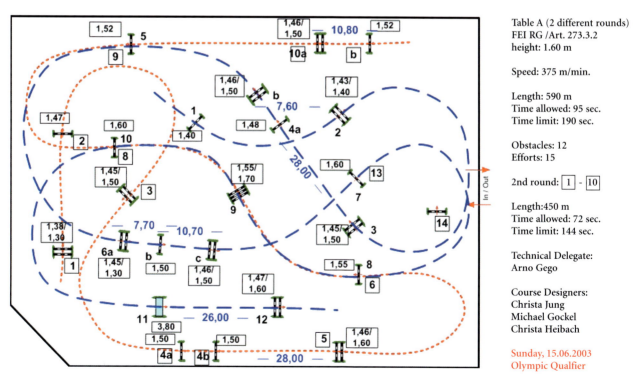

Figure 22.1: *Selection trials for the Olympic Games, Athens 2004.*

It is therefore a good idea to:

- describe the course in all its details (figure 22.1);

- keep an exact penalty record (table 22.3).

Figure 22.2 and table 22.4 are another example of how to analyse a GRAND PRIX.

With today's sophisticated information technology, it is a good idea to produce such overviews automatically and alongside the results list for all high-level championships, Olympic Games and CSI/CSIO.

For the course designer, the aim of the results analysis is to review his original aims and learn from this experience in order to guide his future activities.

Table 22.3 *Analysis and distibution of faults (see figure 22.1)*

Obstacle No.	1. Round					Obstacle No.	2. Round				
	R	E	F	Knock down			R	E	F	Knock down	
1				2	‖	1				1	‖
2				3	‖‖	2	1			9	‖‖‖ ‖‖‖
3				2	‖	3				7	‖‖‖ ‖
4a				2	‖	4a	3	3	1/R	12	‖‖‖ ‖‖‖ ‖‖‖
4b	1			4	‖‖‖	4b	3	1		2	‖
5						5				1	‖
6a				6	‖‖‖ ‖	6	1			2	‖
6b	5			1	‖	7					
6c				4	‖‖‖	8	2	1		3	‖‖‖
7				4	‖‖‖	9				9	‖‖‖ ‖‖‖
8				4	‖‖‖	10a				7	‖‖‖ ‖
9	1			1	‖	10b				2	‖
10	1			4	‖‖‖						
11											
12	1			5	‖‖‖						

Total:						Total:				Grand Total:	
• Starters	38					38				76	
• Knock-downs	42					57				99	
• Knock-down/participant	1.14					1.5				1.3	
• Refusal	9 (23%)					10 (26%)				19 (25%)	
• Elimination	0					5				5	
• Time faults	7 (18%)					7 (18%)				14 (18%)	
• Falls of horses											
• Falls of riders											

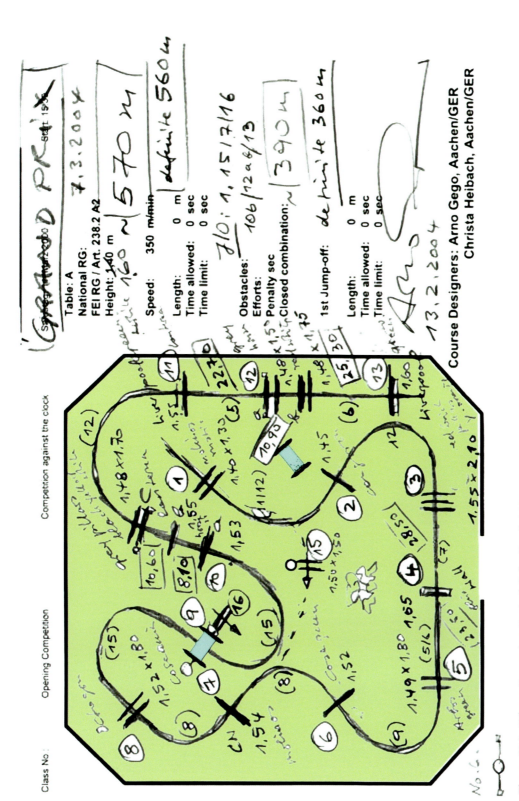

Figure 22.2: *Winter Equestrian Festival, Palm Beach 2004.*

Table 22.4 *GRAND PRIX, Palm Beach, Florida 2004*

No.	Strides	Knock down	Refusal	Various Criteria	Fault Statistics
1	11/12	--			Faults %
2	12	IIII		Starting List 43	0 5
3	7	IШ IШ III		Withdrawn 2	>0...4 6
4	5/6		II	time faults 6	>4...8 7
5	9	IШ IIII	IIII	retired 5	>8...12 10
6	8	IIII		elimination 1	>12...20 6
7	8	II		fall of horse --	>20 3
8	15	IШ II	I	fall of rider --	
9	15	I			
10a	1	IШ III			**Average**
10b	2	IШ			2.2 knock-down/starter
10c	12	IШ IIII		1 Laura Kraut	$\frac{560m}{148} = 3.78$m/stride
11	6	IШ I		2 Beezie Madden	
12a	2	III		3 Chris Kappier	$\frac{84\ sec.}{148} = 0.57$ sec/stride
12b	6	IIII		4 Marley Goodman	
13		IШ IШ IШ I		5 Eric Hasbrouck	f= 1.76 strides/sec.

23 THE COURSE DESIGNER'S REPORT AFTER THE TOURNAMENT

After the tournament, the course designer produces a report for the event organiser, with two objectives:

1   a critical and constructive analysis of the tournament from his viewpoint;

2   suggestions for the future.

With relevance to the tournament that has just finished, the course designer collects comments and information before, during and after the tournament, which will be important for its future development. These concern:

- issues of ground maintenance;

- time scheduling;

- competition schedule;

- organisational processes;

- bottlenecks;

- breakdowns (for example, the lack of reserve obstacle materials);

- issues concerning the atmosphere at the event.

The second part of the report consists of suggestions for the future, relating to:

1   competition schedule (for example, no jump-off for a competition with 90 competitors);

2   time planning (for example, more time is needed to change the course for the final in a small arena);

3   available obstacle material:

- repair and maintenance arrangements;

- suggestions concerning colour;

- suggestions for new obstacles or obstacle sections;

- measures concerning the footing.

Through his report, the course designer fulfils his task of contributing to the development of this tournament and of show-jumping in a positive way. The report can also include suggestions that go beyond the equestrian event. However, the course designer must first and foremost always be an advocate for the sport.

24 ON ACHIEVING VARYING DEGREES OF DIFFICULTY FOR JUMPING COMPETITIONS

The question of the degree of difficulty in jumping competitions can be discussed in a simplified way by using the example of a 1.40-m competition.

The schedule of the CSI**** NOBODIA 2009 may list the following specifications:

arena size: 75 x 125 m

● surface: grass (Lava surface)

● table A, art. 238.2.2 with one jump-off

● height: 1.40 m

● speed: 375 m/min.

The height of 1.40 m given in the schedule represents the following restrictions on dimensions in practice:

1   maximum height: 1.40 + 0.05 = 1.45 m (allowing 5 cm tolerance)

2   minimum height: 1.30 m (exception no. 1)

3 oxer spread: approx. between 1.50 and 1.80 m

The course designer may find that the skill levels of the competitors vary greatly.

The schedule of the jumping class is such that some second- or even third-level horses will be starting. The average level of skill of the competitors can vary greatly from one year to the next. So, before the start of the tournament or the specific jumping class, the course designer must try to get an idea of the level of skill of the competitors. Only then will he decide what mixture of degrees of difficulty he should plan for the particular jumping class (table 24.1). If he just adheres to the simple scheme of:

- three horse/rider levels;

- four different course criteria for selection;

he will arrive at $3^4 = 81$ different possibilities for combining different degrees of difficulty. Table 24.1 shows a varying mix of the degree of difficulty

Table 24.1 *Matrix of possible mix of degrees of difficulty in courses*

Average Level Horse/Rider	Scheme of Different Selection Criteria			
	Design of Obstacles	Dimmension of Obstacles	Concept of Lines	Distances
A LOW	friendly	lower than average	easy	normal
B MEDIUM	a little delicate	medium dimensions	a little difficult	a little delicate
C HIGH	more delicate	higher than average	difficult	delicate

- for a low skill level;

- for a high skill level;

of the respective competitors.

So the course designer has a wide range of instruments at his disposal to design the degree of difficulty of the course.

If the condition of the footing were to be considerably worse than described above, then the course designer would have to reconsider his mix of requirements and probably alter them.

25 SAFETY ISSUES

When it comes to the aspect of safety, there has been very noticeable progress in the last 25 years of jumping.

- Falls of horses in high-level tournaments have become the exception.

- Thanks to substantially improved jumping surfaces, injuries resulting from excess strain, such as damaged ligaments, have decreased markedly.

Of course, event organisers, soil experts or course designers cannot be held responsible if horses sustain injuries because they:

- begin to compete in high-level competitions too soon or too young;

- compete too frequently;

- carry riders who are not skilled enough for the job in hand.

The move towards greater safety in jumping has been underpinned in particular by the following developments:

- noticeably better footings;

- lighter construction of obstacles;

- lighter knock-down behaviour of poles etc.;

- improved safety cups (figure 25.1);

- in some cases, better design in the construction of water jumps – but, unfortunately, the awareness of tournament organisers and course designers of the

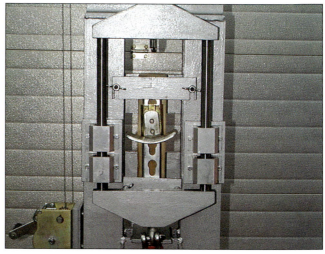

Figure 25.1: *Test machine for FEI-approved safety cups at the ika-Institute of the Aachen University of Technology. Photo: private collection.*

particular rules relating to natural obstacles has not yet developed to the extent that is desirable;

- in particular, the FEI qualification procedure for the Olympic Games and major international championships has helped to improve the safety of the sport, because the best are selected in advance – ideally at a level close to Olympic standard;

- in contrast, the World Cup system appears to continue to operate differently because the selection standards in the various regions can be totally different;

- reduced risk thanks to the high standard of course design in larger tournaments.

There is no need for new FEI committees but it might be worth considering whether the FEI should, in some cases, get outside advice from consultants with a high level of professional, cultural and international expertise on issues such as:

1   improving safety in different disciplines;

2   identifying and exploiting the traditional strengths of equestrian sport to create strategies geared towards positive development;

3   setting limits on the commercialisation of equestrian sport;

4   finding out what equestrian sport can learn from other sports; for example, golf. Golf is, after all, a sport which remains successful without indoor golf tournaments. It is very clearly:

- recognisable as a nature-based sport;

- in which the sponsor presence remains extremely discreetly in the background;

- and its athletes present themselves in a pleasant way — without being plastered from head to foot with dozens of company logos.

26 AACHEN SCHOOL OF COURSE DESIGN ASCD®

Course design is a young and complex creative discipline – a multidisciplinary speciality – which will have a decisive influence on the future development of jumping.

The current training of course designers is characterised by the following measures:

- national and international courses and seminars (one to three days) – often not at a sufficiently high level of training. The regular continued professional development of course designers is not sufficient by any means, or sometimes does not happen at all. Here, however, one should praise the training system for the judges;

- placements for practical assistance at tournaments, which can usually be regarded more as a kind of active 'learning by looking over someone else's shoulder'. Just 'being there', however, cannot be equated with training;

- the formative influence on a few assistants of the rank of co-course designer of working with leading course designers with the status of high-ranking teachers.

In particular, existing national systems for training and continued professional development have not adequately matched the global development and importance of jumping – particularly when compared to developments in other types of sport.

Also, some course designers have deficits in their curriculum vitae such as:

- limited school education;

- limited personal experience of jumping;

- limited knowledge of foreign languages;

- limited capability for team-working and communication.

This must be considered in the context of knowing that the expectations placed on a future FEI course designer are that he is a strong, professionally independent, diplomatic and integrative personality who is also capable of dealing with difficult situations.

After prolonged research and discussions, and with the encouragement of Leopoldo Palacios (1999 in Sydney), the co-chairmen:

- Arno Gego, Aachen, Germany (speaker)

- Leopoldo Palacios, Caracas, Venezuala, second Vice-President of the FEI and

- Olaf Petersen, Munich, Germany, Chairman of the FEI Jumping Committee

in close co-operation with the FEI, decided in January 2004 to found the

AACHEN SCHOOL OF COURSE DESIGN ® • ASCD

Co-operation with other organisations and tournament organisers is under discussion. The ASCD pursues the following main objectives:

- the organisation of a regular high-level 'International Symposium on Course Design', first held in December 2004;

- the annual organisation of one- or two-week high-level training courses, preferably in the winter season when the international show season is predominantly quiet;

- advising and promoting young course designers;

- initiating and/or supervising masters, diplomas and PhD theses/dissertations and studies;

- an annual award for the best master's dissertation at scientific institutions in the field of course design and jumping sport;

Table 26.1 *The organisation of a high-level international symposium on course design, December 2004*

1. INTERNATIONAL SYMPOSIUM ON COURSE DESIGN
Aachen/GER, 08–11.12.2004
Under the umbrella of the FEI and in co-operation with the German NF and other organisations

ASCD ■ AACHEN SCHOOL OF COURSE DESIGN

Co-Chairman	■ Arno Gego	Aachen (Speaker)
	■ Leopoldo Palacios	Caracas
	■ Olaf Petersen	Munich
Management Asst.	■ Christa Heibach	Aachen

TIME	WEDNESDAY	THURSDAY	FRIDAY	SATURDAY
09.00		Leopoldo Palacios and Olaf Petersen — Welcome on behalf of the FEI and FEI-Strategy Activities of the FEI-Jumping Comittee	Michael Mronz — Concept and Planning of the World Equestrian Games, Aachen, 2006	Steve Stephens — Experiences and Concepts of a World Leading Producer of Obstacles
09.45		Arno Gego — History of Equestrian Sport	Olaf Petersen jun. — Obstacles, Decoration, Colours – Important Means of Presentation and Difficulty Degree also dependent on Footing	Paul Weier — History of Equestrian Disciplines within the Olympic Programme since 1900
10.30		Coffee Break		
11.00		Hanfried Haring — Breeding and Equestrian Sport in Germany	Arno Gego — Aesthetics Ethics, Animal Protection and Fair Play and presentation ASCD	Open Forum — Arno Gego, Chairman
11.45		Leopoldo Palacios — Jumping Sport and Course Design in Latin America and Future Aspects	Olaf Petersen — open topic	
12.30		Lunch		Closing Lunch
14.00	Presentation — Aachen University of Technology	John Weier — Natural Grass Stadiums and new Footing Technologies (grass and sand)	Sven Holmberg — Considerations about the Future of Jumping Sport and Course Design	Visit CSI Maastricht/NED 30 minutes by car,
14.45		R. Roth — Cologne Sports University: Contribution of science to the development of Sports	Ron Southern — What does the Organiser of a World Leading Tournament expect from the Course Designer?	Visit on Sunday also possible
15.30		Coffee Break		
16.00	Registration and distribution of printed material in the hotel	Pilar Cepeda — LA SILLA MONTERREY – Facilities, Breeding, Tournaments and its School of Jumping	N.N. — Landscaping, Architecture, Art and Design	Visit to the historical Christmas Market around Cathedral and City Hall of Aachen.
16.45		Olaf Petersen — The Jumping Courses – Olympic Games, Athens/ GRE, 2004	Gabriella Grillo — Horse and Music through the Ages	
17.30		Discussion	Discussion	
18.00	City Hall/Rathaus Aachen Welcome by the Lord Mayor of the City of Aachen	Dinner	Dinner Invitation	
19.00	Walk Christmas Market			

Figure 26.1: *FEI seminar on course design, Warendorf, Germany 1996. Photo: private collection.*

Figure 26.2: *La Baule, France 2002. Photo by Christa Heibach.*

Figure 26.3: *Warendorf, Germany 2000. Photo by Foto Kaup.*

Figure 26.4: *Brussels, Belgium 1998. Photo by Hippo Foto, Dirk Caremanns.*

- an annual competition in course design (best MASTERPLAN of courses, best obstacle design, best design of sponsor obstacles, etc.) .

The ASCD should be seen as a nucleus of a growing school of course design.

Contact address:

AACHEN SCHOOL OF COURSE DESIGN ® ASCD
Arno Gego, Prof. Dr.-Ing.
Aachen/Germany
Phone: +49-241-13 047
Fax: +49-241-172 871
e-mail: arnogego@aol.com
website: www.Aachen-Course-Design
           www.ArnoGego.com

Comité d'Honneur

HRH Princess Haya Bint Al-Hussein	Dubai	UAE
Athina Onassis de Miranda	Athens	GRE
Maestro Luciano Pavarotti	Modena	ITA
Ing. Alfonso Romo	Monterrey	MEX
HRH Prince Tsunekazu Takeda	Tokyo	JPN

Founders
2004

Arno Gego
Aachen/GER

Leopoldo Palacios
Caracas/VEN

Olaf Petersen
Munich/GER

AACHEN SCHOOL OF COURSE DESIGN
ARNO GEGO
LAURENSBERGERSTRASSE 130
52072 AACHEN/GERMANY

Phone:	+49-241-13047
Fax:	+49-241-172871
e-mail:	arnogego@aol.com
Internet:	www.Aachen-Course-Design.com

**Beneficiary Foundation
since 2005**

AACHEN SCHOOL
OF
COURSE DESIGN

Under the Patronage of the

Plan of Regular and Main Activities

1   Intensive Course of Instruction on Course Design –
     Level 1.30/1.50 m, 8 days, theory and practice.

2   International Symposium on Course Design –
     High-level Conferences on various subjects – 1/2 days.

3   Seminars on Course Design, various subjects, 2 days in different
     countries.

4   Academic Postgraduate Studies
     'DIPLOMA IN COURSE DESIGN' and 'DIPLOMA IN CONCOURS
     DESIGN' – in consideration and planning – 21 months, special
     requirements for admission, about 20 International high-level Lectors,
     alternation theory/practice, Diploma-Thesis – in preparation.

5   Competition in Course Design 'Who designs best Courses, Obstacles,
     Layouts, etc.?' – In co-operation with HORSE INTERNATIONAL.

6   ACADEMIC STUDENT PROMOTION AWARD
     3,000 EURO for three best Diplomas or Master-Theses
     (in English or German).

7   Friends of the Aachen School of Course Design, a School of Excellence
     and a School for Life

Become a member of Studbook Zangersheide NOW !

And receive Z-Magazine 6 times a year, the only horse magazine published in four languages

Profit from the many advantages offered by Studbook Zangersheide

Yes I want to be a member of Studbook Zangersheide for Euro 50 per year within Europe (rest of the world: Euro 65)

Name: _____

Address: _____

Postal code/Place: _____

Country: _____

Telephone: _____

Fax: _____

Signature: _____ Date: _____

Please send voucher to: Studbook Zangersheide, Domein Zangersheide, B-3620 Lanaken, Belgium

Zangersheide... the most complete studbook !

APPENDICES

A1 PERSONAL POSTSCRIPT AND ACKNOWLEDGEMENTS

I have lived a very full life so far, in which many different and lucky circumstances have combined to have a lasting influence on my private, professional and equestrian journey.

1   I grew up near Aachen on a farm with horses. I inherited a passion for equestrian sport from my father and grandfather.

2   My French ancestry on my father's side (Jacques Guyot, 1685/1690) contributed towards my love of Latin languages and my preference for Aachen (Aix-La-Chapelle/Aquisgran) as the central point of my life, close to the French-speaking region.

3   The CHIO Aachen, which I have known since 1946, when my father participated in the first post-war national championship in the Soers, and where I have been active in the jumping arena since 1965, as well as through my studies and teaching at the internationally renowned Aachen University of Technology, were also important links to Aachen as a location, with its proximity to Belgium, Holland, Luxembourg and France. I had the great opportunity of getting to know the Aachen jumping stadium as a show-jumper in two national championships in 1962 and 1964.

4   I owe a great deal to the CHIO Aachen and its presidents:

   ● Assessor Albert Vahle

   ● Consul Hugo Cadenbach

- Manufacturer Kurt Capellmann

- Consul Klaus Pavel

as well as to Anton Fischer, the long-time sports director, CHIO-promoter and board member.

5 The same applies to my 'senior' teacher, Colonel H.-H. Brinckmann, whom I first met in 1960/1962 at show-jumping clinics and who gave me a great deal of support.

6 My ability to speak several languages led me to get involved in international professional and sports activities at an early stage.

7 And I always had the luck, both in my profession and in the sport, to be given tasks I enjoyed and with which I could identify. In addition, I owe enormous thanks to my dear wife Christa, herself now internationally active as an FEI International course designer, after long and hard years of training, for the many professional discussions, ideas and suggested improvements in the energy-sapping writing of this book.

8 I had the additional luck of being able to combine my profession as an engineer and the task of course designer, and thus avoid a conflict of interest.

9 And I had the chance and the honour not only to design and build new courses, but also:

- to design new showgrounds, for example, Monterrey and Valkenswaard, often with distinguished colleagues;

- to help new tournaments to find their feet;

- to lead numerous seminars on 'course design' in many countries around the globe, and to help and support many young course designers (women and men) over many years. I am delighted by their incredibly positive progress;

- to work with almost all leading international course designers in one way or another, co-operating and helping to promote the sport (see list below).

10 It is also true that I have worked very closely for many years with some renowned colleagues:

- Olaf Petersen (at the CHIO Aachen 1983-1986 and various German Championships, as course designers with equal status, since 1980 jointly as directors and examiners of the training of German, and later also international, course designers, and in addition, working together at many other top tournaments, such as the CSI Valkenswaard, CSI Monterrey etc.).

- Leopoldo Palacios/VEN (CSI Caracas 1980-1983, Pan-American Games, Caracas/VEN 1983 and Havana/Cuba, 1991, CSI Monterrey/MEX 1989 to the present, CSI Valkenswaard, CHIO Aachen 1981 and 2000, and the 2000 Olympic Games in Sydney).

- With Pilar Cepeda, manager and trainer of LA SILLA Monterrey/MEX and Valkenswaard/NED, former top international rider, I have had a close working relationship and personal friendship for many years. Under the leadership of Alfonso Romo/MEX, we have built new showgrounds, designed new obstacles, and created and established new international tournaments such as Pavarotti International 1991, CSI Monterrey and CSI Valkenswaard.

- In this connection, I particularly want to mention Harry Cornford, a British rider after the Second World War (army of the Rhine), an entrepreneur in Düsseldorf, my longstanding colleague (since 1975) and friend in Aachen and around the globe, to whom I owe a great deal and who has given me a lot of support.

- Linda Allen/USA (CSIO Mexico 1988, CSI Monterrey several times, Mexican Championships Queretaro, CHIO Aachen several times, and many other events).

- Jon Doney/GBR (CSIO Toronto/CAN, CSI Valkenswaard, CSI Monterrey and others).

- Lt-Col. Paul Weier, an extremely knowledgeable representative of the 'art of riding', one of the few true horsemen, a master of many disciplines, successful Olympic rider – who represents the 'classical school'.

- Dr Marcello Mastronardi/ITA, with whom I have exchanged interesting ideas on several occasions, including at the CSI Monterrey, CSIO Rome, etc.

- I have already paid tribute to Dr. h.c. Bertalan de Némethy and Pamela Carruthers as my teachers in chapter 1.

- Col. Luc Hamon/FRA (CSIO Fontainebleau among others) was also a trainer and discussion partner who stimulated my interest.

- In addition, I have for many years maintained warm human relations and fruitful professional contact with a large number of prominent tournament organisers, trainers, coaches, riders, judges, stewards and other sports professionals and representatives of the FEI and national federations. Listing them all by name would exceed the limits imposed by this book.

Below is a list of my teachers and course design colleagues with whom I have been able to collaborate over the last 20 years. My special thanks go to them. I ask for forbearance if I have forgotten anyone.

- Antonio Allegria Simoês/BRA
- Georg Christoph Boedicker/GER

- Linda Allen/USA
- Jürgen Brasse/GER

- Nicolas Alvarez de Bohorques/ESP
- Hans-Heinrich Brinckmann/GER

- Daniel Aeschlimann/SUI
- Giovanni Bussu/ITA

- Hernan Aguirre de Castilllo/BOL
- Cynthia Carlisle/MEX

- Avni Atabek/TUR
- Pamela Carruthers/GBR

- Marina Azevedo/BRA
- Lucini Antonio Castro/ESP

- Ihab Aziz/EGY
- Pilar Cepeda/MEX

- Alan Ball/GBR
- Frank Chapot/USA

- David Ballard/CAN
- Harold (Harry) Cornford/GER

- Angel Ballestrini/VEN
- Marco Cortinovis/ITA

- Alexa Bell/AUS
- Bernardo Costa Cabral/POR

- Frédéric Cottier/FRA
- Cathalina Cruz/MEX
- Werner Deeg/GER
- Jon Doney/GBR
- Henk Jan Drabbe/NED
- Hans Dussler/GER
- Ted Dwyer/AUS
- Horst Ense/GER
- Bob Ellis/GBR
- Neylan Etiman/TUR
- Wolfgang Feld/GER
- Javier Fernandez/MEX
- Lourenço Fernandez/POR
- Natus Ferreira/RSA
- Joberto Pio da Fonseca/BRA
- Danny Foster/USA
- Edith Gabilo/PER
- José Maria (Pepe) Gamarra/BOL
- Michael Gockel/GER
- Robert Gordon Goldswortley/AUS

- David Graham/NZL
- Andrea Greco/HKG
- Luc Hamon/FRA
- Polyana Hardwick Brown/CAN
- Christa Heibach/GER
- Clemencia Herrera/COL
- Steve Hickey/IRL
- Conrad Homfeld/USA
- Serge Houtman/FRA
- Lukasz Jankowski/POL
- Rob Jansen/NED
- Richard Leslie Jeffrey/GBR
- Robert Jolicoeur/CAN
- Leicester B. Jordan/NZL
- Guilherme Jorge Nogeira/BRA
- Christa Jung/GER
- Saad Khalifa/EGY
- Louis Konickx/NED
- Ekkehard Krueger/VEN
- Jochen Kuenneke/GER

- Joaquin Larrain/CHI
- Brian David Lavery/RSA
- Jean Legat/BEL
- Jean-Pierre Lentz/LUX
- Peter Lichtner-Hoyer/AUS
- Heinrich Liegl/GER
- Tarcisio Lima Guedes/BRA
- Jorge Llambi/ARG
- Bernardo Lopez Davidson/ESA
- Carol Lopicich/CHI
- Marcello Mastronardi/ITA
- Eugène Mathy/BEL
- Wolfgang Meyer/GER
- Jennifer Millar/NZL
- Ali Mohajer/IRI
- George Morris/USA
- Luis Moura dos Santos/POR
- Jaime Muñoz de las Casas/ESP
- Luc Musette/BEL
- Bertalan de Némethy/USA

- Luc Nguen Trong/LUX
- Julio E. Orma Carrasco/ARG
- Jorge Osacar/ARG
- Jorge Osacar jun./ARG
- Minoru Osada/JPN
- Levent Özguney/TUR
- Leopoldo Palacios/VEN
- Helio Pessoa/BRA
- Olaf Petersen/GER
- Olaf Petersen jun./GER
- Harold Presston/RSA
- Robert Ridland/USA
- Flavia Rocha Mello de Azevedo/BRA
- Avelino Rodriguez Miravalles/ESP
- Manuel Rodrigues Velis/CHI
- Ferdinand Rosellen/GER
- Sue Ryan/AUS
- Mariano Sanchez Galvez/ESP
- Guilherme Sarmento/BRA
- Hans-Werner Sattler/GER

- Hossein Schafee/IRI
- HRH Prince Tsunekazu Takeda/JPN
- Hauke Schmidt/GER
- Mehves Trak/TUR
- Walter Schmidt/GER
- John Vallance/AUS
- Leeson Serritt/AUS
- Michel Vaillancourt/CAN
- David Sheppard/AUS
- Noel Vanososte/VEN
- Erica Sportiello/BRA
- Jorge Verswyvel Lamizar/COL
- Steve Stephens/USA
- Uliano Vezzani/ITA
- Juan Carlos Tafur/COL
- Daniel Walker Ramos/CHI
- Chrystine W. Tauber/USA
- John Weier/LUX
- Edward Taylor/IRL
- Paul Weier/SUI
- Wilfried Thiebes/GER
- Omar Yilmaz/TUR
- Hans-Joachim Thiede/GER
- Juan Carlos Zegers/CHI

I am particularly pleased that some of the people mentioned above have been among my students.

11 I worked for more than 40 years in the jumping stadium of the CHIO Aachen, 28 of these as a course designer and 22 years as chief course designer. After such a very long commitment in the stadium of the CHIO Aachen, I decided in 1998, on the occasion of the centenary of the ALRV, to relinquish my responsibility as course designer from around 2003, and to give the next generation a chance.

   The reason was not a lack of motivation, nor a decline in intellectual agility. On the contrary, I decided at the same time that from 1993, I would:

- write this book;
- write other books;

- become more involved in the training of the FEI course designers;

- establish the 'AACHEN SCHOOL OF COURSE DESIGN', together with Leopoldo Palacios and Olaf Petersen;

My decision, and the date of 2002, were also significantly influenced by the World Equestrian Games in Aachen in 2006. In my view, the same course designer should not be responsible twice in the same location for world championships. For me, this is an important question of ethics and fair play.

The transition was made easier because I continue to have a variety of responsibilities, as a member of the board of the ALRV (CHIO Aachen) for the development of the jumping stadium, as a member of the four-person sports committee, and as the person responsible for 'ethics, welfare of the horse and fair play'.

12 So I have come back to where I started.

At the age of 20, when I was still a young rider, I built my 'first course' on a plain meadow in my home parish of Laurensberg – 6 km from the jumping stadium of the CHIO Aachen:

- Before the competition, I and two helpers borrowed fences from neighbouring clubs and loaded them on to two trailers;

- I designed all the courses and built them with assistants;

- I rode the main course myself (I came second in the main jumping competition);

- on the Monday after the competition, I and the two helpers loaded all the fences on the trailers again and took them back to the neighbouring clubs by tractor.

All this happened in the vacation when I was a student.

I know, of course, that, even then, the sports rules did not permit a person who builds the courses to simultaneously participate in the competition. It was 47 years ago. I hope that the federations, judges and juries will belatedly forgive me.

A2 NOTES FROM INTERNATIONAL COURSE DESIGNERS

In addition to theoretical considerations and examples of my own activities as course designer, in order to give this book a special touch, I have asked leading international colleagues to present one of their many courses.

I think that this chapter has produced most interesting perspectives on the work of different course designers, especially in showing that each of them has his or her own 'handwriting', philosophy, taste and style.

Jumping sport needs such variety of concepts and a positive and constructive competition between leading course designers as a contribution to further development of our sport on the base of its classical roots.

Any monopolisation of course design, showgrounds and obstacles in countries, regions or worldwide would soon conspire to lower the standards of our sport [200].

I especially appreciate the mixture of courses from different regions like Europe, North America, South America, Arabia or Oceania. Also, the shape, size and footing of different showgrounds might be of interest.

However, I think that the study of the Olympic Nations Cup, Los Angeles 1984 (Course Plan A2.6) leads to particularly interesting observations:

1   no horse falling, no real surprises;

2   fair balance between 1.55/1.60-m verticals and 180/190-m spreads;

3   water jump, 4.60 m, best contruction and design;

4   one interesting, three-stride-distance 14.00 m between two 1.46 x 1.80 m Liverpools, Swedish oxer spreads

5 balanced variation between normal, a little short and a little long distances;

6 normal fluent distances;

7 interesting option 13/14a;

8 % of time faults (length of the course 790 m) – extemely long stadium.

So enjoy the study of courses by 14 different famous course designers.

LINDA ALLEN

1996 Olympic Games, Atlanta – Team Competition

The greatest honour and challenge of my career was serving as course designer at the 1996 Olympic Games in Atlanta. While all three days of show-jumping required questions to be asked that were uniquely suited to the needs of each specific competition, the Team Competition was the one on which I worked longest and hardest.

I felt that because this was a medal event and the winners would remain in the history books forever, the competition must be difficult enough to ensure that the advantage would go to the current best teams in the world. However, at the same time, this was a competition in which riders from all nations would compete and our sport has not yet reached the point at which riders from countries where show-jumping is not a prominent sport have the opportunities to compete regularly over courses of the size and technical difficulty that are the norm at the top levels in, say, Europe or the USA.

It does not make a good impression on today's public to see horses struggling or riders suffering serious falls. Therefore, even while obtaining an honest result among the top riders, I felt I must also consider the less well-prepared combinations and do my best to assure that the majority of competitors would complete the course even if they did not finish anywhere near those who would eventually stand on the podium.

As can be the case in our sport, the day produced two totally unexpected occurrences. One was the fall of Franke Slootaak at the fence following the water in the first round. This looked very serious but did not prevent Franke from returning to produce an excellent second round. The other unpleasant surprise was a drenching thunderstorm nearing the end of the first round. The rain was so hard it turned the sand competition arena into a virtual lake in less than 20 minutes. Thanks to the late Hermann Duckek's excellent preparation of the arena and our ability to drain the surface water off almost immediately after the rain stopped, competition was able to resume with excellent conditions for every competitor!

When the final rider had jumped I was, perhaps, as happy as the riders on the podium. The strong German team took the gold, the American team finished with silver, and the Brazilian team took bronze. With the three medals going to three different continents, how could I have asked for a better outcome?

However, even more satisfying was the fact that out of the 160 total starters for the two rounds there were only four falls, along with three other eliminations and two retirements. My goal of having virtually everyone finish was achieved, even though there was not a single double clear all day (three riders finished with one clear round and one went clear but had time faults).

Personally, I find it very interesting and educational to review the detailed results of every important class. For each competition of these Olympic Games my colleague and good friend Richard Jeffery kindly prepared very detailed statistics. A study of these shows that the water jump produced the most faults of all the obstacles in both rounds. I did not find this surprising as, outside of Europe, water jumps are only seen with any frequency in a few areas, and even then a jump of more than 4 m is unusual.

Table: A art.339
Speed: 400 m p.m.
Time Allowed: 93 seconds
Distance: 620 metres
Time Limit: 186 seconds

Atlanta 1996

No.	Front Height	Back Height	Spread	Distance
1	1.40 m	1.45 m	1.45 m	
2	1.50 m	1.50 m	1.55 m	
3	1.58 m			
4	1.55 m		2.00 m	
				20.70 m
5a	1.50 m			
				7.95 m
5b	1.50 m			
				10.20 m
5c	1.50 m	1.50 m	1.60 m	
				22.50 m
6	1.50 m	1.50 m	1.70 m	
7	1.60 m			
8			4.30 m	
9	1.60 m			
				18.30 m
10	1.51 m	1.51 m	1.70 m	
11	1.60 m			
12a	1.10 m	1.55 m	2.00 m	
				7.65 m
12b	1.57 m	1.57 m	1.50 m	
13	1.60 m			

JUMP OFF:

Fences: 2, 3, 4, 10. 12ab, 13
Distance: 350 metres
Time Allowed: 53 seconds
Time Limit: 106 seconds
Footing: sand
Size about 120 x 120 m

GAMES OF THE XXVth OLYMPIAD - ATLANTA 1996

TEAM COMPETITION - Round 1

NUMBER OF STARTERS: 81

TABLE OF FAULTS

FENCE	1	2	3	4	5a	5b	5c	6	7	8	9	10	11	12a	12b	13
TYPE*	O	O	V	V	V	V	O	O	V	W	V	O	V	T	O	V
				Liver-pool back pole	plank	plank			wall		wall or plank					
KNOCKDOWNS	4	9	1	2	18	10	7	13	13	24	10	9	9	21	30	17
REFUSALS			1	1	2	5	1	1	1		3	1	3	1		2
FALLS											1					
ELIMINATIONS						1					1					
RETIREMENTS											1					
FENCES WHERE RIDERS WITH SINGLE PENALTIES INCURRED FAULTS	-	1	-	-	-	-	1	3	-	2	1	-	-	3	1	3

*V = vertical, O = oxer, T = triple bar, W = water

ANALYSIS OF INDIVIDUAL ROUNDS

Clear	Clear/time	4 faults	4 faults/time	8 faults	8 faults/time	11 faults/time	12 faults	12 faults/time	Others
8	2	11	4	1	13	4	13	1	24
9.90%	2.50%	33.60%	5.00%	1%	16.00%	5.00%	16.00%	1.20%	29.60%

% OF RIDERS WITH TIME FAULTS (not counting those with refusals or falls): 15%

The fences in the combinations and the lines related to the combinations also took their toll. In general, the results were better in the second round. There were fewer faults in the combinations and the number of clear rounds and clear rounds with time faults went from ten to 14 competitors. I like it when the horses do better at their second attempt.

Paying attention to all aspects of a competition helps me to become a better course designer. I believe it hones that all important 'natural instinct' for designing that is needed when the time comes to decide if an obstacle should be set a couple of centimetres higher or wider, or if a distance is truly correct for the particular circumstances.

I am very pleased that I can look back on my courses for the Atlanta Olympic Games and remain satisfied with both the courses and the sport that took place over them. Together with a wonderful team of assistants and arena crew, it was possible to produce the results that I hoped for and also have fun in the process.

TABLE OF FAULTS

FENCE	1	2	3	4	5a	5b	5c	6	7	8	9	10	11	12a	12b	13
TYPE*	O	O	V	V	V	V	O	O	V	W	V	O	V	T	O	V
				Liver-pool back pole	plank	plank			wall		wall or plank					
KNOCKDOWNS	3	3	3	5	13	7	10	11	7	21	9	13	13	10	16	11
REFUSALS				3	2	2									1	1
FALLS				1		1									1	
ELIMINATIONS																1
RETIREMENTS																1
FENCES WHERE RIDERS WITH SINGLE PENALTIES INCURRED FAULTS		1		1			2	1	2	1			1		4	4

*V = vertical, O = oxer, T = triple bar, W = water

ANALYSIS OF INDIVIDUAL ROUNDS

Clear	Clear/time	4 faults	4 faults/time	8 faults	8 faults/time	11 faults/time	12 faults	12 faults/time	Others
10	4	14	3	15	2	2	5	2	22
12.70%	5.10%	17.70%	3.80%	19%	2.50%	2.50%	6.30%	2.50%	27.80%

% OF RIDERS WITH TIME FAULTS (not counting with refusals of falls): 17.7%

FREDERIC COTTIER

Show-jumping, VIII Pan Arab Games July 1997

I have chosen the drawing of the team competition of the Pan Arabian Games of 1997. It is not the course of which I am most proud, nor is it an important competition sports wise. However, these days 'equestrian-developing' nations are appearing more and more on the international scene and the job of the course designer then becomes that of an instructor and trainer. In this context, a course of reasonable height but with enough technical difficulties will enable these riders to progress in joining the world elite, thanks to an increase in experience offered by good course designing.

The increasing professionalism of the riders, the improved quality in breeding and training of the horses, who now command very high prices,

demand of course designers a high level of competence and finesse. As a rider myself, I have been witness to this evolution over the last 30 years.

My first thought would be that the 1984 Olympic Games in Los Angeles, designed and built by Berthalan de Némethy, were the beginning of real research into the design of fences, but also the beginning of similarities in the difficulties presented by the different course designers. Before this date, courses were all very different whether they were in Germany, Great Britain, the United States or elsewhere.

There is now a common language from one continent to the next. So the implementation of technical and tactical difficulties for the riders and horses, which must be addressed through training and intelligence while still preserving physical integrity, should be the guideline for course designers. Not forgetting the avoidance of monotony through the use of imagination and creativity.

I wish here to touch on a subject which, to my knowledge, needs to evolve. I wish to talk about the place of the water jump in competitions today.

The water jump is neglected in the training of too many horses as they mature, so that, as time goes by, this jump is made shallower in order for it to be less dangerous.

VIII ᵉ Jeux Pan Arabes Saut d'obstacles
Date: 24 Juillet 1997.
Lieu: FAQRA - LIBAN.
Epreuve: Coupe des Nations

VIII Pan Arab Games Show-jumping
Date: 24 July 1997.
Location: FAQRA - LEBANON
Competitions: Nations Cup

Course designer:
Chef de piste:
Frédéric Cottier

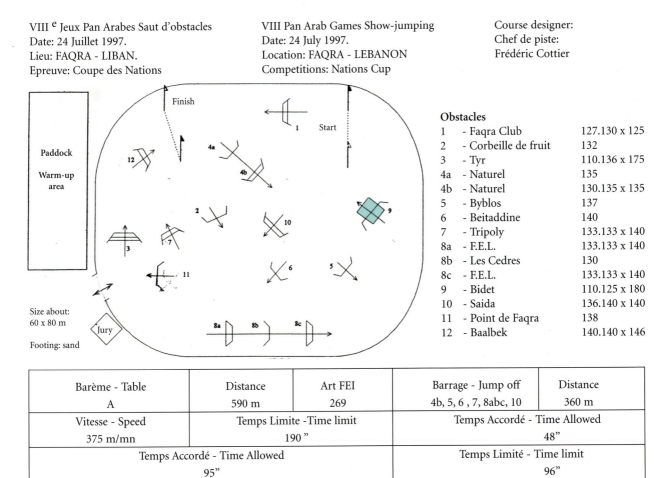

Obstacles

1	- Faqra Club	127.130 x 125
2	- Corbeille de fruit	132
3	- Tyr	110.136 x 175
4a	- Naturel	135
4b	- Naturel	130.135 x 135
5	- Byblos	137
6	- Beitaddine	140
7	- Tripoly	133.133 x 140
8a	- F.E.L.	133.133 x 140
8b	- Les Cedres	130
8c	- F.E.L.	133.133 x 140
9	- Bidet	110.125 x 180
10	- Saida	136.140 x 140
11	- Point de Faqra	138
12	- Baalbek	140.140 x 146

Size about:
60 x 80 m

Footing: sand

Barème - Table		Distance	Art FEI	Barrage - Jump off	Distance
A		590 m	269	4b, 5, 6 , 7, 8abc, 10	360 m
Vitesse - Speed		Temps Limite -Time limit		Temps Accordé - Time Allowed	
375 m/mn		190 "		48"	
Temps Accordé - Time Allowed				Temps Limité - Time limit	
95"				96"	

The take-off and landing zones are often in poor shape when it is raining, badly delineated, and the side decorations often not properly thought out, sometimes even causing the decision of a judge to be challenged. Those factors cause me to reflect on the need to make important changes to this fence.

Why not have a type of triple bar placed above the water at a height of 1.15 m, with a spread of 3 m or more, with the fault being sanctioned by the fall of the pole?

I would like to thank Arno Gego for his skill in helping me, as well as my horses, to improve over all these years of jumping his courses, especially in Aix la Chapelle. Through this book, he will also encourage other course designers to excel both now and into the future, for this sport is not frozen and is far from having reached its limits.

It is for us to strive to meet these expectations while always respecting the horses.

JON DONEY

World Equestrian Games, The Hague 1994

I have designed many courses all over the world over many many years and it is very difficult to select just one.

I have chosen Table C at The Hague World Games – which stands out for me because it produced a good start to the championships and the horses looked happy and in good order at the end of the course (and, in fact, even at the end of the games).

In general, the course was not too high (1.50 m) but was quite technical, with a number of options.

Fence 1   Parallel – wide enough so that the rider had to ride forward from the start.

Fence 2   Vertical – a narrow fence which was difficult to jump across to save time from fence 1 to 3.

Fence 3   Triple bar – high front – if the horse cut in too much it was possible to have the front rail down or not make the spread.

Fence 4   Vertical – inside or outside an island – if the horse cut in too tightly, it made the distance to the next fence long.

Fence 5a & b Parallel to vertical – if ridden too strongly from the previous fence, the distance was short.

Fence 6	Vertical – inside or outside an island.
Fence 7	Triple bar – wide – the rider needed to ride forward from the previous fence
Fence 8	Parallel – wider on one side than the other. This enabled the competitor to ride inside obstacle 1. Because the previous two fences needed forward movement, the distance could ride short – but the rider needed to ride short if he or she wanted to turn inside obstacle 1.
Fence 9	Liverpool – poles towards the back. If the rider cut in short from fence 8 to fence 9, the water was sometimes a surprise.
Fence 10	Option – parallel – narrow fronted but quite wide, was the quicker route, or a vertical wall 10 cm higher than the parallel gave a longer route – approx. 50/50 each fence. Turn back to 11.

World Equestrian Games

THE HAGUE 1994

Table: C	Speed:	400 m/min.	Obstacles:	14
National RG:	Length:	665 m	Efforts:	17
FEI RG / Art. 239/268+309	Time allowed:	100 sec.	Penalty sec:	7
Height: 1.50 m	Time limit:	200 sec.	Closed combinaton:	

No.	Front	Back	Spread	Distance
1	1.40 m	1.45 m	1.50 m	
2	1.50 m			
3		1.50 m	1.80 m	
4	1.50 m			
5a	1.45 m	1.45 m	1.70 m	
				7.50 m
5b	1.50 m			
6	1.50 m			
				17.70 m
7		1.50 m	2.00 m	
				14.60 m
8	1.45 m	1.45 m	1.50 m	
9	1.50 m			
10	1.60 m			
10	1.50 m	1.50 m	1.50 m	
11	1.45 m	1.45 m		
				25.00 m
12			4.00 m	
13	1.50 m	1.50 m	1.60 m	
14a	1.50 m			
				10.70 m
14b	1.50 m			
				7.80 m
14c	1.45 m	1.50 m	1.70 m	

Size about 95 x 120 m

Footing: sand

Fence 11   Parallel – if the rider cut into this, it made it very long to 12 – the water.

Fence 12   Water jump – low front fence. The previous fence had a big bearing here. Some riders took a stride out from the previous fence.

Fence 13   Parallel – riders' decision when to turn.

Fence 14a b c Vertical (option) – vertical – parallel. 14a could be jumped at the side which was the quickest route. Because of the type of the competition and as the course generally rode forward, the line from a to b could ride a little short.

SERGE HOUTMAN

C.S.I.O. de France, La Baule 2002

LA BAULE le: 10 mai 2002   GRAND PRIX DE LA VILLE DE LA BAULE
Epreuve: 7   GRAND PRIX   2 eme MANCHE
Barème: Barème A au chronometre
Article no: 238.2.2.3.3   Obstacles: 14 - 5 - 6 ab - 7 - 8-9 - 11b - 12 ab - 13
Distance: 670 m   Vitesse: 400 m/Mn   Distance: 490 m
Temps Acc : 101 sec.   Temps Lim: 202 sec.   Temps Acc: 74 sec.   Temps Lim: 148 sec.

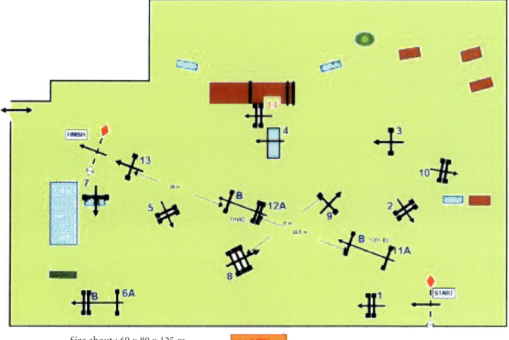

Size about : 60 x 80 x 125 m
Footing: grass
Course Designer: Serge Houtmann/FRA

No.	Nature	Hauteur	Largeur
1	Oxer	140 x 145	140
2	Oxer	145 x 147	150
3	Vertical	154	
4	Riviere		400
5	Oxer	143 x 150	110
6a	Vertical	150	
6b	Oxer	148 x 147	150
7	Vertical	155	
8	Spa	150	195
9	Vertical	155	
10	Oxer	148 x 148	160
11a	Vertical	158	
11b	Vertical	155	
12a	Oxer	147 x148	150
12b	Vertical	155	
13	Vertical	159	
14	Oxer	140 x 145	140

MARCELLO MASTRONARDI

World Equestrian Games, Roma 1998

Table: C
National RG:
FEI RG / Art. 239/268+309
Height: 1.50 m

Speed: 400 m/min.
Length: 680 m
Time allowed: 102 sec.
Time limit: 204 sec.

Obstacles: 14
Efforts: 17
Penalty sec: 7
Closed combinaton:

No.	Front	Back	Spread	Distance
1	1.40 m	1.45 m	1.35 m	
				30 m
2	1.50 m			
3	1.45 m	1.46 m	1.45 m	
4		1.50 m	1.90 m	
				16.80 m
5	1.51 m			
				22.50 m
6	1.47 m	1.49 m	1.70 m	
7	1.50 m			
8	1.47 m	1.47 m	1.70 m	
8	1.54 m	1.55 m	1.60 m	
9a	1.50 m			
				11.10 m
9b	1.50 m			
				7.80 m
9c	1.48 m	1.50 m	1.70 m	
10		4.00 m		
11	1.50 m	1.50 m	1.80 m	
12		1.50 m	1.70 m	
				25.50 m
13a	1.46 m	1.48 m	1.70 m	
				7.50 m
13b	1.50 m			
14	1.47 m	1.49 m	1.65 m	

Size about 80 x 120 m
Footing: sand
Course designer: Marcello Mastronardi/ITA

BERTALAN DE NEMETHY

Games of the XXIIIrd Olympiad, Los Angeles 1984

TEAM COMPETITION

Table: A	Speed:	400 m/min.	Obstacles: 15	1st Jump-off: 1, 2, 11, 12abc, 14a, 15	
National RG:	Length:	790 m	Efforts: 18	Length:	390 m
FEI RG / Art.	Time allowed: 119 sec.		Penalty sec:	Time allowed:	59 sec.
Height: 1.60 m	Time limit:	238 sec.	Closed combination:	Time limit:	118 sec.

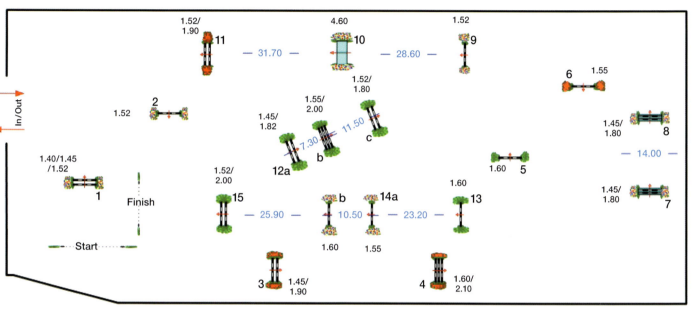

Size about 75 x 175 m
Footing: sand

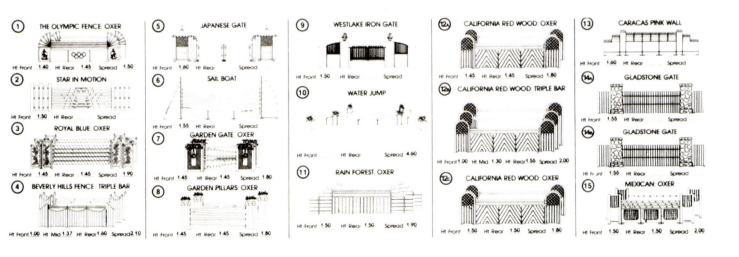

Course designer Bertalan de Némethy and technical delegate Arno Gego.

A 2.7.2 S3 (Nahons Cup): Distribution of Faults

Obstacle No.	1. Round R	E	F	A	Knock down	Obstacle No.	2. Round R	E	F	A	Knock down
1	--	--	--	1	‖	1	--	--	--	1	ǀ
2	--	--	--	3	‖‖	2	1	--	--	5	卌
3	1	--	--	6	卌 ǀ	3	--	--	--	5	卌
4	--	--	--	1	ǀ	4	--	--	--	1	ǀ
5	1	--	--	11	卌 卌 ǀ	5	3	1	--	5	卌
6	--	--	--	4	‖‖	6	--	--	--	3	‖‖
7	1	--	--	18	卌 卌 卌 ‖‖	7	--	--	--	8	卌 ‖‖
8	2	--	--	7	卌 ‖	8	--	--	--	6	卌 ǀ
9	3	--	1	3	‖‖	9	4	--	1	5	卌
10	--	1	1	9	卌 ‖‖	10	--	1	1	13	卌 卌 ‖‖
11	1	--	--	12	卌 卌 ‖	11	--	--	--	10	卌 卌
12a	3	1	--	34	卌 卌 卌 卌 卌 卌 ‖‖	12a	--	--	--	13	卌 卌 ‖‖
12b	2	--	--	10	卌 卌	12b	--	--	--	4	‖‖
12c	2	--	--	10	卌 卌	12c	--	--	--	7	卌 ‖
13	--	--	--	5	卌	13	--	--	--	3	‖‖
14a	3	--	--	31	卌 卌 卌 卌 卌 卌 ǀ	14a	1	--	--	6	卌 ǀ
14b	1	--	--	22	卌 卌 卌 卌 ‖	14b	--	--	--	15	卌 卌 卌
15	--	--	--	22	卌 卌 卌 卌 ‖	15	--	--	--	14	卌 卌 ‖‖

	Total:		Total:	Grand Total:
• Starters		60	48	108
• Knock down		210 (3.5 per start)	124 (2.58 per start)	334
• Time fault		21 (35%)	13 (27%)	34
• Falls of horses		--	--	--
• Falls of riders		1	--	1
• Retired		1	4	5
• Eliminated		3	2	5

LEOPOLDO PALACIOS

Olympic Games, Sydney 2000

Table: A
National RG:
FEI RG / Art.283 / 2.3
Height: 1.60 m

Speed: 400 m/min.
Length: 650 m
Time allowed: 98 sec.
Time limit: 196 sec.

Obstacles: 12
Efforts: 15
Penalty sec: 7
Closed combination:

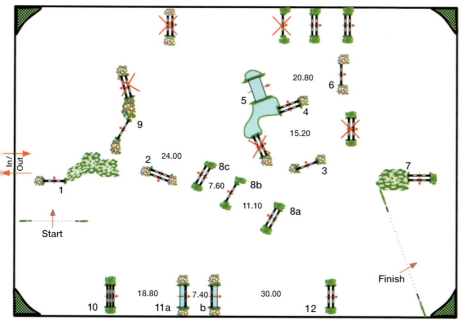

Size about 80 x 120 m
Footing: sand

No.	Front	Back	Spread	Distance
1	1.48 m			
2	1.49 m	1.49 m	1.60 m	
3	1.60 m			
				16.80 m
4	1.48 m	1.48 m	1.65 m	
5			4.30 m	
				20.80 m
6	1.60 m			
7	1.50 m	1.50 m	1.80 m	
8a	1.49 m	1.50 m	1.70 m	
				11.10 m
8b	1.55 m			
				7.80 m
8c	1.51 m	1.52 m	1.70 m	
				24.00 m
9	1.59 m			
10		1.55 m	2.00 m	
				18.80 m
11a	1.53 m			
				7.40 m
11b	1.55 m			
				30.00 m
12	1.46 m	1.48 m	1.70 m	

OLAF PETERSEN

European Championship, Donaueschingen 2003

GRAND PRIX are not necessarily the only events where we can see particularly exciting or enjoyable competitions. One of my favourite courses is the speed class at the 2003 European Jumping Championship in Donaueschingen. It is held on an arena measuring 100 x 120 m, whose perfect grass surface is an invitation to galloping.

What is a course designer's aim when designing a course for speed classes? First of all, testing the scope of the horses over longer lines, and their responsiveness in tight turns by providing alternative tracks – and by asking the same number of questions, of equal difficulty, on both reins. Then we ask different questions in combinations, by creating shorter or longer distances; but in a championship class one should also not

forget to test the horses' jumping ability and stamina.

And since I consider jumping as a team sport in which the horse and rider form the team, I also want the rider to be challenged by offering alternatives in the lines of the course. Which route is the fastest? How much of a risk can I take? Which shorter alternative would it be better not to take, because there is too great a danger of a pole down?

Finally, we should make use of the whole showground in such a way that every spectator has a chance to be very close to some fences. This is often particularly difficult to achieve with large arenas.

If we look at this speed class in Donaueschingen, we can see that it is possible to gain speed over fences No. 1 and No. 2 on a straight line. The

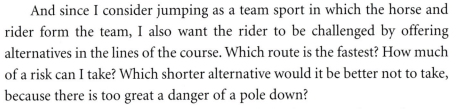

right turn to the wide oxer, No. 3, is left up to the rider, while the next left turn requires the first big decision: either to follow the safe way around the trees and straight to No. 4, or go on the inside at a flat angle, which involves risk but saves time.

A free approach to the double oxer No. 5a, b. This combination is built for two forward-ridden strides, and the rider can further increase the speed to the water jump, No. 6.

After that, the rider has to take a second decision on this course, because there is a choice of two combinations: the right-hand side leads along the longer line to No. 8, but that is the safer way. The combination is less demanding in terms of height and width, and is built for two friendly strides. It also has the advantage that the longer distance can be ridden at greater speed.

The left-hand combination is quite a challenge in terms of the dimensions – it is high and wide and can only be cleared with a big jump. Here, the rider needs a real jumping horse. And the subsequent turn to the double *staccionata*, No. 8, is not easy either; it has to be ridden very precisely.

When deciding on the measurements of the line from the water jump, No. 6, to the double *staccionata*, No. 8, I made sure that the right-hand alternative takes exactly 3

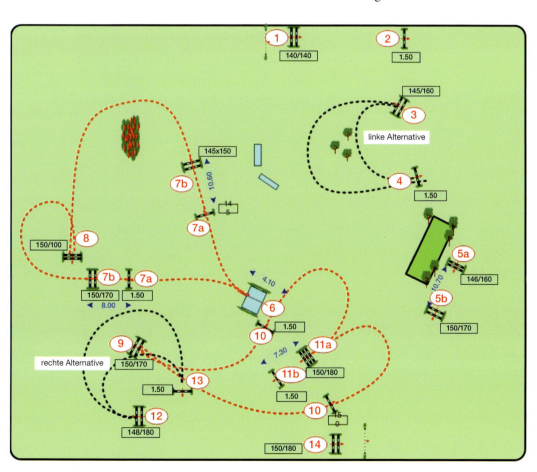

Class No.: 01

1st Qualification

Competition against the clock

Thursday 21 August 2003

Start 13.45

Table: C
National RG:
FEI RG / Art. 239, 263, 325.5
Height: 1.50 m
Speed: 400 m/min.
Length: 0 m
Time allowed: 0 sec.
Time limit: 180 sec.
Obstacles: 14
Efforts: 17
Penalty sec: 4

Size about 100 x 120 m   Course designer: Olaf Petersen – Hans Dussler – Olaf Pertersen Jr
Footing: grass

seconds longer. But when taking the left track, there is a risk of knocking a pole down, which incurs 4 faults. So which is the best way?

The third decision has to be made after fence No. 9: go across the left or the right of No. 10 to reach the narrow combination, No. 11a, b? The left- and right-hand tracks are exactly the same distance. Here, the rider has to choose the track that is most suitable for his horse.

The fourth decision has to be made after obstacle No. 12 (whether to pass No. 9 on the inside or outside?), before starting on the long final line to No. 14.

I love speed classes, because they are full of energy and variation, and can become a sort of chess game between riders and course designers.

JOBERTO PIO DA FONSECA

Sociedade Hipica Brasileira – CSI-W Rio de Janeiro

No.	Front	Back	Spread	Distance
1	1.30 m			
				28.50 m
2	1.30 m	1.35 m	1.40 m	
3	1.35 m	1.35 m	1.50 m	
				26.80 m
4	1.35 m			
5		1.35 m	1.80 m	
				23.00 m
6a	1.35 m			
				7.40 m
6b	1.35 m			
				7.90 m
6c	1.35 m	1.35 m	1.80 m	
7	1.35 m	1.35 m	1.70 m	
8	1.35 m			
9a	1.35 m	1.35 m	1.70 m	
				11.00 m
9b	1.35 m			
				20.50 m
10	1.35 m			
11	1.40 m	1.40 m	1.00 m	

For the first competition, I designed fences under the maximum height (up to 1.35 m, jump-off) concentrating the difficulties on distances and time. In my opinion, it is not a good idea to start a show (especially the top classes) with fences that are too big.

Vitor Alves Teixeira was the winner, riding the European gelding Jolly Boy.

Table: A   Speed: 375 m/min.   Obstacles: 11   1st Jump-off: 1, 2, 7, 8, 9a, 9b, 11   2nd Jump-off
National RG: Length: 530 m   Efforts: 14   Length: 280 m   Length: 0 m
FEI RG / Art. 238.3 AM5S   Time allowed: 85 sec. Penalty sec: Time allowed: 45 sec.   Time allowed: 0 sec.
Height: m   Time limit: 170 sec.   Closed combination: Time limit: 90 sec.   Time limit: 0 sec.

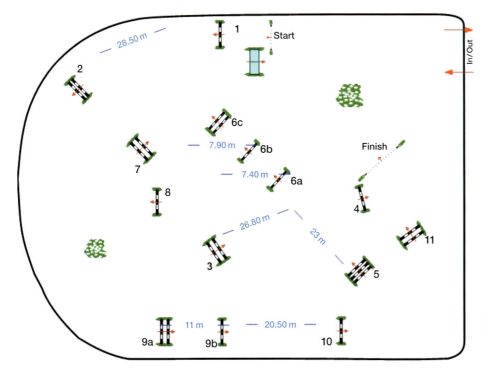

No.	Front	Back	Spread
1	1.30 m		
2	1.30 m	1.35 m	1.40 m
3	1.35 m	1.35 m	1.50 m
4	1.35 m		
5		1.35 m	1.80 m
6a	1.35 m		
6b	1.35 m		
6c	1.35 m	1.35 m	1.80 m
7	1.35 m	1.35 m	1.70 m
8	1.35 m		
9a	1.35 m	1.35 m	1.70 m
9b	1.35 m		
10	1.35 m		
11	1.40 m	1.40 m	1.00 m

Size about 70 x 90 m
Footing: sand
Course designer: Joberto Pio da Fonseca

AVELINO RODRIGUEZ MIRAVALLES

Spain, World Championshps 2002

For the last two years we have been working in close collaboration with the Organising Committee to get everything ready for the start of competition, as well as to create a championship with personality. In this sense, the design of the jumps is fundamental. Following a broad exchange of ideas, we have created a type of design that is very typical of Jerez and Andalusia.

From a technical point of view, as course designer of these World Championships, I have chosen to give the rider-horse partnership centre stage, with courses that will enable us to select the best and in which the strong points of the former can make up for the shortcomings of the latter, and vice versa.

In order to reach our objective we must consider that the first test, the speed and handiness class, is very important in shaping how the championship will develop because we have to think very hard about the options to make sure that it really is the best pair that win.

The second individual qualifying round also counts towards the final team classification and the aim should be to keep the jumps low while emphasising technical difficulties. The best team must win but without the less-competitive ones being humiliated.

However, I want the courses in the third qualifying round to involve both kinds of difficulty, i.e. size and technical aspect, because, by then, the top 25 horses and riders will have been selected and this round will be crucial in deciding the four finalists.

Lastly, I think that the final course must not be too high, but should be technically difficult. Bearing in mind the difficulty of having to ride other people's horses and the tension that always reigns in a final, those factors will be enough to enable us to watch an exciting competition and select the best – the World Champion.

TEAM FINAL 2nd. Qualifier
TABLE: A Two Rounds Art. No 310   LENGTH: 510 mts
SPEED: 400 mts/min.   TIME ALLOWED: 77 sec.

Course designer: Avelino Rodriguez Miravalles

| No. | Dimension | Obstacle | | | 1. Round | |
		R	E	F	A	Knock-down
1	1.50				4	IIII
2	1.55				18	LHT LHT LHT III
3	1.45 x 1.47 x 1.70				14	LHT LHT IIII
4	1.60	2	1		10	LHT LHT
5	1.59 x 2.00	1		R	23	LHT LHT LHT LHT III
6	1.60		1		8	LHT III
7a	1.46 x 1.48 x 1.60		2		5	LHT
7b	1.55				9	LHT IIII
7c	1.50 x 1.51 x 1.60	1	1	2H	29	LHT LHT LHT LHT LHT IIII
8	1.60	1			18	LHT LHT LHT III
9	1.50 x 1.52 x 1.70				9	LHT IIII
10a	1.55	2			33	LHT LHT LHT LHT LHT LHT III
10b	1.48 x 1.50 x 1.65	2			24	LHT LHT LHT LHT IIII
11	4.20				59	LHT LHT LHT LHT LHT LHT LHT LHT LHT LHT LHT IIII
12	1.50 x 1.52 x 1.80				28	LHT LHT LHT LHT LHT III

Total:	1. Round	2. Round	Grand Total:
Starters	96	40	136
Knock-down	291 (3.03 per start)	44 (1.1 per start)	335
Time fault	20 (28.8%)	5 (12.5%)	25
Falls of horses	2	2	
Falls of riders	1	--	2
Retired	5	--	5
Elimination	--	1	1

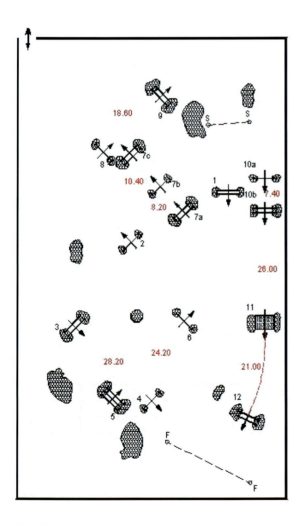

Size about 80 x 120 m
Footing: sand

HAUKE SCHMIDT

CSIO Calgary Spruce Meadows – Masters – September 8th, 1991

Table: A
National RG:
FEI RG / Art. 283 / 2.3
Height: 1.60 m

Speed: 400 m/min.
Length: 0 m
Time allowed: 0 sec.
Time limit: 0 sec.

Obstacles: 14
Efforts: 17
Penalty sec:
Closed combination:

2nd round: 1, 2, 3, 7, 6, 12bc, 13, 14
Length: 0 m
Time allowed: 0 sec.
Time limit: 0 sec.

Jump-off: 3, 7, 11, 12bc, 13, 14
Length: 0 m
Time allowed: 0 sec.
Time limit: 0 sec.

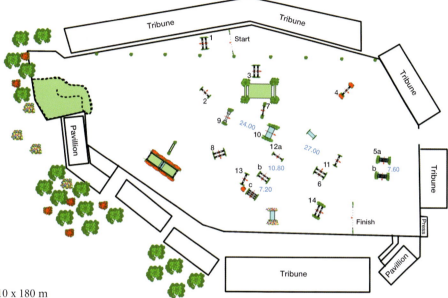

Size about 110 x 180 m
Footing: grass
Course designer: Hauke Schmidt/GER

The GRAND PRIX of Spruce Meadows in 1991.

1. round 36 Starters

2. round 12 Starters

1	Double Clear
5	4 faults
1	4.5 faults
4	8 faults
1	16 faults

Winner 1991: Ian Millar and Big Ben

No.	Description	Front	Back	Spread	Distance
1	Oxer	1.45	1.50	1.70	
2	Vertical	1.55			
3	Oxer	1.45	1.45	1.90	
4	Vertical	1.60			
5a	Liverpool	1.50	1.50	1.80	
					7.60 m
5b	Liverpool		1.50	1.60	
6	Oxer	1.55	1.55	1.80	
7	Plank Vertical	1.60			
8	Oxer	1.50	1.50	1.90	
9	Wave Wall	1.60			
					24.00 m
10	Water Jump	0.50		4.30	
					27.00 m
11	Vertical	1.60			
12a	Vertical	1.55			
					10.80 m
12b	Oxer	1.55	1.55	1.80	
					7.20 m
12c	Triple Bar		1.55	2.00	
13	Small Gate	1.60			
14	Oxer	1.55	1.55	1.90	

STEVE STEPHENS

American Invitational, Tampa 2004

Table: A	Speed: 375 m/min.	Obstacles:	1st Jump-off: 3, 4, 5, 6BC, 9, 12A, 13, 14
National RG:	Length: 600 m	Efforts:	Length: 330 m
FEI RG / Art. 238.2.2	Time allowed: 96 sec.	Penalty sec:	Time allowed: 53 sec
Height: 1.60 m	Time limit: 192 sec.	Closed combination:	Time limit: 106 sec

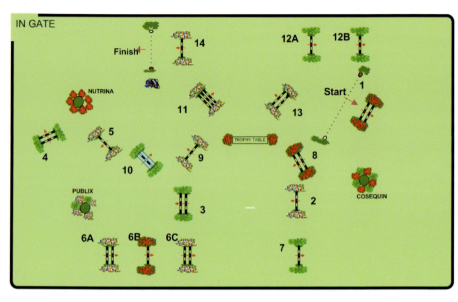

No.	Front	Back	Spread	Distance
1	1.35	1.40	1.45	
2	1.50			
				23.40
3	1.45	1.47	1.60	
4	1.47	1.47	1.60	
5	1.52			
6a	1.45	1.47	1.60	
				7.50
6b	1.52			
				7.90
6c	1.50	1.50	1.70	
				19.50
7	1.55			
8	1.47	1.47	1.60	
				21.00
9	1.55			
10	1.53			
				19.65
11		1.60	2.00	
				33.00
12a	1.47			
				10.60
12b	1.60			
13	1.47	1.47	1.70	
14	1.60			

Size about 60 x 100 m
Footing: grass
Course designer: Steve Stephens/USA

JOHN VALLANCE

Sydney Royal Easter Show, 2003

This course was designed as the second competition of the Australian Championships. As such, I felt it needed to be quite demanding as there was one round and a jump-off.

The opening four obstacles were not too demanding, particularly from a distance point of view, and allowed the riders and their horses to establish the fluency and rhythm required for a championship course.

The first related line of obstacles, 5 to 6ABC, required the riders to have a sound understanding of their horse's capabilities as they made either seven or eight strides. Many early riders opted to make the seven strides but found the B element came up short. Later riders tried the eight strides and found that they didn't have impulsion to make the back rail of the C element.

The line 9AB to 10 caused a great deal of discussion amongst the riders when they walked the course and proved difficult in the riding. With the speed of the course at 400 m/min., the riders could not afford to be too generous in their approach to the

Class No.: 739   Australian Championships   Competition with one jump-off   Sunday, April 20, 2003   Start 10.30

Table: A	Speed: 400 m/min.	Obstacles: 13	1st Jump-off: 1, 8, 15, 6b,6c, 3, 12, 13	2nd Jump-off:
National RG:	Length: 580 m	Efforts: 16	Length: 290 m	Length: 0 m
FEI RG / Art. 238.22	Time allowed: 87 sec.	Penalty sec:	Time allowed: 44 sec.	Time allowed: 0 sec.
Height: 1.60 m	Time limit: 174 sec.	Closed combination:	Time limit: 88 sec.	Time limit: 0 sec.

Course diagram:

11 — 1.55
3 — 1.45/1.60
5 — 1.55/2.00 — 29.20m
6a, 6b, 6c — 7.5m, 7.6m — 1,45/1,50 — 1.50 — 1,45/1,60
12 — 1.50/1.70
4
15 Jump-off only — 1,50
10 — 1.55 — 21.0m
2 — 1.45
7 — 3.8 — 27.0m — 25.5m — 31.0m
8 — 1.55/1.00
13 — 1.60
9b — 1.50/1.60 — 10.8m
9a — 1,50
Finish
1 — 1.40/1.50
Start

In / Out

Fence No.	Rails	Refusals
1	1	0
2	2	0
3	3	0
4	1	0
5	1	0
6a	6	0
6b	10	0
6c	2	0
7	1	1
8	1	0
9a	5	0
9b	9	0
10	14	0
11	2	0
12	10	0
13	2	0

Size about 70 x 120 m
Footing: grass

Starters	31
Total Penalties	280
Av Penalties/Starter	9
Time Penalties	10
0 Penalties	1
1-4	5
5-8	13
9-12	4
13-16	2
17-20	1
20+	4
Elim	1

A element and, as such, found the B element a long way off and struggled to clear the back rail. Fence 10, which was set at 21 metres from the combination, should have been a holding five strides but many riders over-rode the distance either as a result of the impulsion generated from the combination distance or because of the nature of obstacle 10, the Sydney Harbour Bridge, from the 2000 Olympic Games. Many combinations came too deep to the Harbour Bridge and found the 1.60-metre wall too high. Those riders who trusted their horse to jump the bridge and allow it to back their horse off had much more success.

The final line of obstacles, 12 to 13, seemed quite easy after the two previous major lines but had a decisive role in the final placings. Some horses appeared to switch off after obstacle 11 while some others were showing the effects of their previous efforts and were far too forward to safely negotiate these final obstacles.

Although there was only one clear round over the course, I was pleased with the way the course rode as the questions asked throughout the course all worked and were all solvable.

PAUL WEIER

European Jumping Championships, St Gallen, Switzerland 1987
Aims:

1   Art. 263.1,2,3 (268 before 2003).

2   Using the whole natural arena, extending the length of the course to maximum (700 m).

3   A galloping track with the opportunity to shorten and cut the track and save important metres, without losing and changing the rhythm.

4   Giving a real chance to the best ridden, most balanced horses and the 'thinking' riders throughout the course.

5   Using some of the natural fences (Liverpool, Trakehner, water jump).

6   Presenting the fences in the colours and aspects of the participating nations.

Winner: Pierre Durand with Japeloup, in a splendid round, riding the shortest possible track (saving 168 m).

No.	Description	Front	Back	Spread	Distance	Faults	Alternative No.	Used Alternatives
1	St Andrew's oxer	0.70 m	1.45 m	1.60 m		3		
							1	24
2	Irish rails	1.47 m				2		
							2	36
3	Belgian railway barriers	1.50 m				1		
4	Nizza oxer	1.45 m	1.50 m	1.60 m		2		
							3	9
5	Trakehner rustic poles	1.50 m				4		
							4	12
6a	Dutch windmill	1.45 m				1		
					7.60 m			
6b	Dutch oxer	1.45 m	1.45 m	1.50 m		7		
7	English park gate	1.50 m				2		
7	Rustic, paddock gangway	1.50 m	1.50 m	1.30 m		3	5	16
8a	Swiss triple bar	0.90 m	1.40 m	2.10 m		1		
					8.00 m			
8b	Zurich blue-white planks	1.50 m				4		
							6	8
9	Italian birch rails	1.48 m				7		
10	Water jump with small wall			4.00 m		2		
							7	38
11	French Tour d'Eiffel	1.50 m				1		
							8	9
12a	St Gallen bridge over river	1.45 m	1.45 m	1.45 m		3		
					10.80 m			
12b	Appenzell cattleway	1.45 m	1.50 m	1.40 m		5		
							9	32
13	Irish gate	1.50 m				4		
14	German oxer	1.45 m	1.48 m	1.60 m		15*		

* long way, towards the exit

Table: C
National RG:
FEI RG / Art. 239 / 268
Height: 1.5 m

Speed: 400 m/min.
Length: 700 m
Time allowed: 105 sec.
Time limit: 210 sec.

Obstacles: 14
Efforts: 17
Penalty sec: 7
Closed combination:

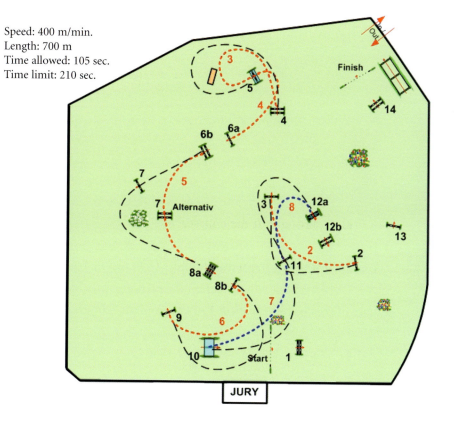

A3 PLANING A MAJOR TOURNAMENT: THE WORLD JUMPING CHAMPIONSHIPS, AACHEN 1986

This section is provided to show in just how much detail such an important world event has to be planned. The responsibility of being the course designer for the World Jumping Championships in the prestigious jumping stadium of CHIO Aachen is a great privilege and honour but it needs still a great amount of:

- spiritual and emotional effort;

- systematic planning;

- regular communication;

with the people involved (for example, the FEI – on this occasion especially with Fritz O. Widme, the technical delegate, the media, sponsors, the course design team, etc.).

A course designer has to define in advance the general objectives and write them down (table A3.1). The schedule for the design for planning the World Jumping Championships, Aachen 1986 (table A3.2) and the official FEI-approved schedule (table A 3.3) are the basic framework of the planning process. The date of each design step is the date of concept completion. Other systematically structured charts are listed as follows:

A 3.4   combinations plan (20.04.1986);

A 3.5   MASTERPLAN for the structure of courses (preliminary at 07.06. because final lengths not yet known);

A 3.6   structure of combinations;

A 3.7   concept of strides' distribution in combinations;

A 3.8   optional competition;

A 3.9   MASTERPLAN 1. qualifier (speed competition);

A 3.10   MASTERPLAN 2. qualifier (Nations Cup);

A 3.11   MASTERPLAN 3. qualifier (GRAND PRIX, rounds 1 and 2);

A 3.12   MASTERPLAN, Final;

A 3.13   distribution of faults (S2 and S5);

A 3.14   distribution of faults (S3);

A 3.15   distribution of faults (S4).

The third qualifier is a very interesting competition:

1   only for the best 20 participants;

2   big and demanding course;

3   very good results:
     a   far fewer faults than the Nations Cup;
     b   far fewer time faults;
     c   only 1 refusal;
     d   no elimination;
     e   still one double clear (Pierre Durand/Japeloup).

A3.1: General Objectives for the Competitions of the World Jumping Championships, Aachen 08-13.07.1986

1   **General Design Objectives**

1.1   Classical courses with obstacles which correspond to the character and size of the Aachen Stadium.

1.2   The degree of difficulty (level) should not pose unsolvable tests for the 12 leading teams.

1.3   Aesthetically pleasing and imposing obstacles.

1.4   No major optical problems or surprises.

1.5   Difficult sections mainly recognised from the Aachen Shows of recent years.

1.6   Sufficient use of decorative material such as trees, flowers, etc. (typical for the Aachen Show).

1.7   Standards (used in Aachen since 1979):
a) poles: 4 m length and 10 cm diameter
b) open metal cups 2.2 cm (same as in LA), special hanging gates, planks, etc. special cups for hanging gates, etc.

1.8   Sufficient use of obstacle design variation.

1.9   No artificially created or 'not-sensible' problems/difficulties.

1.10 Growing demand of difficulty and dimension from competition 1 to 3.

1.11 No extreme tests.

2   **Concept of Distances/Combinations**

2.1   Fairly balanced tests in combinations (no one-sided questions, alternation of fairly long, normal, fairly short; no exaggerations, no tricks).

2.2   Free approach to the water jump (more than 6 strides).

2.3   First obstacle after the water jump minimum 5 strides or more.

2.4 Use of all classical obstacle types in combination.

2.5 Alternation/variation of the entrance type of the provided combinations.

2.6 Alternation of 1- and 2-stride distances.

3   Concept of Tracks/Lines

3.1 Inviting starting line with limited dimensions and questions for each competition.

3.2 Classical design of lines with a maximum variety of track elements and variation of obstacle type sequences.

3.3 Minimum one sequence of related obstacles in a mainly straight line with distance tests (5 strides or more, except first qualification).

3.4 Fairly balanced alternation of different difficulties in the respective courses.

3.5 Alternation of combinations with free approach and in line (related distance).

A3.2: Schedule of design for planning the World Jumping Championships, Aachen 1986

No.	MASTERPLAN	Date and Place of Design	Competition Date
1	Definite Combinations Plan	20.04. Aachen	08.07
2	Optional Competition	22.06. Aachen	08.07
3	1st Qualifier, Table C	27.01. Flight Santiago de Chile – Kansas/USA	09.07
4	2nd Qualifier, Nations Cup	17.04. Aachen	10.07
5	3rd Qualifier ● Round A	20.01. Santiago de Chile	12.07
	● Round B	24.04. Aachen	
6	Final	20.01. Santiago de Chile until 31.01. Kansas/USA (flight to Germany)	13.07
●	Visit TD Bertalan de Némethy	27- 30.04 Inspection of the Aachen showground and facilities. Presentation and discussion of all MASTERPLANS, courses, combinations, etc.	

A3.3: Specification of the competitions of the World Jumping Championships, Aachen, 08-13.07.1986

Date	Competition	Rules	Speed m/min.	Obstacles				Combi-nations	Length m	Remarks
				Number m	Height m	Spread m	Water jump m			
1 08.07	Optional	Table A	350 238.2A2		1.40	--				1 Liver-pool
2 09.07	1st Qualifier, Speed Competition	Table C 239 +268+ 282.1.5	400	12…14	1.50	2.00	4.00	1D+1T or 3D	700/800	--
3 10.07	Nations Cup Final Teams	Table A 282.2.1 Appendix 1.9.3.1 282.2.2	400	12…14	1.60	2.00	4.50	1D+1T or 3D	650/800	2 equal rounds
4 12.07	3rd Qualifier Round A Round B	Table A, 238.1	400	10…12 8	1.60	2.00	4.50	1D+1T or 3D 1T or 3D	500/600 400/500	2 different rounds 20 partici-pants
5 13.07	Final	Table A, 282.4.6	350	8	1.30… 150	1.80	--	1T or 1D	400/500	4 partici-pants

As produced by Arno Gego, Flight Paris – Buenos Aires, 14.01.1986

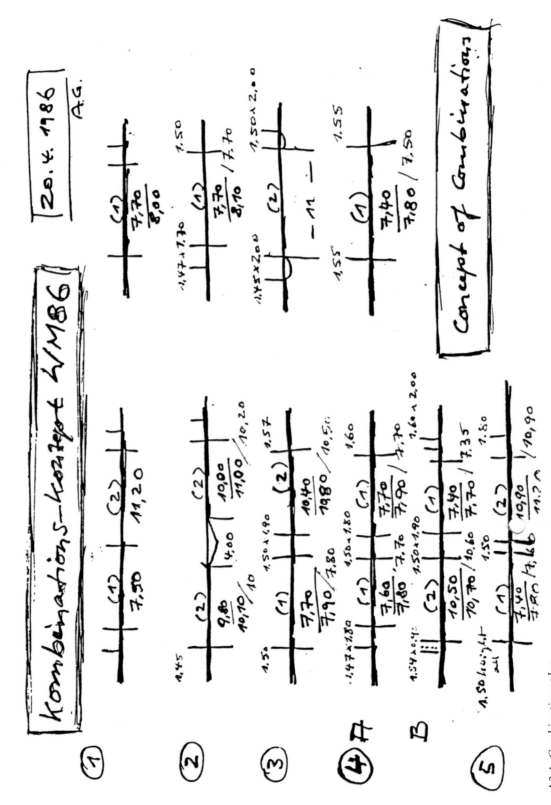

A3.4: *Combinations plan.*

A3.5: MASTERPLAN for the structure of courses, World Jumping Championships, Aachen, 08–13.07.1986 (preliminary 07.06.1986)

| Criteria | Structure of Competitions | | | | |
	1. Qualifier Table C	2. Qualifier Nations Cup	3. Qualifier Round A	Round B	Final
Starting rein	left	right	free	free	left
Changes of rein	5 or 6	3 + (3/2)	3	3	3 + (2/2)
Number of obstacles	14	14	12	8	8
Number of efforts	17	17	15	10	10
Triple combination	1	1	1	1	1
Double combinations	1	1	1	--	--
Type of first obstacle	Triple bar	Vertical	Oxer	Oxer	Intermediate
Type of last obstacle	Oxer	Vertical	Oxer	Vertical	Oxer
Water jump	1	1	1	--	--
Liverpool	1	2	--	1	--
Length of the course	700	730	580	450	450
Average m/effort	41	43	39	45	45

A3.6: Structure of combinations, World Jumping Championships, Aachen 08–13.07.1986

Type of Obstacle in Combinations	Total Number 3 Qualifiers	Final	Type of Entrance 3 Qualifiers	Obstacle Final	Optional
1 Normal vertical	7	1	3	1	--
2 Wall	--	--	--	--	1
3 Parallel	6	1	2	--	1
4 Obstacle over water	2	--	1	--	--
5 Triple bar	1	--	--	--	--
6 Intermediate	1	1	1	--	--
7 Open water jump	1	-	--	--	--
Total number of combinations			7	1	2

A3.7: Concept of stride distribution, World Jumping Championships, Aachen, 08–13.07 1986

Criteria	Number of Strides 1 stride	2 strides	Number of Distances in Combinations
1 Optional competition	2	1	3
2 Three qualifiers	5	5	10
3 Final	1	1	2
Total (6 courses)	8	7	15

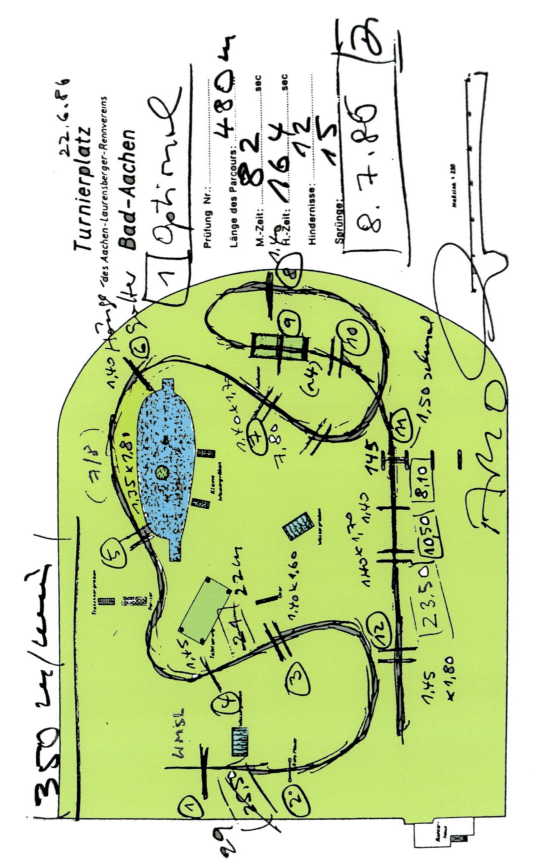

A3.8: Optional competion.

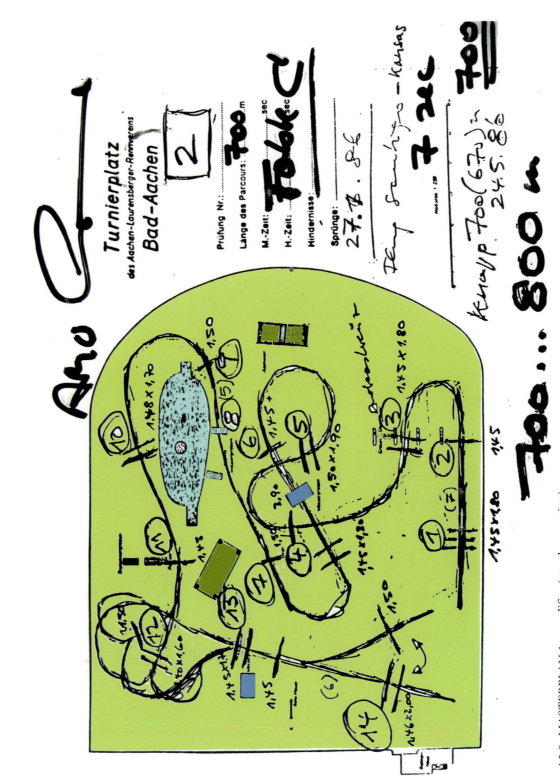

A3.9: *MASTERPLAN 1 – qualifier (speed competion).*

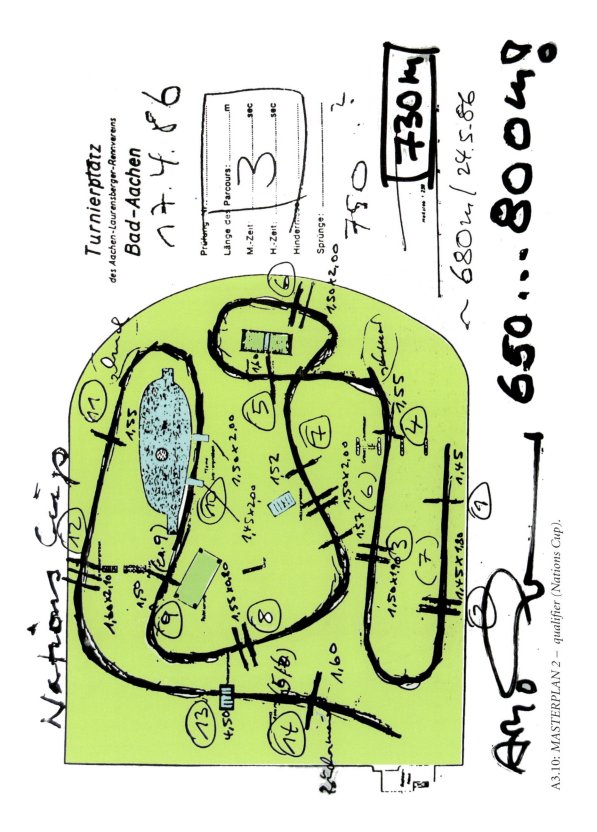

A3.10: MASTERPLAN 2 – qualifier (Nations Cup).

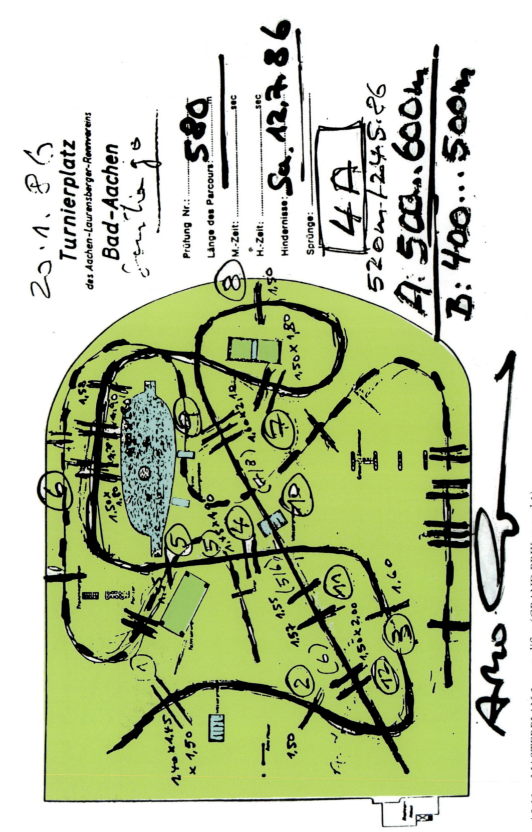

A3.11a: MASTERPLAN 3 – qualifier (GRAND PRIX, round 1).

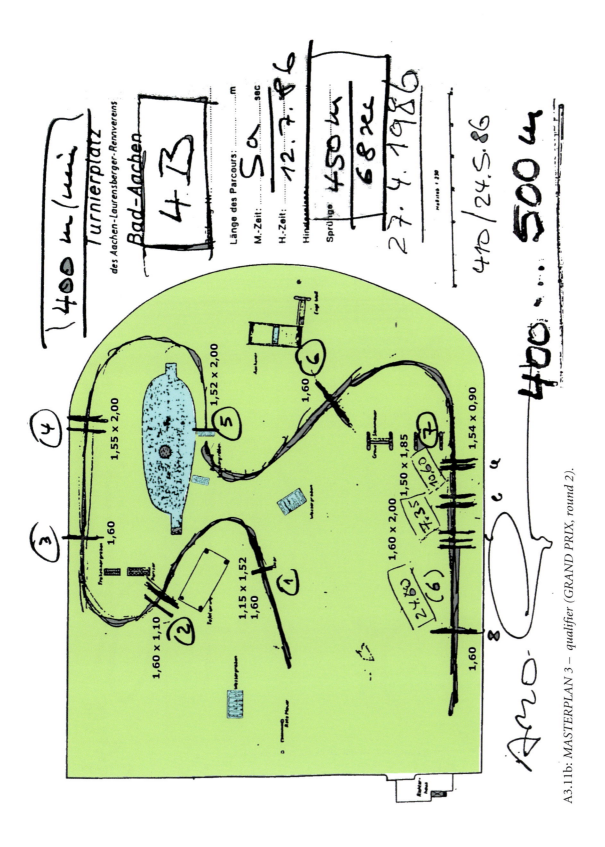

A3.11b: MASTERPLAN 3 – qualifier (GRAND PRIX, round 2).

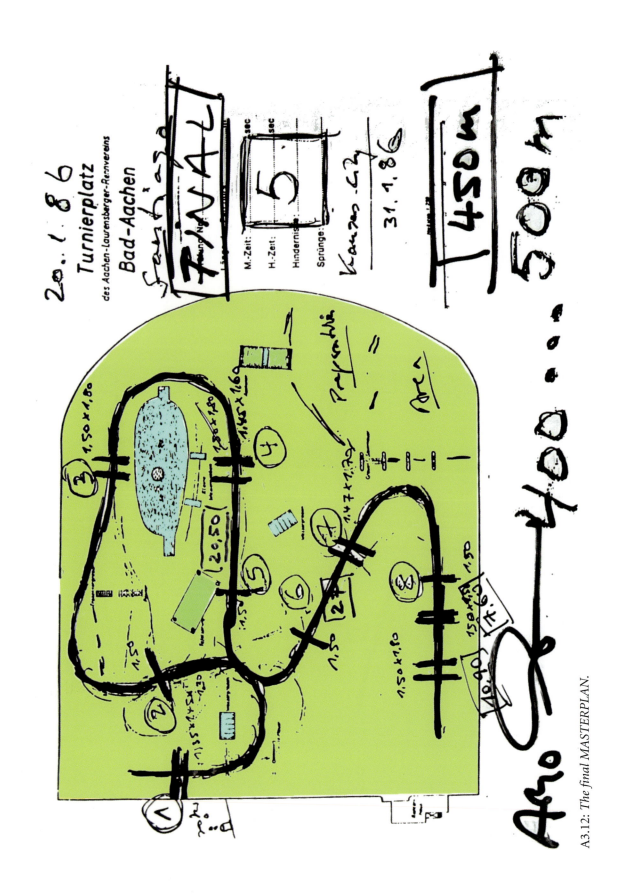

A3.12: *The final MASTERPLAN.*

Distribution of Faults

Obstacle No.	S2 Speed Class, Table C, 1. Qualifier				
	R	E	F	A	Knock down
1	1			3	III
2				2	II
3				3	III
4				10	卌 卌
5				12	卌 卌 II
6a				8	卌 III
6b	2			22	卌 卌 卌 卌 II
6c				19	卌 卌 卌 IIII
7				9	卌 IIII
8	6			8	卌 III
9				4	IIII
10				6	卌 I
11				2	II
12	3			5	卌
13a	1			12	卌 卌 II
13b				2	II
14				25	卌 卌 卌 卌 卌

Obstacle No.	S 5 Final			
	R	E	F	Knock down
1				--
2			1	I
3			1	I
4				--
5			2	II
6				--
7				--
8a			1	I
8b			4	IIII
8c			2	II

Total:
- Starters — 72
- Knock-down — 144 (2 per start)
- Time fault — 2
- Falls — --
- Retired — --
- Eliminated — --
- Refusals — 2

Total:
4 x 4 = 16
11 (0.7 per start)
1 (6%)
--
--
--
1

(Nations Cup) Distribution of Faults

Obstacle No.	1. Round				
	R	E	F	A	Knock down
1				1	I
2				4	IIII
3	1			13	卌 卌 III
4				5	卌
5	1			18	卌 卌 卌 III
6				4	IIII
7a				11	卌 卌 I
7b				16	卌 卌 卌 I
7c	1			13	卌 卌 III
8				5	卌
9				12	卌 卌 II
10a	8			26	卌 卌 卌 卌 卌 I
10b	2			11	卌 卌 I
11		1	R	3	III
12				4	IIII
13				3	III
14	1			31	卌 卌 卌 卌 卌 卌 I

Obstacle No.	2. Round				
	R	E	F	A	Knock down
1				4	IIII
2				4	IIII
3	1			13	卌 卌 III
4				5	卌
5				19	卌 卌 卌 IIII
6				6	卌 I
7a	2			10	卌 卌
7b	2	1	RR	10	卌 卌
7c				14	卌 卌 IIII
8				3	III
9	3			9	卌 IIII
10a	3			20	卌 卌 卌 卌
10b	3	1	R	6	卌 I
11				2	II
12				4	IIII
13				6	卌 I
14	2			28	卌 卌 卌 卌 卌 III

Total:
- Starters — 68
- Knock-down — 189 (2.8 per start)
- Time fault — 33 (49%)
- Falls of horses — --
- Falls of riders — 1
- Retired — 4
- Eliminated — 1

Total:
63
163 (2.6 per start)
25 (40%)
--
3
3
3

Grand total:
131
352
58
--
4
7
4

(GRAND PRIX, Third Individual Competion) Distribution of Faults

Obstacle No.	1. Round					Obstacle No.	2. Round			
	R	E	F	A	Knock down		R	E	F	Knock down
1				--		1				--
2				2	II	2				--
3				2	II	3				5 ИН
4				1		4				4 IIII
5				--		5				--
6a				--		6				--
6b				5	ИН	7a				1 I
6c				--		7b				1 I
7				2	II	7c				4 IIII
8				1	I	8				--
9				--						
10a				--						
11a	1			1	I					
11b				--						
12				3	III					

Total:			Grand total:
• Starters	19	19	38
• Knock-down	17 (0.9 per start)	15 (0.8 per start)	32
• Time fault	4 (21%)	--	4
• Falls of horses	--	--	--
• Falls of riders	--	1	1
• Retired	--	--	--
• Eliminated	1	--	1

SUMMARY

The jumping competitions of the World Jumping Championships, 8–13 July 1986 in Aachen could be considered as a great success.

Notably:

1 There were no falls involving horses, nor any serious accidents.

2 All teams finished the Nations Cup

3 The ground conditions during the whole event could be considered to have been optimal.

4 All competitions fulfilled public expectations.

5 All competitions had a most exciting atmosphere and dramaturgy.

6   The general objectives (20.05.1986/AG) were achieved.

7   The system of cups and poles was fair and effective (same as at the Olympic Games in Los Angeles 1984).

The MASTERPLANS of the course were discussed on the occasion of the visit of the technical delegate, Dr h. c. Bertalan de Némethy, to Aachen from 24–27 April 1986 and were mailed without any major modification on 28 May 1986 to the technical delegate.

With regard to the results of the different competitions of the World Jumping Championship, there has always been a very clear outcome:

1   The first qualifying competition (S2, Table C) ended with a difference of nearly two seconds between each of the three first places (winner Paul Schockemöhle with Deister).

2   There was **one competitor** in the Nations Cup (S3) who had **two clear rounds** (Gail Greenough with Mr T).

3   There was again **one competitor** who had **two clear rounds** in the third qualifying competion (S4) – Pierre Durand with Japeloup.

4   Only **one competitor went clear four times** in the Final (Gail Greenough).

A4 SOME OF MY OWN MASTERPLANS

The author believes that an international course designer with long-standing experience and responsibility should document a representative selection of major MASTERPLANS, in order to:

- prove that his written statements and beliefs are in accordance with what he does in reality; and

- to give a fair chance of comparison with former and later MASTERPLANS and courses of other course designers

But this only works with honest course designers who do not create illusions like:

Obstacle type	'official course plan'	'effective' dimension
triple bar	1.60 x 2.20 m	1.55 x 2.00 m
oxer	1.52 x 1.80 m	1.50 x 1.65 m
vertical	1.60 m	1.56 m
water jump	4.30 m	4.00 m
length of the course	630 m	660 or 580 m?

This type of deception gives a totally wrong picture of the 'reality'.

With seldom-justified exceptions (like extremely bad weather situations) the author has always tried to verify his original MASTERPLAN as precisely as possible.

Nevertheless, each course designer makes mistakes. The author has tried to minimise mistakes by creating the best teams of assistants (co-course designers). On the other hand, with a representative collection of MASTERPLANS, the course designer gives a real picture of his 'creations' and his contribution to the art of course design.

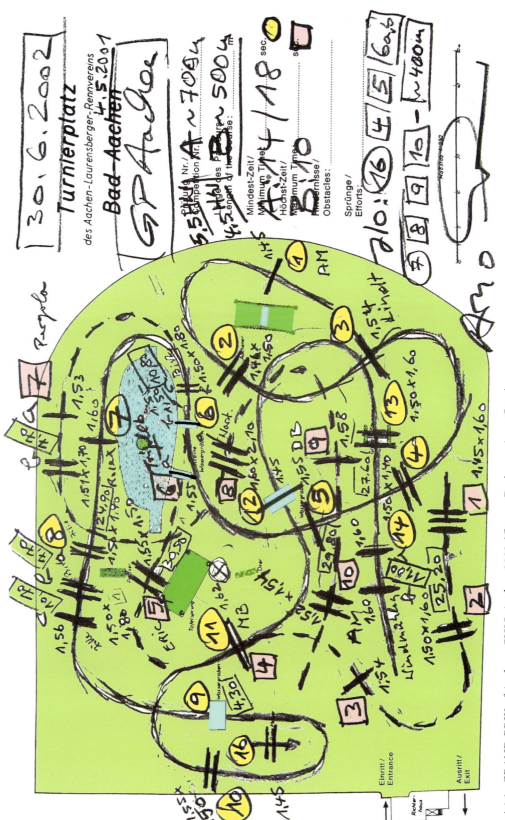

A4.1: GRAND PRIX of Aachen, CHIO Aachen 2002 (Course Designer: Arno Gego).

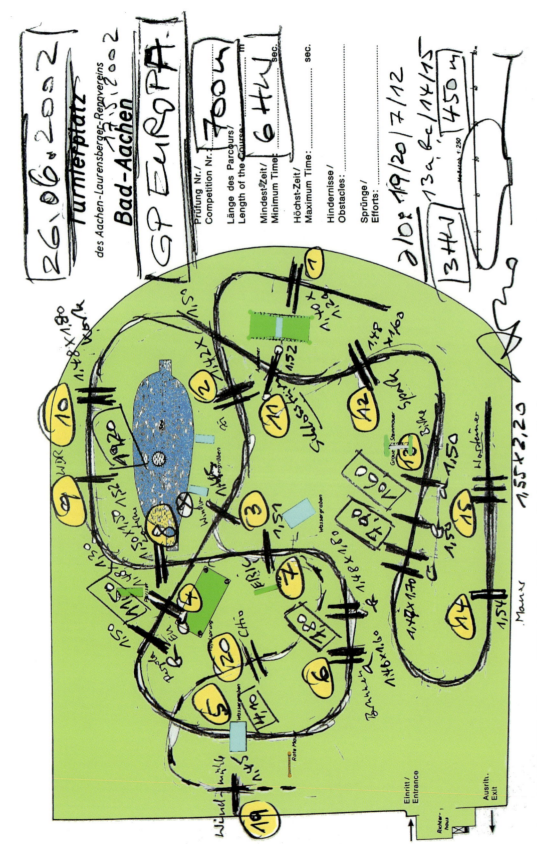

A4.2: GRAND PRIX of Europe, CHIO Aachen 2002 (Course Designer: Arno Gego).

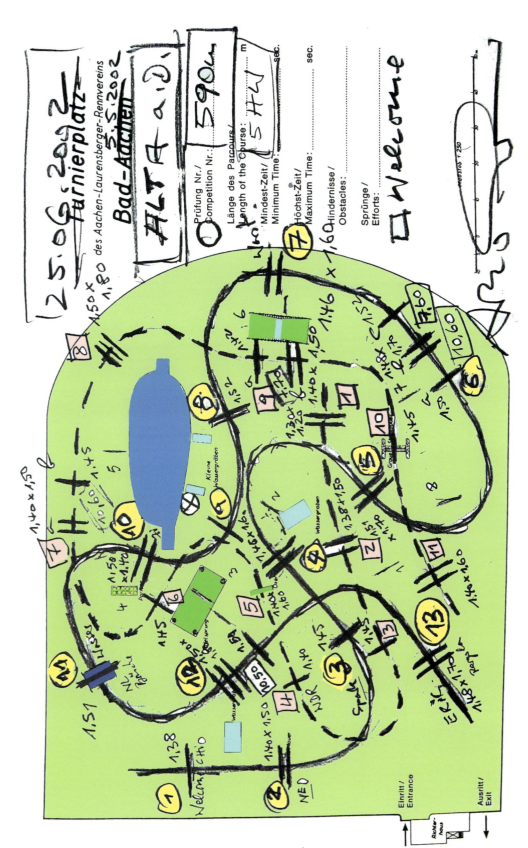

A4.3: First qualifier for the GRAND PRIX of Aachen 2002, CHIO Aachen 2002 (Course Designer: Arno Gego).

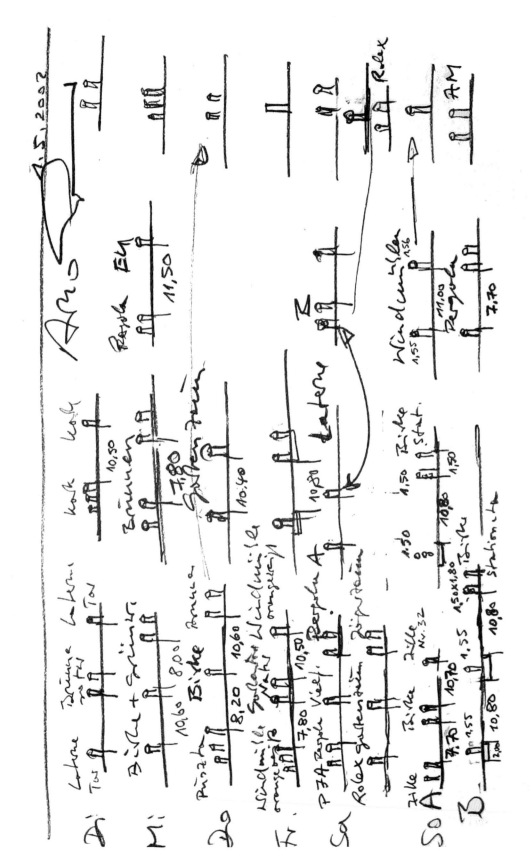

A4.4: Combination Plan, CHIO Aachen 2002 (Course Designer: Arno Gego).

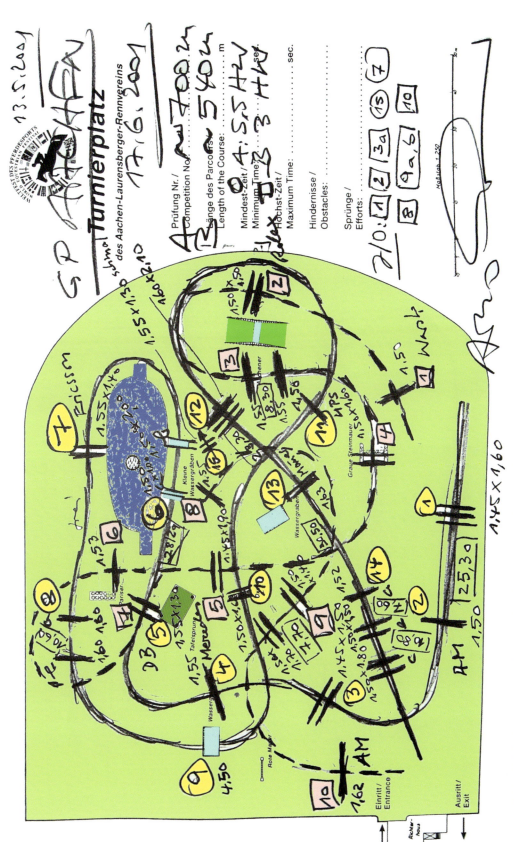

A4.5: GRAND PRIX of Aachen, CHIO Aachen 2001 (Course Designer: Arno Gego).

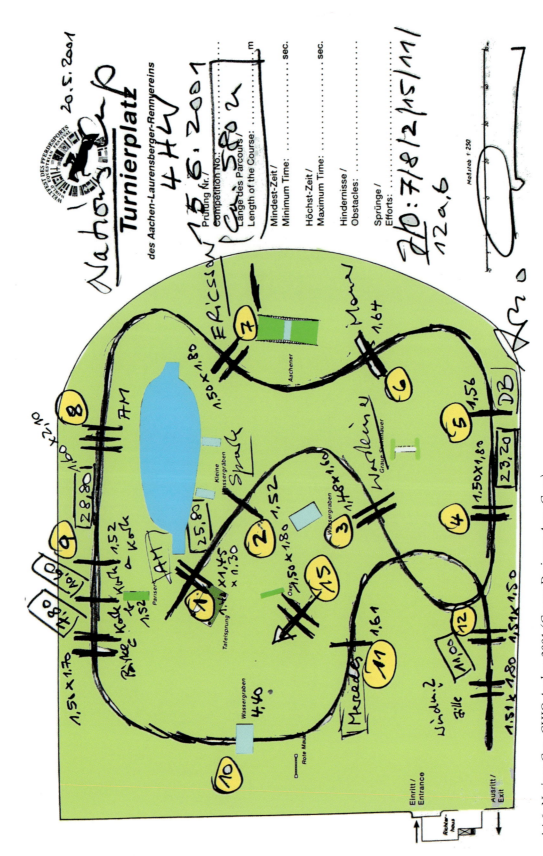

A4.6: *Nations Cup, CHIO Aachen 2001 (Course Designer: Arno Gego).*

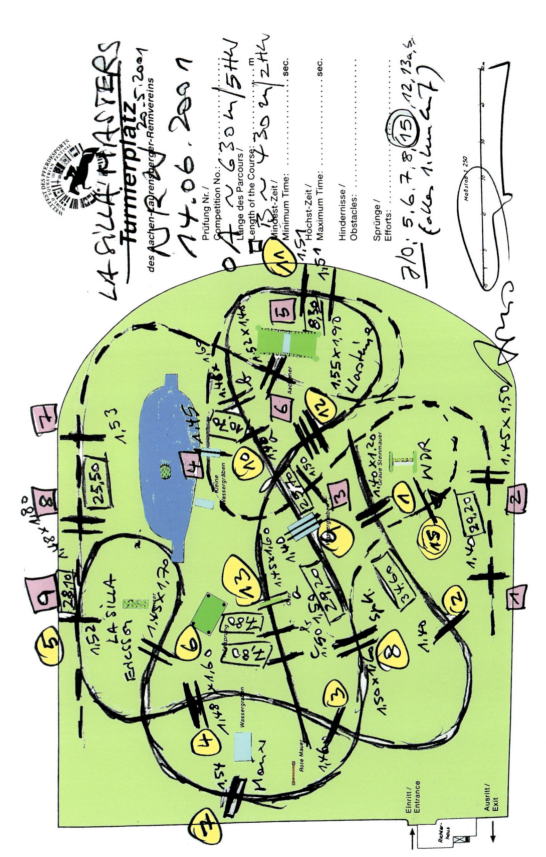

A4.7: La Silla Masters, CHIO Aachen 2001 (Course Designer: Arno Gego).

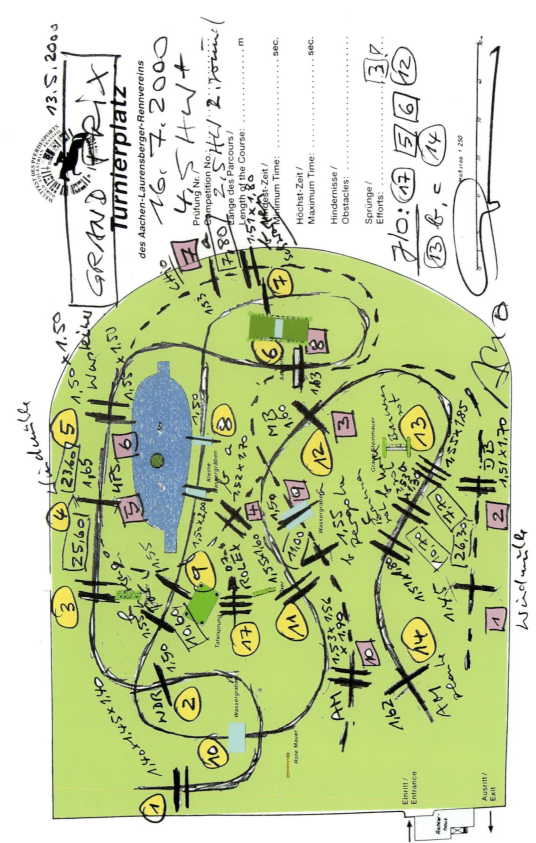

A4.8: *GRAND PRIX of Europe, CHIO Aachen 2001 (Course Designer: Arno Gego).*

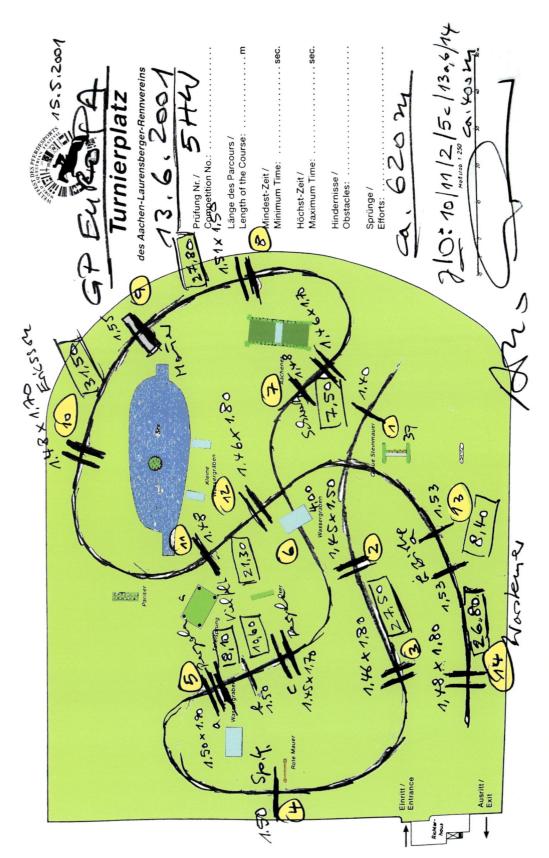

A4.9: *GRAND PRIX of Aachen, CHIO Aachen 2000 (Course Designer: Arno Gego).*

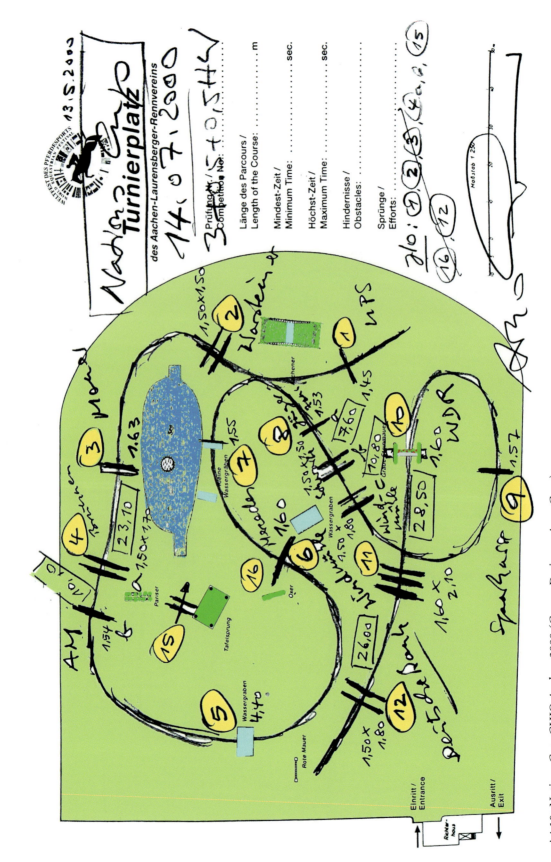

A4.10: *Nations Cup, CHIO Aachen 2000 (Course Designer: Arno Gego).*

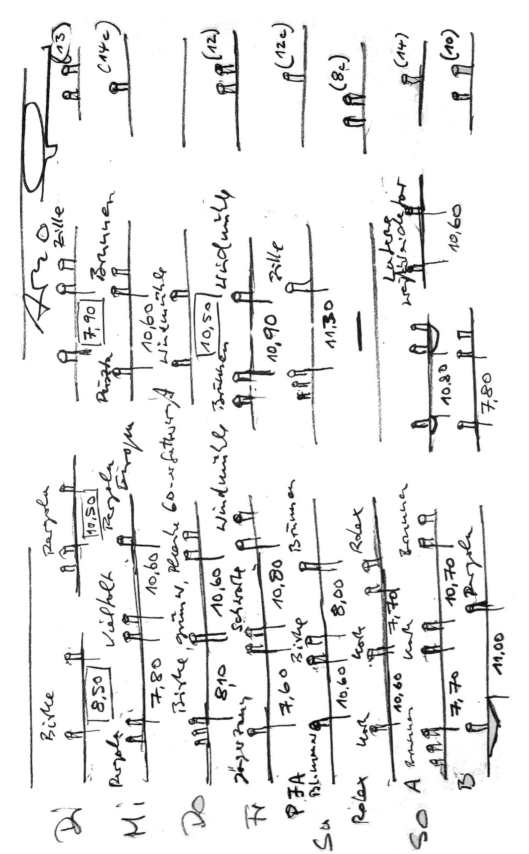

A4.11: *Combinations Plan, CHIO Aachen 2000 (Course Designer: Arno Gego).*

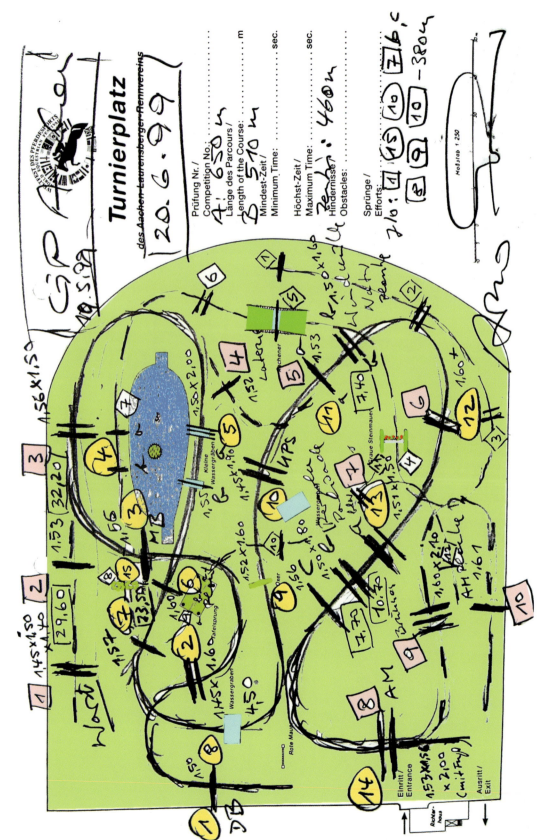

A4.12: *GRAND PRIX of Aachen, CHIO Aachen 1999 (Course Designer: Arno Gego).*

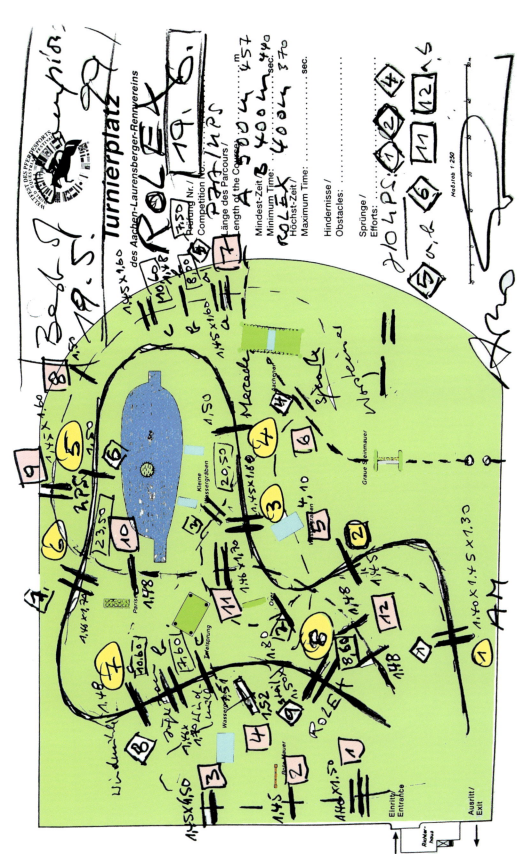

A4.13: *Rolex Best of Champions, CHIO Aachen 1999 (Course Designer: Arno Gego).*

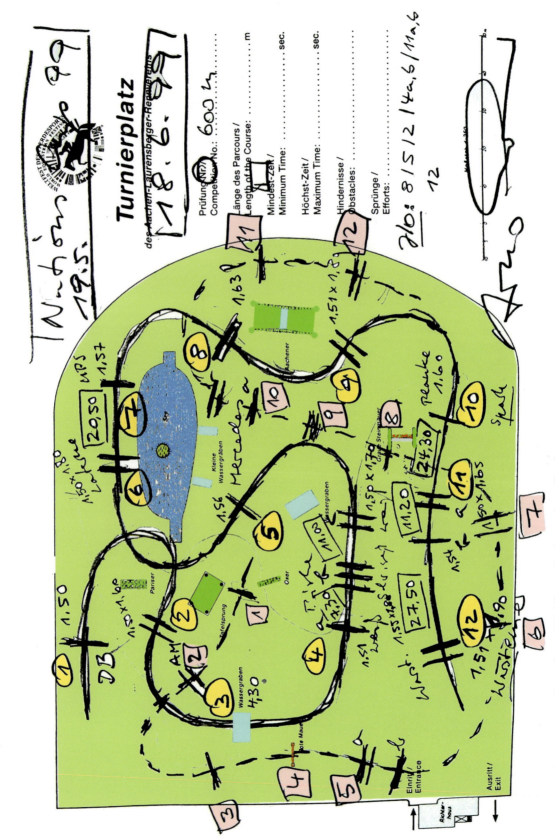

A4.14: *Nations Cup, CHIO Aachen 1999 (Course Designer: Arno Gego).*

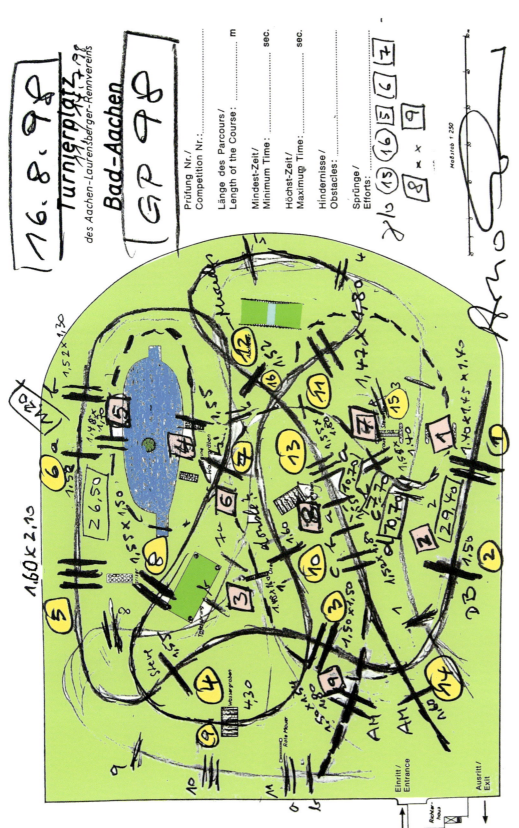

A4.15: *GRAND PRIX of Aachen, CHIO Aachen 1998 (Course Designer: Arno Gego).*

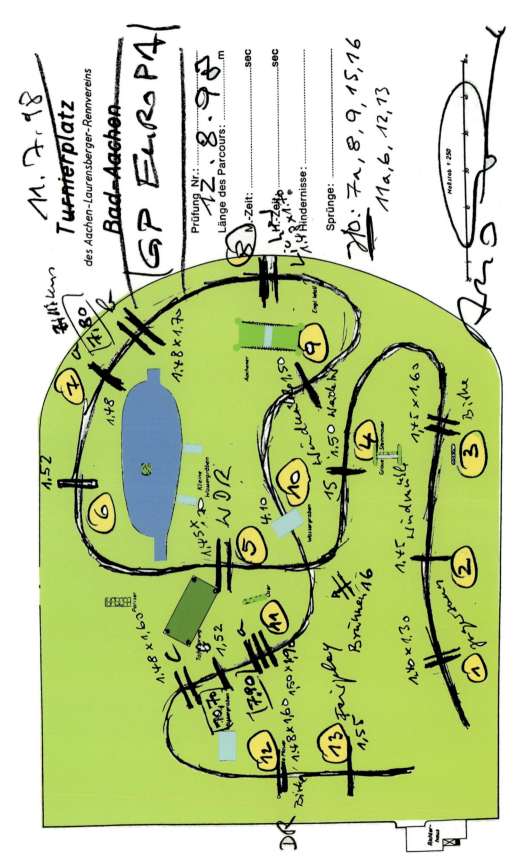

A4.16: *GRAND PRIX of Europe, CHIO Aachen 1998 (Course Designer: Arno Gego).*

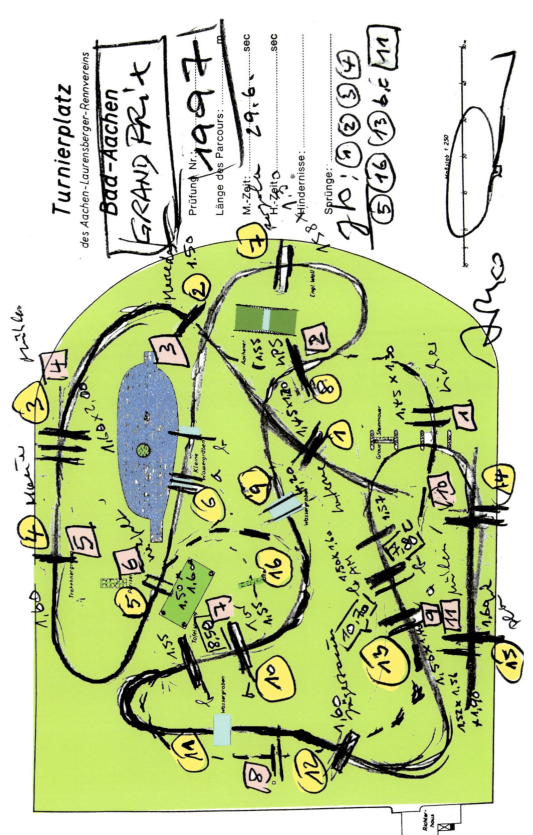

A4.17: *GRAND PRIX of Aachen, CHIO Aachen 1997 (Course Designer: Arno Gego).*

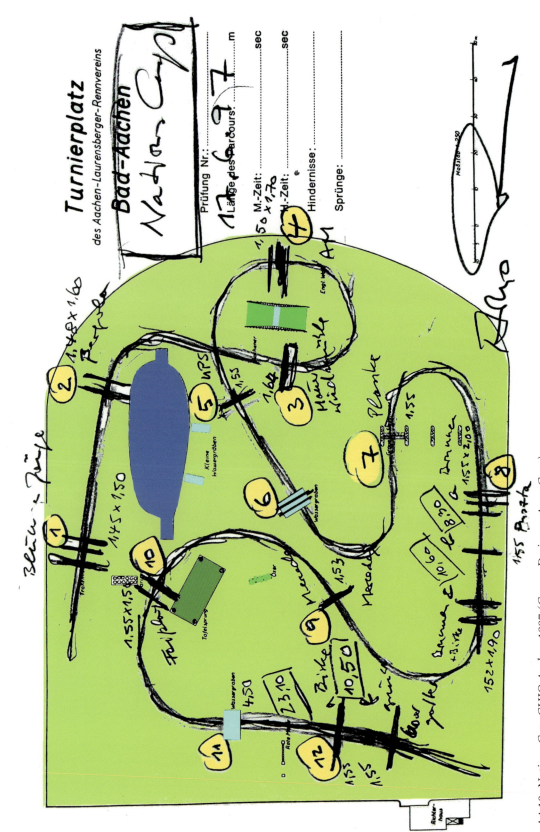

A4.18: *Nations Cup, CHIO Aachen 1997 (Course Designer: Arno Gego).*

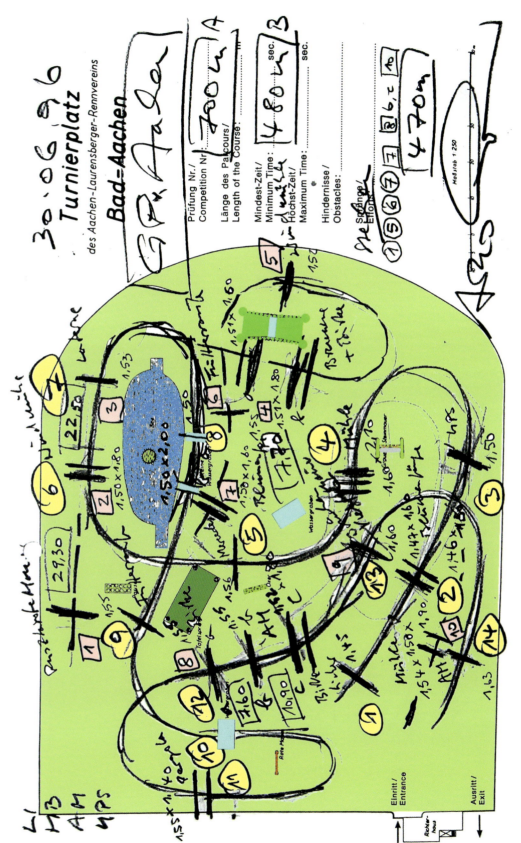

A4.19: *GRAND PRIX of Aachen, CHIO Aachen 1996 (Course Designer: Arno Gego).*

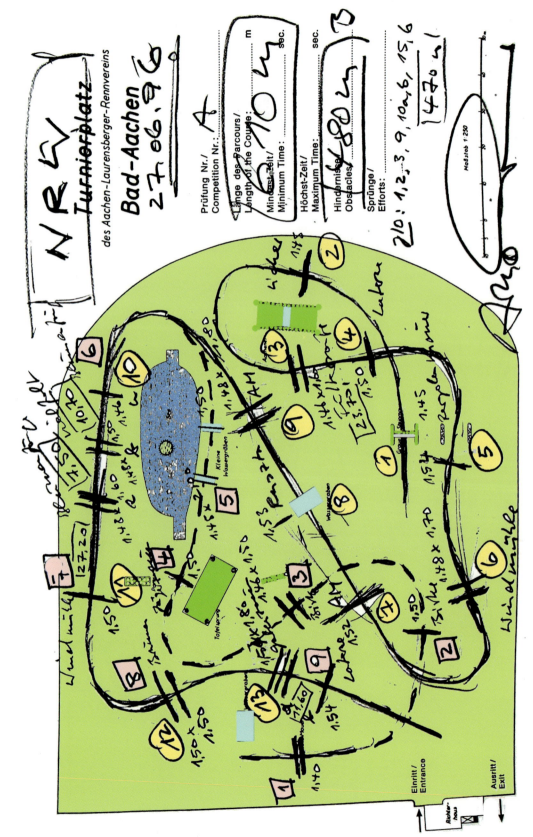

A4.20: *GRAND PRIX of Nord-Rhein-Westfalen, CHIO Aachen 1996 (Course Designer: Arno Gego).*

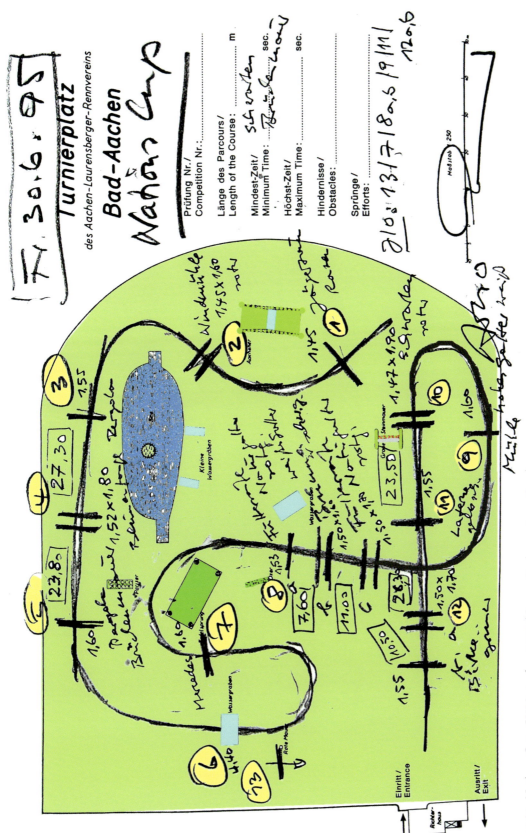

A4.21: *Nations Cup, CHIO Aachen 1995 (Course Designer: Arno Gego).*

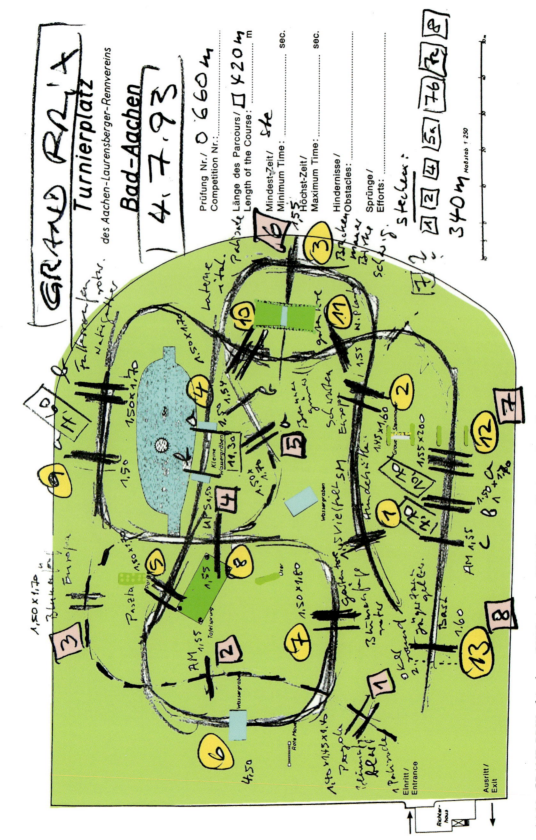

A4.22: *GRAND PRIX of Aachen, CHIO Aachen 1993 (Course Designer: Arno Gego).*

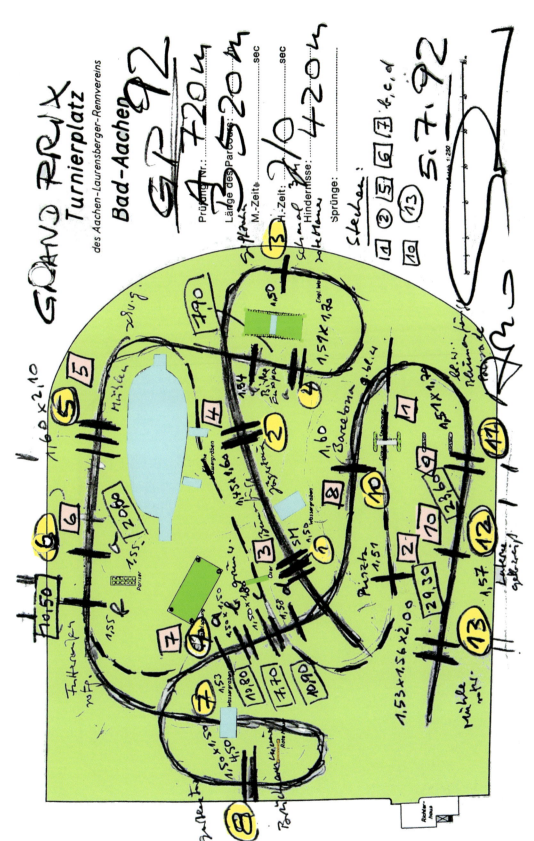

A4.23: *GRAND PRIX of Aachen, CHIO Aachen 1992 (Course Designer: Arno Gego).*

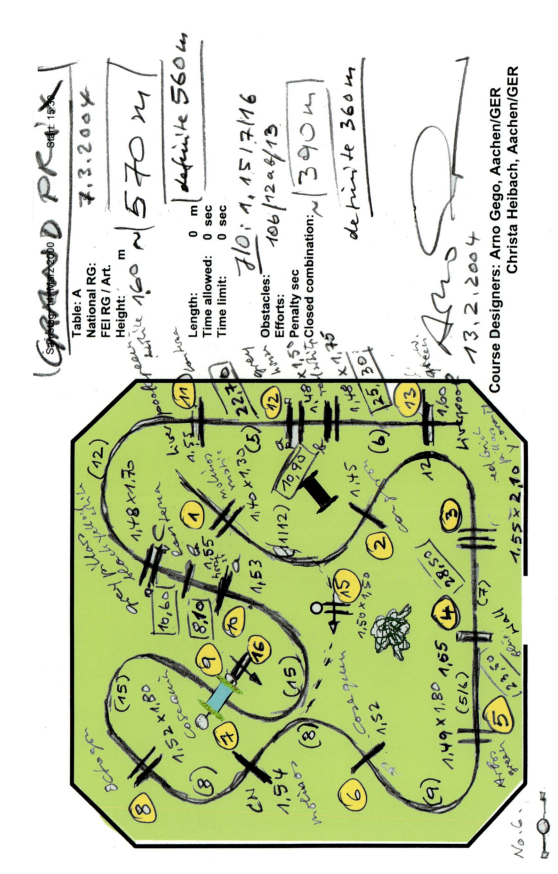

A4.24: *GRAND PRIX of Palm Beach, Winter Equestrian Festival 2004 (Course Designer: Arno Gego).*

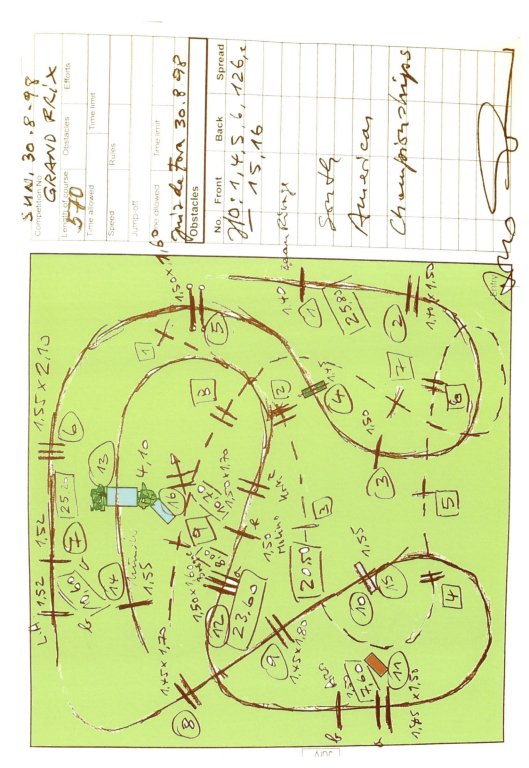

A4.25: *South American Championships 1998, GRAND PRIX (Course Designer: Arno Gego).*

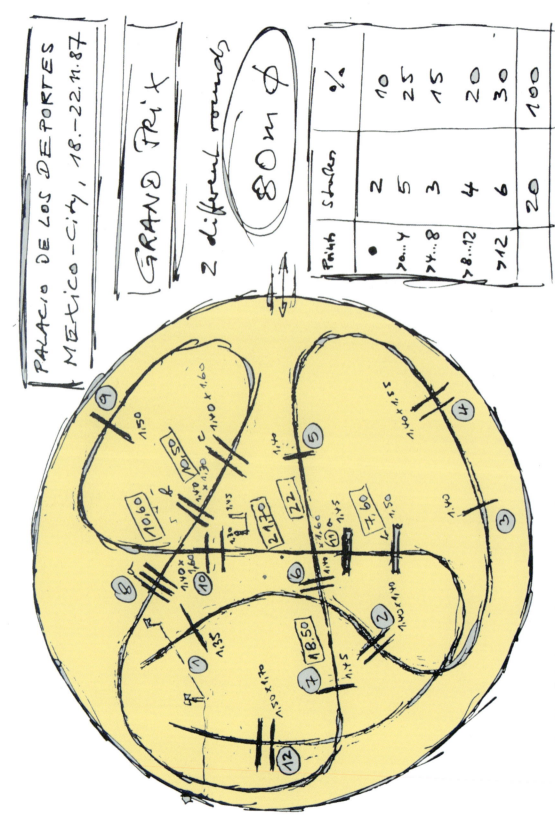

PALACIO DE LOS DEPORTES
MEXICO-City, 18.-22.11.87

GRAND PRIX

2 different rounds

80m ⌀

Faults	Strokes	%
•	2	10
>0...4	5	25
>4...8	3	15
>8...12	4	20
>12	6	30
	20	100

A4.26: GRAND PRIX of Mexico City, CSI Mexico City 1987 (Course Designer: Arno Gego).

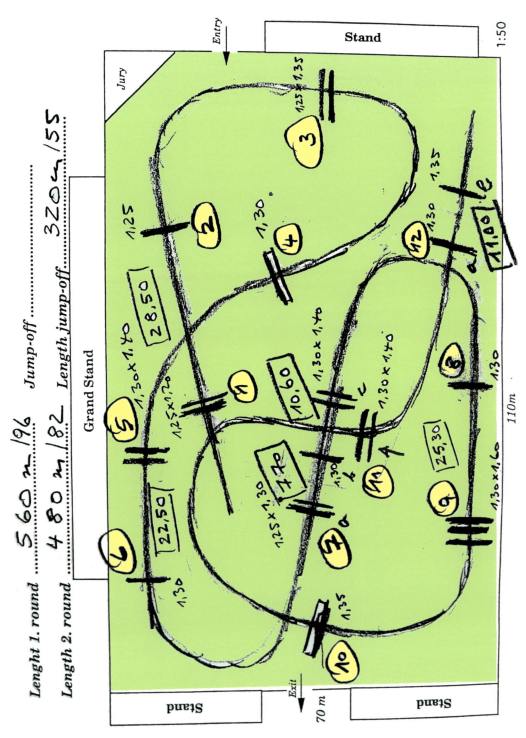

Lenght 1. round ..... 560 m /96 Jump-off ..... 320m /55

Length 2. round ..... 480 m /82 Length jump-off

1:50

A4.27: GRAND PRIX, Qatar Show Jumping 1997 (Course Designer: Arno Gego).

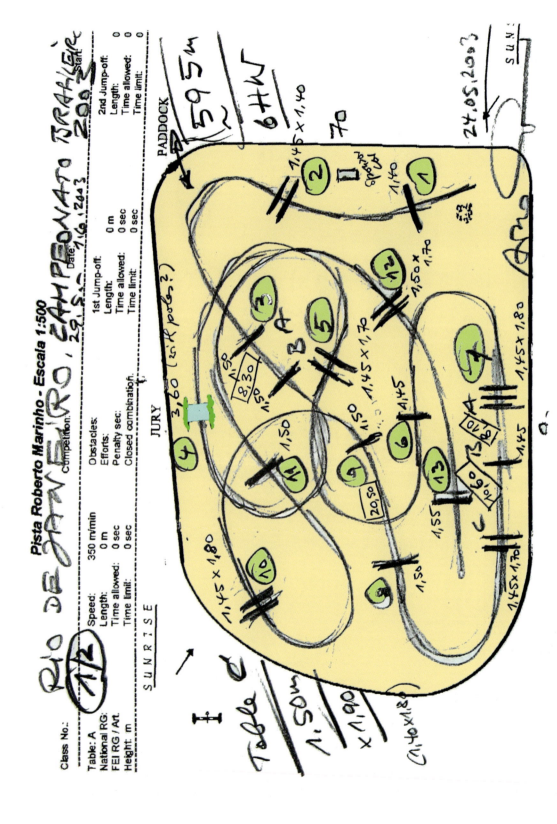

A4.28: *Brazilian Championships 2003, first qualifier (Course Designer: Arno Gego).*

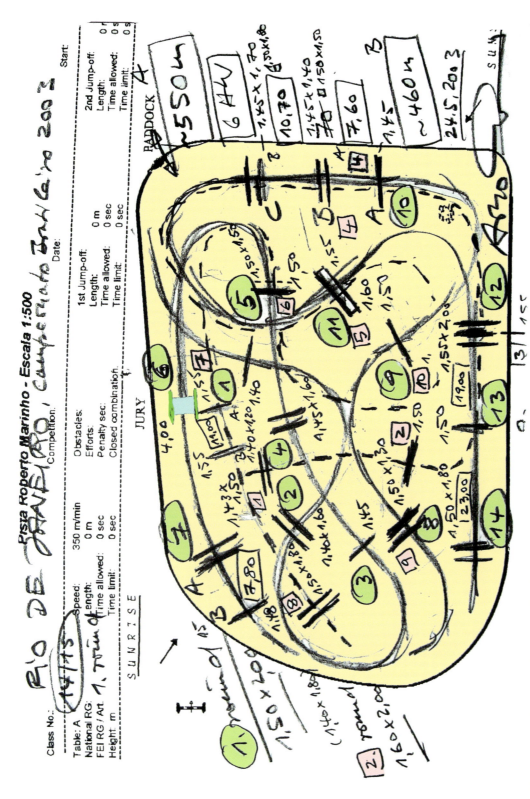

A4.29: *Brazilian Championships 2003, Final (Course Designer: Arno Gego).*

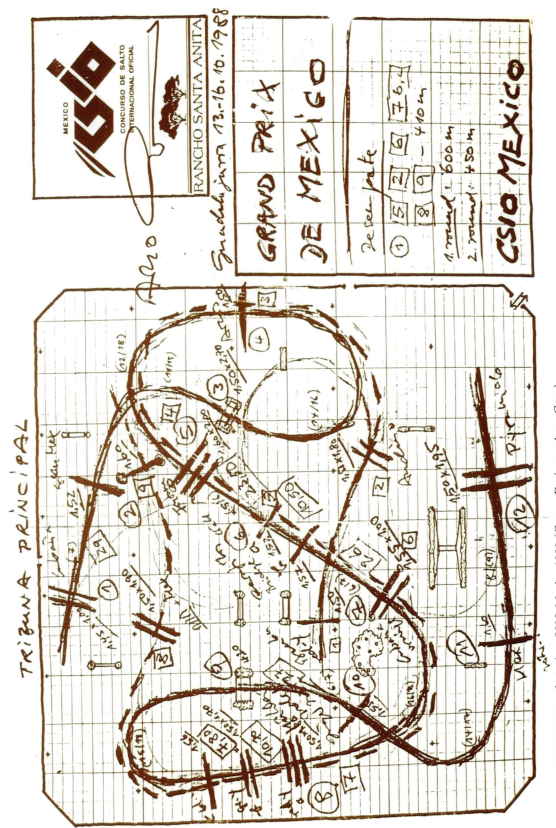

A4.30: *GRAND PRIX of Mexico, CSIO Mexico 1988 (Course Designer: Arno Gego).*

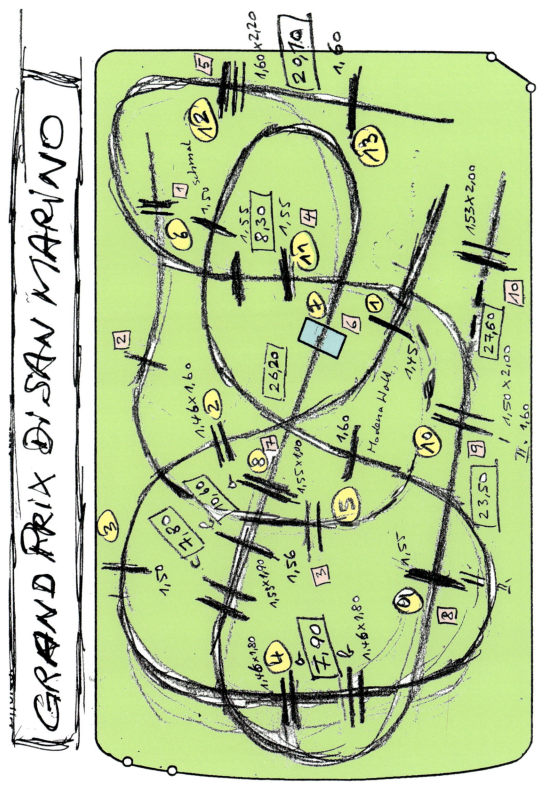

A4.31: GRAND PRIX di San Marino, first Pavarotti International 1991 (Course Designer: Arno Gego).

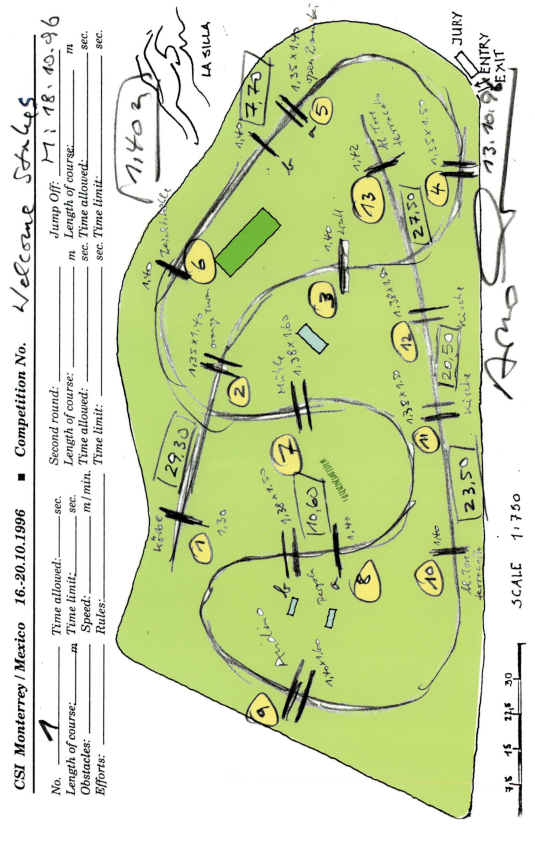

CSI Monterrey / Mexico   16.-20.10.1996   ■   Competition No.

Welcome Stakes

Jump Off: M: 18. 10. 96

No.	1		Second round:	
Length of course:	——— m	Time allowed:	——— sec.	Length of course: ——— m
Obstacles:		Time limit:	——— sec.	Time allowed: ——— sec.
Efforts:		Speed:	——— m/min.	Time limit: ——— sec.
		Rules:		

A4.32: *Welcome Stakes, CSI Monterrey 1996 (Course Designer: Arno Gego).*

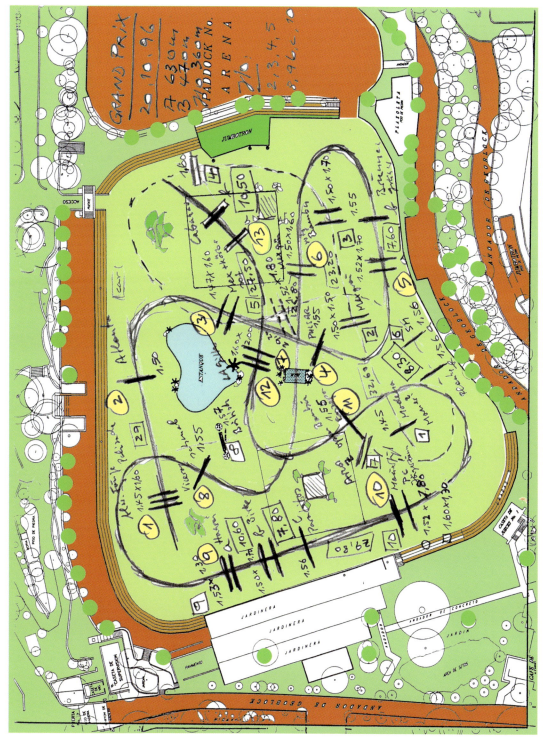

A4.33: GRAND PRIX of Monterrey, CSI Monterrey 1996 (Course Designer: Arno Gego).

A4.34: GRAND PRIX of Istanbul, Istanbul Horse Show 1998 (Course Designer: Arno Gego).

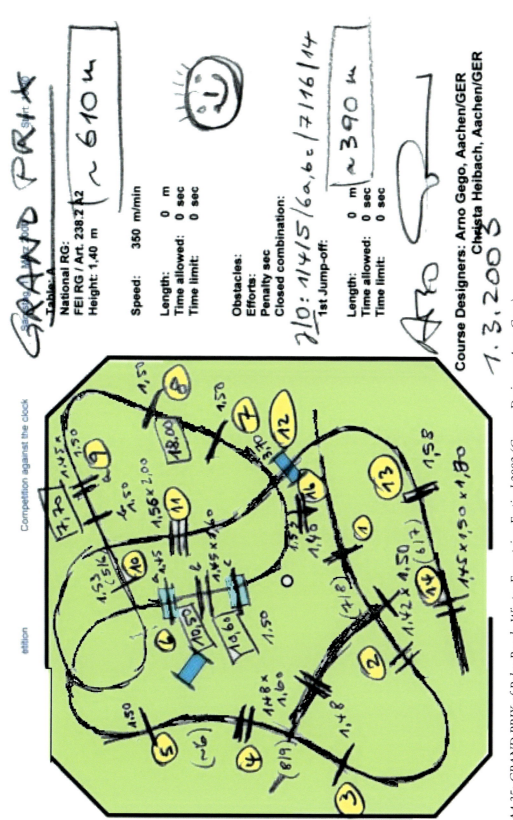

A4.35: *GRAND PRIX of Palm Beach, Winter Equestrian Festival 2002 (Course Designer: Arno Gego)* .

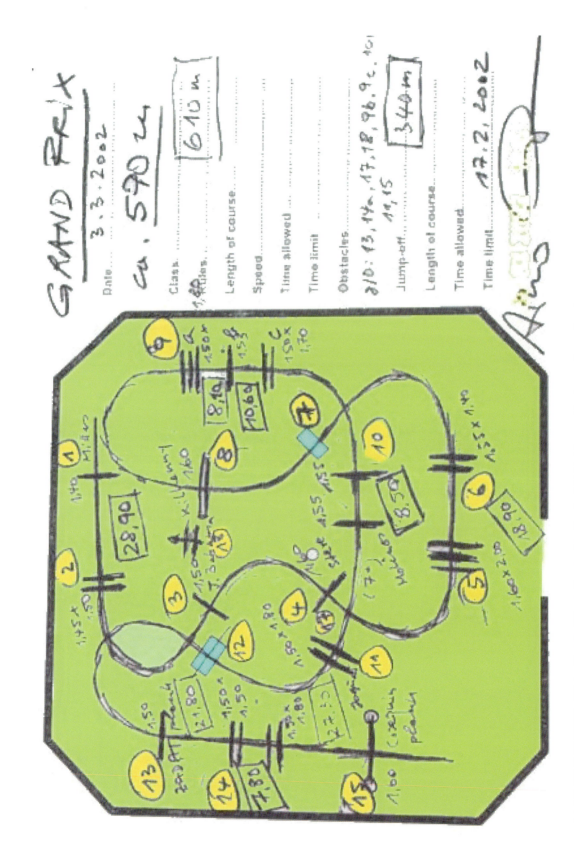

A4.36: *GRAND PRIX of Palm Beach, Winter Equestrian Festival 2003 (Course Designer: Arno Gego)* .

BIBLIOGRAPHY

[001] Adriani, Götz, Evelyn Benesch, Ingrid Brugger
PICASSO Figur und Portrait
2000 Kulturforum Wien/AUT
ISBN 3-932353-42-0

[002] Aebi, Ernst
Ein Querschnitt durch den Parcoursbau
ca. 1985 Parcoursbau-Kommission
Schweizerischer Reit- und Fahrsportverband,
Berne/SUI

[003] Allen, Linda
101 Jumping Exercises for Horse and Rider
2002 Storey Books, North Adams, MA/USA
ISBN 1-58017-465-5

[004] Allen, Linda
Clinic about Course Design – Olympic Games, Atlanta, 1996
CD-ROM, USA

[005] Allmeroth, Jörg
'Für das heutige Tennis würde ich kein Geld ausgeben' – Der große Björn Borg - über fehlende Ästhetik auf dem Centre-Court und das Phänomen Wimbledon - Interview
07/2003 No. 27, WELT AM SONNTAG, Springer Verlag, Hamburg/GER

[006] Amman, Max E.
Buchers Geschichte des Pferdesports
1976 Luzern/SUI
ISBN 3-7658-0223-9

[007] Amman, Max E.
The Top Events 1998, Show Jumping Outdoor
1998/99 L'ANNEE HIPPIQUE, BCM, Best,/NED

[008] Amman, Max E.
The Volvo World Cup – Twenty Years 1978 – 1998
1998 Geiger AG, Berne/SUI

[009] Amman, Max E.
The Horse in Outside Art
2003/2004 L'ANNEE HIPPIQUE, Eindhoven/NED

[010] Andreae, Hans-Joachim
Hindernisbau
1962 Verlag St. Georg, 2. Auflage, Düsseldorf/GER,

[011] Anesty, Susan, Max. E. Ammann
Ethics and the Equestrian Sports
1996/97 L'ANNEE HIPPIQUE, Best/NED

[012] Armstrong, Carol
Degas Skizzenbuch
2001, Stiebner Verlag, Munich/GER
ISBN 3-8307-0169-1

[013] Bahr, Gerhard.
Olympia 1956 in Stockholm 1956
1956 No. 2, Jahres-Sport-Meister, Nürnberg/GER

[014] Barber, Barrington
The Fundamentals of Drawing
2001 Arcturus Publishing Ltd., London /GBR
(4. edition)
ISBN 3-8112-2095-0

[015] Barnekow, Marten von
Die Ausbildung des Springpferdes
1950 2. Auflage, Verlag St. Georg, Neuss/GER

[016] Bartels, Joep
The ACADEMY – Global Dressage Forum
2002 Hooge Mierde/NED

[017] Basche, Arnim
Geschichte des Pferdes
1999 SIGLOCH EDITION, Deutschland
ISBN 3-89393-172-4

[018] Bazin, Germain
Geschichte der Gartenbaukunst
1990 Du Mont Buchverlag, Cologne/GER
ISBN 3-93366-01-1

[019] Beazky, Mitchell
The World Atlas of Architecture
1984 Octopus Publishing Group, London/GBR
ISBN 3-572-01302-X

[020] Becher, Rolf
Hindernisse, Parcours, Geländereiten
1982 FN-Verlag, Warendorf, ca. 1965, Eigen-Verlag

[021] Begunowa, Alla
*W ZWONKOM TOPOTE KOPYTPROSCHLOE
I NASTOJASCHTSCHOJE*
Im Klang der Pferdehufe – Über die Vergangenheit und
Gegenwart des russischen Pferdesports
1989 Moskwa, Fisikultura i Sport
ISBN 5-278-00078-3

[022] Beier, Harm-Eckart, Alfred Niesel, Heiner Pätzold
*Lehr-Taschenbuch für den Garten-, Landschafts- und
Sportplatzbau*
2003 Eugen Ulmer, Stuttgart/GER
ISBN 3-8001-4447-6

[023] Benderup, Bent, Eberhard Kern
*Barockes Reiten nach F.R. de la Guérinière. Über die
Ausbildung des Pferdes.*
2000 CADMOS Verlag, Lüneburg/GER
ISBN 3-86127-342-X

[024] Bernaerts, Gustave
Souvenirs Hippiques 1959
Fédération Royale Belge des Sports Equestres

[025] Beyer, Andreas, Markus Lohoff
*Bild und Erkenntnis – zur Funktion von "Bildhandeln"
und Anschaulichkeit in Wissenschaft und Technik*
2003 RWTH Themen, Nr. 2, Aachen University of
Technology, Aachen/GER

[026] Bissinger, Rudolf, Willy Haupts
500 Jahre Pferdesport in Aachen
1961 Limpert Verlag, Frankfurt/GER
Verlag-Nr.: 6137

[027] Boden, A.M. n J. Wimmer
Hippologisches Lexikon
1961 2. Auflage, Limpert-Verlag Berlin/GER

[028] Boulet, Jean-Claude
Vocabulaire multi-lingue du Cheval
1995 Bibliothèque Nationale du Canada, Québec
ISBN 2-9804600-1-X

[029] Boulet, Jean-Claude
Dictionaire multi-lingue du Cheval (français, english,
español)
1995 Bibliothèque Nationale du Canada, Québec
ISBN 2-9804600-1

[030] Brand, Salli *et. al.*
The Ultimate Book of Paint Effects
2000 Merehurst Ltd. London/GBR
ISBN 817-2635-4453-6271

[031] Brunnert, Andreas
*Entwurf, Berechnung und Bau einer Testeinrichtung für
Sicherheits-Auflagen (Safety-Cups)*
1998 Aachen University of Technology, Aachen/GER

[032] Carruthers, Pamela
'Show Jumping Courses' *in Designing Courses and
Obstacles*
1978 John H. Fritz, Houghton, Mifflin Company,
Boston
ISBN 0-395-26304-02

[033] Catoir, Barbara
Miró auf Mallorca
1995 Prestel, Munich, London, New York

[034] Clifford, Derek
History of Gardens
1962 Faber and Faber, London/GBR

[035] Coldrey, Christopher
Courses for Horses
1991 Revised Edition, J.A.Allen, London/GBR
ISBN 0-85131-541-0

[036] Compton, Susan
Marc Chagall – Mein Leben – Mein Traum
1997 Prestel Munich/GER
ISBN 3-7913-1419-X

[037] Cooper, Guy, Gordon Taylor
Moderne Paradiese – Private Gärten unserer Zeit
1997 Deutsche Verlags-Anstalt, Stuttgart/GER
ISBN 3-421-03152-5

[038] Cooper, Guy, Gordon Taylor
Gardens for the Future – Gestures against the wild
1997 Conran Octopus, Ltd. London/GBR

[039] Cortesi, Isotta
Parcs Publics, paysages 1985-2000
2000 Actes Sud/Motta, Arles/FRA
ISBN 2-7427-2854-6

[040] Csete, Gabor
A Lovaspálya (Course Design)
1996 Horváth Jenö/HUN
ISBN 963-04-8079-4

[041] Decker, Wolfgang
Sport und Spiel im alten Ägypten
1987 Verlag Oscar Beck, Munich/GER
ISBN 3-406-31575-5

[042] Dossenbach, Monique, Hans D. Dossenbach
König Pferd
1989 Bechtermünz Verlag/GER
ISBN 3-8289-1568-X

[043] Dragisie, Milena
Art and Life belong to Horses
2003/2004 L'ANNEE HIPPIQUE, Einhoven/NED

[044] Droste, Magdalena
Bauhaus, 1919-1933
2002 TASCHEN-Verlag, Cologne/GER
ISBN 3-8228-2102-0

[045] Düchting, Hajo
Paul Klee, Malerei und Musik
2001 Prestel, Munich/GER, London/GBR, New York/USA
ISBN 3-7913-1853-5

[046] Edwards, Betty
Zeichnen Lernen – Die Befreiung unserer schärfsten Gestaltungs-Kräfte (The New Drawing on the Right Side of the Brain – A Course in Enhancing Creativity and Artistic Confidence)
2000 Rowohlt Verlag GmbH, Hamburg/GER
(insgesamt 20. Auflage, davon 17 in USA)
ISBN 3-498-01669-5

[047] Eller-Rüter, Ulrika-Maria
KANDINSKY - Bühnenhauskomposition und Dichtung als Realisation seines Synthese-Konzepts
1990 Georg Olms AG, Hildesheim/GER
ISBN 3-487-09387-1

[048] d'Endrödy, A.L.
Give Your Horse a Chance
First published 1959, 8 reprints
1999 J.A. Allen Ltd., London/GBR
ISBN 0-85131-741-3

[049] Enthöfer, Anke
Umgestaltung der Reitanlage Weissenfelde – Diplom-Arbeit
2003 Fachbereich Landschafts-Architektur Fachhochschule Osnabrück/GER

[050] Fehlau, Ria
Traumberufe rund ums Pferd
1993 Kosmos Verlag, Stuttgart/GER
ISBN 3-440-06673-8

[051] Ferreira, Renyldo
História Do Hipismo Brasileiro
1999 Brazilian Equestrian Federation, Rio de Janeiro/BRA

[052] Ferrier, Jean-Louis
Paul Klee
2001 Finest S.A./Edition Pierre Terrail, Paris/FRA
ISBN 3-89836-193-4

[053] Fischer, Ernst Peter
Gäste der Wissenschaft ('ohne Ästhetik keine Ethik')
2003 Zeitschrift "Forschung und Lehre" des Deutschen Hochschul-Verbandes
Ausgabe 11/2003, Bonn/GER

[054] Friell, Charlotte, Peter Friell
Graphic Design for the 21st Century
2003 TASCHEN-Verlag, Cologne/GER
ISBN 3-8228-1605-1

[055] Gandhi, Mahatma
Die Kraft der Wahrheit – In Worten und Gedanken
1999 Benno Verlag, Leipzig/GER
ISBN 3-7462-1325-8

[056] Gego, Arno, Hauke Schmidt
Parcours-Gestaltung
1982 FN-Verlag, Warendorf/GER
ISBN 3-88542-013-9

[057] Gego, Arno, Hauke Schmidt
Hindernisse und Hindernisteile
1979 FN-Verlag, Warendorf/GER

[058] Gego, Arno
The Art of Course Design
2003 Practical Horseman, Vol. XXXI, No. 6, June 2003, PRIMEDIA PUBLICATION,
Editor: Mandy Lorraine, Unionsville, PA, USA

[059] Gego, Arno
Merkblatt für Parcours-Chefs
1977 Aachen/GER

[060] Gego, Arno
Anmerkungen zur Entwicklung des Parcoursbaus
2003 Mitteilungsblatt der Deutschen
Richtervereinigung für
Pferdeleistungsprüfungen e.V., Nr. 145, Warendorf/GER

[061] Gego, Arno
*Collection of the Design of New Stadiums and Natural
Obstacles*
1994 Aachen/GER

[062] Gego, Arno
CSI Monterrey – Paper for Discussion
1994 Monterrey/MEX

[063] Gego, Arno
CSI Valkenswaard – Report
1994 Aachen/GER

[064] Gego, Arno
Documentation of an FEI-Seminar on Course Design
2003 Canberra/AUS

[065] Gego, Arno
*Information about the Jumping Competitions, Los
Angeles/USA*
GAMES OF THE XXIII OLYMPIAD
1984 Report to the FEI, Berne/SUI

[066] Gego, Arno
JUEGOS DEPORTIVOS PANAMERICANOS
Documentation about the Jumping Competitions
1983 Caracas/VEN

[067] Gego, Arno
Parcours-Design CHIO Aachen
Unpublished Study
2001/2002 Aachen/GER

[068] Gego, Arno
PAVAROTTI INTERNATIONAL, CSIO SAN MARINO
1991 Report to PULSAR INTERNACIONAL S.A. de
C.V.,
Monterrey/MEX

[069] Gego, Arno
*Séminaire 'COURSE DESIGN'– FEI, à l'occasion du
CSIO LA BAULE*
2002 La Baule/FRA

[070] Gego, Arno
Summary Report of the Technical Delegate:
WORLD CUP FINAL, Tampa/Florida/USA/04/1989
1989 Report to the FEI, Berne/SUI

[071] Gego, Arno
WORLD JUMPING CHAMPIONSHIPS, Aachen
1986 Documentation, Aachen/GER

[072] Griesbauer, Judith M. – Manfred Kröplien
Vom Bauhaus.....
1992 Edition Cantz, Stuttgart/GER
ISBN 3-89322-383-5

[073] Grillo, Gabriela
'The history of riding to music'
Publication in: *The World Cup Dressage. The first ten
years.*
1995 Dr. Joep Bartels, BCM, Best/NED

[074] Grube, Frank, Gerhard Richter
Pferdesport
1975 Hoffmann und Campe Verlag, Hamburg/GER
ISBN 3-455-08976-3

[075] de la Guérinière, François Robinchon
Ecole de Cavalerie
1733 Versailles/FRA
School of Horsmanship (English translation)
1994 J.A. Allen Ltd., London/GBR
ISBN 0-85131-575-5

[076] Harrison, Hazel
Drawing with Pencils and Pastels
1999 Lorenz Books/GBR
ISBN 3-332-01061-1

[077] Heibach, Christa, Arno Gego
Selection Trials for the Olympic Games Athens 2004
Aachen/GER 12.-15.06.2003
2003 Summary Report

[078] Hoffmann, Gerlinde, Hans-Dieter Wagner
Reitanlagen – und Stall-Bau
1992 FN-Verlag, Warendorf/GER
ISBN 3-88542-243-5

[079] Hoffmann, Gerlinde, Hans-Dieter Wagner
Orientierungshilfen, Reitanlagen – und Stall-Bau
2001 FN-Verlag, Deutsche Reiterliche Vereinigung,
Warendorf/GER
ISBN 3-88542-243-3

[080] Hogarth, Burne
Hogarth's Zeichenschule
2001 TASCHEN-Verlag, Köln/GER
ISBN 3-8228-1614-0

[081] Hounour, Hugh, John Fleming
Weltgeschichte der Kunst
2000 Prestel Verlag, Munich/GER, London/GBR, New York/USA
ISBN 3-7913-2425-X

[083] Isenbart, Hans-Heinrich
Das Königreich des Pferdes
1983 6. Auflage, Verlag Bucher, Luzern/SUI
ISBN 3-7658-0413-4

[084] Jolicoeur, Robert, Robert Murphy
Progress Report No. 2 on Footing Research
L.I.F.E. – List of International Footing Experts
1997 Montréal/CAN

[085] Joray, Marcel
Vasarely I–IV
1974 Editions du Griffon, Neuchâtel/SUI

[086] Kadatz, Hans-Joachim
Lexikon der Architektur
2001 Seemann Verlag, Leipzig/GER
ISBN 3-363-00613-6

[087] Kandinsky, Wassily
Du Theâtre
1999 Du Mont Buchverlag, Cologne/GER
ISBN 3-7701-4702-2

[088] Kandinsky, Wassily
Über das Geistige in der Kunst
2004 revidierte Neuauflage, 1952 Nina Kandinsky, Neuilly-Sur-Seine/FRA
ISBN 3-7165-1326-1

[089] Klimke, Reiner, Werner Ernst
Olympia der Reiter – Barcelona 1992
1992 FN-Verlag der Deutschen Reiterlichen Vereinigung GmbH, Warendorf/GER
ISBN 3-88542-253-0 / 3-7843-2513-0

[090] Klimke, Reiner, Frantisek Jandl, Werner Lutz
Reiterspiele Mexico 1968 – Olympiade
1968 Aschendorff – Verlag, Münster/GER

[091] Kohle, Hubertus, Katja Kwastek
Computer, Kunst und Kunstgeschichte
2000 Deubner Verlag, Cologne/GER
ISBN 3-937111-01-8

[092] Kühnst, Peter
SPORT – Eine Kulturgeschichte im Spiegel der Kunst
1996 Verlag der Kunst, Dresden/GER
ISBN 90-5705-001-3

[093] Kurras, Lotte
Das Große Buch der Turniere
Alle 36 Glanzvollen Ritterfeste des Mittelalters
1996 Beizer AG, Stuttgart/GER und Zürich/SUI
ISBN 3-7630-5633-5

[094] Le Corbusier
Mein Werk – Mon Oeuvre
2001 Fondation Le Corbusier, Paris, Hatje Crantz Verlag, Ostfildern/GER
ISBN 3-7757-1072-8

[095] Legat, Jean
La piste est-elle prête? – Souvenirs Hippiques 1959
1959 Fédération Royale Belge des Sports Equestres

[096] Lenz, Helmut
Auf Olympischem Parcours
1989 4. Auflage, VEB Deutscher Landwirtschaftsverlag, DDR, Berlin
ISBN 3-331-00513-4

[097] Lichtner-Hoyer, Peter
Cavaletti-Training
1985 Müller-Verlag, Zürich/SUI
ISBN 3-275-00864-1

[098] Linkenbach, Hermann
Olympische Reiterkämpfe, London, 1948
1948 St. Georg Kunstverlag, Düsseldorf/GER

[099] Llewellyn, Jean
SAUMUR – City of the Horse
1999/2000 L'ANNEE HIPPIQUE, BCM; Best/NED

[100] Lloyd Jones, David
Architektur und Ökologie – Zeitgenössische Bioklimatische Bauten
1998 Deutsche Verlagsanstalt, Stuttgart/GER
ISBN 3-421-03155-X

[101] Lütteken, Karsten
Vergleichende Video-gestützte 2D-Bewegungs-Analyse von Reiter-Pferd-Kombinationen der Weltelite beim Springreiten 'CHIO Aachen, Diplom-Arbeit
2001 Deutsche Sporthoch-Schule, Cologne/GER

[102] Mader, Günter
'Gartenkunst des 20. Jahrhunderts'
Garten- und Landschafts-Architektur in Deutschland
1999 Deutsche Verlags-Anstalt, Stuttgart/GER
ISBN 3-421-03200-9

[103] Maur, Karin von
Vom Klang der Bilder (About sound of paintings)
1999 Prestel, Munich/GER, London/GBR, New York/USA
ISBN 3-7913-2098-X (Deutsche Ausgabe)
ISBN 3-7913-2082-3 (English Edition)

[104] de Menten de Horne, Chevalier H.
Souvenirs Hippiques 1960/61
1961 Fédération Royale Belge des Sports Equestres

[105] Meyer, Wolfgang
Unveröffentlichte Messungen über Flugkurven, Tempo, Absprung- und Lande-Distanzen – Studie in Zusammenarbeit mit Arno Gego
2002/2003 Diehlo/GER

[106] Meyer zu Hartum, Christine
Kunst kommt von Können,
2004 St. Georg, No. 2, Hamburg/GER

[107] Mielke, Rita, Wilhelm Stein
Aachen-World Equestrian Festival 1898–1998 – Germany
1998 Project Co-ordination Arno Gego
ISBN 96-5433-115-1

[108] Montanerella, Lucia
'The Maestro' – Marcello Mastronardi
2003/2004 L'ANNEE HIPPIQUE, Eindhoven/NED

[109] Morgen, Wilhelm
Parcours-Pläne zum 11. Internationalen Reit-, Spring und Fahrturnier. Persönliche Aufzeichnungen
1935 CHIO Aachen/GER

[110] Morscheck, Karl-Heinz
Federzeichnungen
2000 Englisch Verlag, Wiesbaden/GER
ISBN 3-8241-0978-6

[111] Mossdorf, Carl Friedrich
Kavallerieschule Hannover
1986 FN-Verlag, Warendorf

[112] Mossdorf, Carl Friedrich
Preis der Nationen – 30 deutsche Teilnahmen von 1952 bis 1956
1957 Sonderheft des REITER UND FAHRER MAGAZIN,
Kornett Verlag, Verden/Aller/GER

[113] Muñoz de las Casas, Jaime
EL JEFE DE PISTA
1965 Edition Muñoz, Madrid/ESP
ISBN 84-605-4498-2

[114] de Némethy, Bertalan
The de Némethy Method
1988 Doubleday Group, New York/USA
ISBN 0-385-23620-4

[115] de Némethy, Bertalan
Bertalan de Némethy's Impressions,
World Cup Final, Gothenburg/SWE, 1988
1988/89 L'ANNEE HIPPIQUE, Best/NED

[116] de Némethy, Bertalan
The Technical Delegate Views Aachen – World Jumping Championships 1986
1986/87 L'ANNEE HIPPIQUE, Best/NED

[117] Newsum, Gilliam
Educating, training and legislation to create a better world for the Horse
2001/2002 L'ANNEE HIPPIQUE, Best/NED

[118] Nickel, Eckhart
DAS GROSSE EGAL – Essay
07/2003 GQ Gentlemen's World, Condé Nast Verlag GmbH, Munich/GER

[119] Nicolaisen, Dörte
Das andere Bauhaus
1996/97 Berlin/GER
ISBN 389-181-406-2

[120] N.N. (Author unknown)
Art et Métiers du Cheval – Kunst und Pferd
2003/2004 L'ANNEE HIPPIQUE
Eindhoven/NED

[121] N.N.
100 Jahre Tour de France
2003 Deutscher Sportverlag, Cologne/GER

[122] N.N.
Achse, Rad und Wagen – Beiträge zur Geschichte der Landfahrzeuge 2.
1992 Museum Bergische Achsenfabrik, Wiehl/GER
ISBN 3-88265-177

[123] N.N.
Architecture
2001 The Pepin Press, Amsterdam/NED
ISBN 90-5496-077-9

[124] N.N.
Area of Individual Experience in Different Sports
1992 Soko Institut/EMNID
Deutsches Sportfernsehen Medienforschung,
Sport-Freund-Studie

[125] N.N.
Code of Ethics of Engineers, In: Guide of Consultants
2003 ASAE – The Society for Engineering in Agricultural,
Food and Biological Systems, St. Josephs,
Minnesota/USA

[126] N.N.
Equestrian Sport Fact Sheet and Official Result Book
2000 The GAMES OF THE XXVII OLYMPIAD,
Sydney/AUS

[127] N.N.
FEI-Code of Conduct for the Welfare of the Horse
2003 FEI-Bulletin 4/2003, Lausanne/SUI

[128] N.N.
Heeres-Dienst-Vorschrift (HDV 12)
1912 Deutsche Heeres-Reit-Schule Reitvorschrift,
Reprint 1937 und 1983 Verlag Mittler, Herford/GER
ISBN 3-8132-0171-6

[129] N.N.
Contribution of the 'International League for the Protection of Horses, ILPH',
2001/2002 L'ANNEE HIPPIQUE, Best/NED

[130] N.N.
Deutsches Spring-, Dressur- und Fahr-Derby
1965 Eigen-Verlag, Hamburg/GER
Norddeutscher und Flottbecker Reiterverein

[131] N.N.
Dinner for Architects
Servietten-Skizzen für das Architektur-Museum in der
Pinakothek der Moderne in München (10.04.-
18.05.2003)
2003 Deutsche Verlags-Anstalt, Stuttgart-München/GER
ISBN 3-421-03472-9

[132] N.N.
FAIR PLAY AND EQUESTRIAN SPORT
General Assembly, FEI
1999 Doha/QATAR

[133] N.N.
LPO-Leistungsprüfungs-Ordnung
2000 FN-Verlag, Deutsche Reiterliche Vereinigung,
Warendof/GER

[134] N.N.
Marktanalyse Pferdesportler in Deutschland
2001 IPSOS, GER

[135] N.N.
SANKT GEORG, Deutsche Sportzeitung
1927 Berlin/GER, Nr. 14

[136] N.N.
Show Jumping
1953 British Show Jumping Association
Foreward by: Col. M.P. Ansell, Chairman and
International Course Designer

[137] N.N.
The Bain Report: The Equestrian Sport within the Olympic Movement, Sponsored by Alfonso
Romo/Mexico and presented to the FEI General
Assembly in Rio de Janeiro, 03/1993
1993/94 L'ANNEE HIPPIQUE, Best/NED

[138] N.N.
Universal-Lexikon der Kunst
2001 Gondrom Verlag, Bindlach/GER

[139] van Ommen Guijlik, J.H.
Het parcours is vrijgegeven
1962 Dé Hoefslag, Den Haag/NED

[140] Otte, Michaela
Geschichte des Reitens – von der Antike bis zur Neuzeit
1994 FN-Verlag Warendorf/GER
ISBN 3-88542-255-7

[141] Palacios, Leopoldo
The Evolution of Course Design
1999/2000 L'ANNEE HIPPIQUE, Best/NED

[142] Palacios, Leopoldo
SYDNEY 2000, OLYMPIC GAMES
2000 Documentation about the Jumping Competitions, Caracas/VEN

[143] Pavarotti, Luciano
Gesangs-Examen an der Opera di Modena
05/1991 Modena/ITA

[144] Petersen, Olaf
The Volvo World Cup Twenty Years 1978–1998
1988/1999 L'ANNEE HIPPIQUE, Best/NED

[145] Petersen, Olaf
Parcoursreiten, Parcoursbau und – Gestaltung
1999 St. Georg, Video,
Copyright/Sales: Waldhausen, Cologne/GER

[146] Petersen, Olaf
Course Building during morning silence – Jumping in Seoul
1988/89 L'ANNEE HIPPIQUE, Best/NED

[147] Petersen, Olaf
Olympia der Reiter –Seoul
1988 FN Verlag Warendorf/GER
ISBN 3-88542-199-2

[148] Petersen, Olaf
World Equestrian Games, Stockholm/SWE, 1990 – Documentation Show Jumping
1990 Münster/GER

[149] Petersen, Olaf
Olympic Games Seoul/Korea – Documentation of the Course Designer for the Jumping Competitions
1990 Münster/GER

[150] Pevsner, Nikolaus, Hugh Honour, John Fleming
Lexikon der Weltarchitektur
1992 Prestel-Verlag, 3. Auflage, Munich/GER
ISBN 3-7913-2095-5

[151] Phillips, Tom
Music in Art
1998 Prestel-Verlag Munich/GER, London/GBR, New York/USA
ISBN 3-7913-1864-0

[152] Popp, Birgit
Preserving the Future of the Baroque – The Spanish Riding School and the Austrian Federal Stud Farm at Piber
2003/2004 L'ANNEE HIPPIQUE, Eindhoven/NED

[153] Prette, Maria Carla, Alfonso de Giorgis
Was ist Kunst n Leggere L'ARTE – Storia, Linguaggi, Epoche, Stili (ital. Original-Title)
1999 Giunti Gruppo Edizionale, Florenz/ITA
2000 Deutsche Ausgabe

[154] Podhajsky, Alois
Die klassische Reitkunst:
Reitlehre von den Anfängen bis zur Vollendung
1998 KOSMOS-Verlag, Stuttgart/GER
ISBN 3-440-07527-3

[155] Riese, Brigitte
Seemanns kleines Kunst-Lexikon
2001 E.A. Seemann Verlag, Leipzig/GER
ISBN 3-363-00612-8

[156] Schels, Walter, Sabine Schwabenthan
Die Seele der Tiere
2000 Mosaik-Verlag, München/GER
ISBN 3-576-11376-2

[157] Schneider, Helga
Die Nutzung, Planung und Modifikation des Baus einer Gelände-Strecke für den Reitsport
2002 Diplom-Arbeit, Deutsche Sport-Hochschule, Cologne/GER

[158] Schnitzer, Ulrich
Reitanlagen
1970 KTBL, Frankfurt/GER

[159] Schöbel, Heinz
Olympia und seine Spiele
2000 Econ Ullstein List Verlag, Sportverlag Berlin/GER
ISBN 3-328-00866-7

[160] Seunig, Waldemar
Von der Koppel bis zur Kapriole
1960 Freetz & Wasmuth Verlag AG, Zürich/SUI

[161] Sluyter, Frits
Welfare of Horses in FEI Competitions
2003/2004 L'ANNEE HIPPIQUE, Eindhoven/NED

[162] Stecken, Albert, Reiner Klimke, Helmut Müller
München 1972 – Olympische Reiterspiele
1972 Aschendorff Verlag, Münster/GER
ISBN 3-402-06371-9

[163] Steinbrecht, Gustav
Das Gymnasium des Pferdes
2001 Cosmos Verlag, Lüneburg/GER
ISBN 3-86127-357-8

[164] Steiner, Rudolf
Wandtafelzeichnungen 1919–1924
1999 Kunsthaus Zürich/SUI
ISBN 3-7701-5057-0

[165] Steinhart, Matthias
Töpferkunst und Meisterzeichnung
1996 Verlag von Zabern, Mainz/GER
ISBN 3-8053-1896-0

[166] Steinkraus, William
Riding and Jumping
1961 Doubleday, Inc., New York/USA
ISBN 3-275-004-476

[167] Stierlin, Henri, Dietrich Wildung
Weltarchitektur
2001 TASCHEN Verlag, Köln/GER
JSBN 3-8228-1224-2

[168] Stürzebecher, Peter, Sigrid Ulrich
Architecture for Sport
2002 Wiley-Academy, Chichester/GBR
ISBN 0-470-84698-4

[169] Summerhay, R.S.
Show-Jumpers, Horses and Ponies in Pictures
ca. 1965 J.A. Allen, London/GBR

[170] Swaffield, Simon
Theory in Lanscape Architecture
2002 University of Pennsylvania, Press,
Philadelphia/USA
ISBN 0-8122-1821-3

[171] The German Equestrian Federation
Olympia der Reiter 1984
1984 pro Sport GmbH, Munich/GER
ISBN 3-88181-007-2

[172] The German Equestrian Federation
Olympia der Reiter – Atlanta 1996
1996 FN-Verlag, Warendorf/GER
ISBN 3-88542-282-4

[173] The German Equestrian Federation
Sport Equestre 1980 – MOCKBA – GOODWOOD – ROTTERDAM – FONTAINEBLEAU - WINDSOR
1980 pro Sport GmbH, München/GER

[174] Trees, Wolfgang, Arthur Stürmann
Soers
1987 Triangel-Verlag, Aachen/GER
ISBN 3-922974-03-1

[175] Tupitsyn, Margarita
EL LISSITZKY – Jenseits der Abstraktion
1999 Schirmer/Mosel, Munich/GER
ISBN 3-88814-917-7

[176] Veltjens–Otto-Erley, Catharina
Olympic Equestrian Games – Sydney 2000
2000 The German Equestrian Federation,
Warendorf/GER
ISBN 3-88542-368-5

[177] Voorn, Albert
Albert Voorn francophile – Interview on Olympic
Jumping
2003 GRAND PRIX No. 18, Paris/FRA

[178] Voorn, Albert
Keep horses naturally – Interview, Calgary, Alberta/CAN
2000 November, Nr. 47, Breeding News,

[179] Vos, Marinus, Daan Nanning, Christel ter Horst
Parcoursbouw en Springtraining
2001 Tirion Uitgevers BV, Baarn/NED
ISBN 9-05210-441-7

[180] Weis, Richard
The Feel Factor – Contribution to the Art of Riding
09/2003 HORSE INTERNATIONAL, BCM
Eindhoven/NED

[181] Wimmer, Joachim
Reiter-Olympia Rom 1960
1960 *Pferd und Reiter* – Die Peitsche, Ausgabe Oktober
1960,
Limpert-Verlag, Frankfurt/GER

[182] Wingler, Hans M.
Das Bauhaus, Weimar, Dessau, Berlin
2002 Du Mont, 4. Auflage Köln/GER
ISBN 3-8321-7153-3

[183] Wittenius, Julia
Lehren und Lernen in Kavallerie-Schulen and Diplom-Arbeit
2001 Deutsche Sporthochschule, Cologne/GER

[184] Xenophon (400 v. C.)
Peri Hippikes – Über die Reitkunst
1962 Hoffmann Verlag, Heidenheim/GER

[185] Zdenek, Felix
Joan Miró-Zeichnungen und Skulpturen 1945-1983
1996 Verlag Gerd Hatje, Osterfilden-Reut/GER
ISBN 3-7757-0624-0

ADDENDUM

[186] Decker, Wolfgang
*Sport in der Griechischen Antike – Vom minoischen
Wettkampf bis zu den Olympischen Spielen*
1995 Beck-Verlag, Munich/GER
ISBN 3-406-39669-0

[187] Sinn, Ulrich
Das antike Olympia – Götter, Spiel und Kunst
2004 Beck-Verlag, Munich/GER
ISBN 3-406-51558-4

[188] Kapitzke, Gerhard
Pferdesport von A bis Z
1961 Verlag C. J. Bucher, Luzern/SUI

[189] Nash, Steve
*Ein Stratege der Golfplatz-Architektur, Interview mit
Gary Player*
05/2004 Perpetual Spirit – Golf-Mazagin von ROLEX,
Genève/SUI

[190] N.N. (Author unknown)
*Summary Report of the High-Levelled FEI-Seminar on
Course Design*
1989 Utrecht/NED

[191] N.N.
Lexikon für Pferdefreunde
1961 Verlag C. J. Bucher, Luzern/SUI

[192] N.N.
*Affinitäten 2 – Wertigkeit, Sympathie und persönliche
Nähe von Marken und Sport*
2003 SPORTFIVE GmbH, Hamburg/GER

[193] N.N.
*Summary Report of the 2. High-Levelled FEI-Seminar on
Course Design*
1978 German NF, Warendorf/GER

[194] Hollein, Max, Biazenska Perica
The visions of Arnold Schöneberg – The painting years
2002 Hatje Verlag, Ostfildern/GER
ISBN 3-7757-1133-3

[195] Jones, Chrystine W.
Course Design 1983 as compared to 1966
1983/84 L'ANNEE HIPPIQUE, Best/NED

[196] Mill, Daniel, Kathryn Nankervis
Equine Behaviour: Principles and practice.
1999 Blackwell Science, London/GBR
ISBN 0-632-04878-6

[197] Doney, Jon
*Documentation of the Courses and Results of the World
Equestrian Games*
1994 Den Haag/NED

[198] Gego, Arno
*Project 'DERBY LA BAGNAIA/ITA' Layout and Plans for
Natural Obstacles*
1992 Documentation, Aachen/GER

[199] Gego, Arno
Couloir de Deauville – Ferme de la Bernière, Lisieux/FRA
1993 Project Study, Aachen/GER

[200] Pollmann-Schweckhorst, Elmar
Springpferde-Ausbildung heute
2002 FN-Verlag, Warendorf/GER
ISBN 3-88542-371-5

[201] Niesel, Alfred
*Bauen mit Grün – Die Bau- und Vegetationstechnik des
Landschafts-und Sportplatzbaus*
1999 Verlag Parey, Berlin/GER
ISBN 3-489-54322-X

[202] Fansa, Marmoun, Stefan Burmeister
*Rad und Wagen – Der Ursprung einer Innovation Wagen
im Vorderen Orient und Europa*
2004 Verlag von Zobern, Mainz/GER
ISBN 3-8053-3322-6

[203] Treue, Wilhelm
*ACHSE, RAD und WAGEN- Fünftausend Jahre Kultur-
und Technik-Geschichte*
1986 Vandenhoeck & Ruprecht, Gottigen/GER

[204] Jodidio, Philip
Santiago Calatrave
2003 TASCHEN GmbH, Cologne/GER
ISBN 3-8228-2354-6

[205] Welsh, Norbert, Clus Chr.Liebmann
Farben-Natur-Technik-Kunst (Theory of Colours)
2003 ELSEVIER, Spektrum Akademischer Verlag,
Tubingen/GER

[206] N.N.
Das goldene Buch von Rom
1995 Casa Editrice Bonechi
ISBN 88-7009-446-4

[207] Schwarz, Andreas
Die Lehren von der Farbenharmonies (Theory of Colours Harmony) Eine Enzyklopadie zur Geschichte und Theorie der Farben Harmonielehren
1999 Muster-Schmidt Verlag, Gottingen/GER,
Zurich/SUI
ISBN 3-7881-40-53-4

[208] Budianski, Stephen
The Nature of Horses – Exploring Equine Evolution, Intelligence and Behaviour
1997 The Free Press, New York/USA
ISBN 0-684-82768-9

[209] Wines, James
Grüne Architektur
2000 TASCHEN Verlag, Cologne/GER
ISBN 3-8228-0811-3

[210] Garlett, Jörn
Ecole des Beaux Arts in Paris
2003 Ernst Wasmuth Verlag Tübingen, Berlin/GER
ISBN 3-8030-4025-6

[211] Brem, Gottfed *et. al.*
Canto d'Amore – Classicism in Modern Art and Music 1914-1935
1996 Catalogue, Museum of Arts, Basel/SUI

[212] Holland, Betty Lane
Kevin Bacon, Australia's Extraordinary Horseman
2002 The Waterman Press, Sydney, Australia
ISBN 0-949-284-62-9

[213] Dwyer, Ted
Showjumping in Australia
2004 National Library of Australia
ISBN 0-646-44193-0

[214] Graham, David
Course Design for Showjumping
2004 David Graham and Equestrian Systems, Tauranga,
New Zealand
ISBN 0-473-08502-X

[215] de Pluvinel, Antoine
Le Manège Royal
1989 English translation, J.A Allen & Co Ltd. London
ISBN 0-85131-867-3

[216] Gaviâo Gonzaga, Paulo
A History of the Horse
2004 J.A. Allen, London
ISBN 0-85131-452-X

[217] Etherington-Smith, Mike
Cross Country Course Design and Construction
2003 J.A. Allen, London
ISBN 0-85131-844-4

[218] Scali, Marion
Caprilli et Danloux – Les Grands Maîtres Expliqués
2003 Editions Berlin, Paris
ISBN 2-7011-3637-7

[219] Lodge, Ray, Susan Shanks
All-weather Surfaces for Horses
1994, 1999, 2005 J.A. Allen, London
ISBN 0-85131-913-0

[220] Mezendorf, W. Kavalkade
Herausberger: Hans-Joachim von Killisch-Horn
Kornett Verlag/GER

[221] Sankt Georg Almanach
Verlag Sankt Georg GmbH, Dusseldorf/GER

[222] von Langen, Carl Friedrich
Reitet fur Deutschland
Adolf Sponhotz Verlag/GER

INDEX

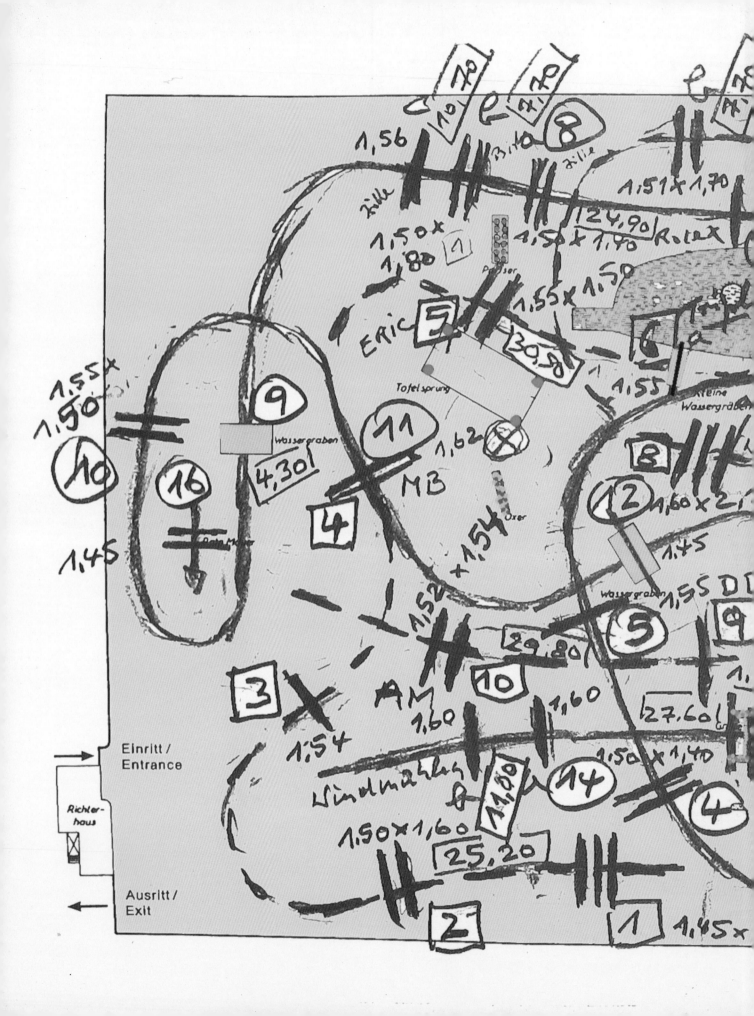